History in the Making

HISTORY IN THE MAKING

Raymond Williams,
Edward Thompson and
Radical Intellectuals 1936–1956

Stephen Woodhams

MERLIN PRESS
FERNWOOD PUBLISHING
PLUTO PRESS AUSTRALIA

First published 2001 by The Merlin Press Ltd.
P.O. Box 30705, London WC2E 8QD
ISBN: 0-85036-494-9 paperback
0-85036-493-0 hardback

Published in Canada by Fernwood Publishing
ISBN: 1-55266-042-7 paperback

Published in Australia by Pluto Press Australia
ISBN: 1-86403-123-9 paperback

British Library Cataloguing in Publication Data
is available from the British Library
•

Canadian Cataloguing in Publication Data
Woodhams, Steven.
History in the Making
ISBN 1-55266-042-7 paperback
1. Great Britain – Intellectual life – 20th century. 2. Historians – Great
Britain – Biography. 3. Socialists – Great Britain – Biography. 4. Political
activists – Great Britain – Biography. I. Title
DA3 A1W66 2000   941.084   COO-950219-X

Typeset by Bruce Brine • Printed in the UK

CONTENTS

Stephen Woodhams is a Visiting Fellow in Politics at Birkbeck College. He lives in East London where he continues to write on cultural history.

For

Margarida Sousa, who bore more of this work than anyone will ever know.

Shalini Nagaraj, whom I love more than she will ever know.

ACKNOWLEDGEMENTS

During the writing of this book I have incurred many debts. First, I am grateful to Birkbeck College for the granting of a Visiting Fellowship which enabled completion of this work. I am grateful to Merryn Williams who, despite receiving so many enquiries, still found time to answer mine. My thanks go to the late Martin Eve for his support for the book when research was at a comparatively early stage.

Margaret McLean was of invaluable help with recollections not only of war-time and post-war adult education but also of personal relations with the Williams family during summer schools at Oxford and elsewhere. I am also indebted to her for copies of recordings of Tony McLean's teaching experiences.

I am grateful to Victor Kiernan, who in correspondence led me to pursue the connection between religious and political commitment which has lain behind the thinking of the whole project. My thanks to John Vickers for his time and thoroughness in discussing his period as Warden of the Wedgwood Memorial College, and particularly his suggestion that the disputes there may have been as much to do with educational politics as with cold-war politics.

I am very grateful to Noreen Branson for her recollections of time in the Communist Party and wise remarks about how history comes to be written. Jim Fyrth was not only very considerate with his time and conversations about adult education in the Communist Party, not to mention a helpful warning against seeing inter-war student radicalism as only a Cambridge phenomenon, but also very generous in sending me a copy of a personal chronography.

The late Douglas Hyde was generous with his time, personal recollections and correspondence in which he pointed me towards the importance of Methodist Bible classes as a learning environment. An insight I have continued to follow for future writing. Alas, his intriguing reference to politically radical musicians proved one too many leads to follow. Another day.

I am indebted to Tish Newland for an interesting discussion of the generation on which this book is based, and her observation of the remarkable knowledge that these earlier writers and teachers could bring to a subject introduced at random. I should also say a big thank you to Tish for her assistance as the Librarian of the Marx Memorial Library.

Andy Croft generously allowed me to use his research into arguments about culture in the Communist Party press, which appears in a discussion of a *Daily Worker* article, 'Culture or Snobology', in chapter eight. Raphael Samuel offered great encouragement by correspondence, but was, alas, too unwell to talk in person.

My thanks to Roger Fieldhouse, John McIlroy, Tom Steele and Lionel Elvin for their assistance by way of various communications, and to Dai Smith and Dorothy Thompson for help with the cover photographs.

ACKNOWLEDGEMENTS

For assistance in researching internal matters in the Communist Party in 1956, I am grateful to Francis King and George Mathews, the one-time custodians of the Party's archive. I should add that unpublished papers in the bibliography may be found in the Circulars 1956 Box and the Historians' Group Box, both of which are in the CPGB archives.

There are also those who helped and supported, at different times and in different ways, including Kathy Burton, Kate Robinson, Alison Assiter, Anthony Stone, Ifor Edwards, Bill Schwarz, Mike Rustin, John Solomos, Tony Marriott, Roger Woods and Soraya Shah. I would also like to thank the Committees of both the Socialist History Society and the Raymond Williams Society. One very special place has to be mentioned: Birkbeck College, not least for a great bar and some good nights.

Although my stay in Pandy was far shorter than I would have liked, I am very grateful to those who gave so freely of their time and knowledge. Finally, those without whom there would not have been a book: its interlocutor Paul Hirst, Tony Zurbrugg and Adrian Howe of The Merlin Press, and the book's supporter, Patricia Eve.

chapter one

HISTORY, CULTURE AND COLLECTIVE BIOGRAPHY

1. People and Their Time

History in the Making is a collective biography of a number of radical intellectuals covering the period from the middle of the nineteen-thirties to a point where the fifties were turning into the beginning of the nineteen-sixties. The choice of period is set by two dimensions. It was during the middle-thirties that the generation which forms the subject of this book was propelled into rapid maturity and early adulthood. The end of the nineteen-fifties by contrast takes us to the years of the first phase of CND, by which time they had established themselves as figures of respect across a wide range of educational and political fields. Their future influence though would have to exert itself into an altering structure of feeling, as the culture that formed this generation slowly declined in the years after the Second World War.

From the experience of maturing in the inter-war period this generation carried forward a belief not only in the possibility of change, but its inherent rightness. Faced with what they perceived to be a fundamentally immoral social order, they determined to commit themselves to its transformation into a new order governed by principles drawn from ethical socialism and Marxist-Leninism. Before the Second World War, Marxist-Leninism, manifested in the Communist Party of Great Britain (CPGB), was a powerful attraction to these young people then at university. After the war when several became members of the party's historians group, Marxist-Leninism continued to serve as a weapon in the 'battle of ideas'. However, the current of ethical socialism never waned. Its most eloquent expression was in moral outrage, whether aimed at poverty on the streets, the sacrifice of democracy in Spain, the treatment of peoples across the Empire, or the sheer inhumanity of the Bomb. The last structures the final years of the story, when many found a new cause to which they could dedicate themselves. Adult education sits alongside these more obviously political actions as a calling where the demonstration of commitment, voluntary work, self-help, revolutionary zeal and protestant nonconformity got mixed-up to form a cocktail which served to inspire and guide what, in retrospect, was a remarkable formation.

In this first chapter I want to set out a longer history and some earlier writings against which to place the figures with whom the rest of the book is concerned. The first section is a brief discussion of who the book is about.

1

Section two examines historical and contemporary influences forming these figures, particularly adult education. In the third section, I discuss a small number of works with which the present book bears some affinity, though also where they differ from the present book. Finally, in section four, I provide an outline of the book, setting down briefly the contents of each chapter and an indication of the conclusion finally drawn.

The title *History in the Making* is intended to convey the emphasis I place on the extent to which people forged their identity and their lives, against or even in spite of the circumstances in which they lived. If the events influencing their lives included the poverty of the thirties, the politics of the Spanish Civil War, the Second World War the cold war and finally the emergence of the Campaign for Nuclear Disarmament, then *History in the Making* is intended to mark how they jointly and individually responded to those events. If the Communist Party and adult education form two parts of the background from which these figures came, Cambridge University forms a third. The choice of Cambridge is because for much of the thirties the place nurtured a certain political radicalism, and because choosing one place enhances the similarity of experience for those who make up the story. Of course, responses to circumstances varied widely, and it is this second feature which I seek to emphasise in the choice of Raymond Williams, for reasons I shall explain shortly, as the central figure around which to wrap the book.

Cambridge, the Communist Party and adult education are then means by which I select most of those discussed in the book. Here I shall not attempt to go into the detail of each character, but rather introduce them. I have already cited Raymond Williams's difference from the other figures as a reason for using him as the central figure around which the work is woven. Political affiliation was certainly one factor in his difference from other people in the book. Equally important though was his thinking through of the idea of culture and change in British society, in the after-war years, which others were only to address at the end of the fifties. Just the point in time when what came to be called the New Left emerged, and Williams found himself between those of his own generation and those younger people with whom he shared closer interests and perceptions.

Our second figure, the historian Edward Thompson, was a Cambridge student, a Communist Party member and an adult education tutor. Edward Thompson, however, was not only a participant in each of these, he was also active in the two movements which take up the later chapters of the book: the Campaign for Nuclear Disarmament and the New Left. Alongside Edward Thompson are several other historians who also attended Cambridge. Eric Hobsbawm and Dorothy Thompson both had their studies similarly disrupted by war. While Dorothy Thompson elected to enter industry for her war service, Eric Hobsbawm pursued educational work, teaching in the Army Education Corp. After the war, Hobsbawm pursued a career inside the university, while Dorothy Thompson taught for a few years as an adult education tutor, before moving to internal academic work at Birmingham University.

By contrast Tony McLean remained in Oxford Extra-Mural teaching throughout his working life. Margaret McLean, meanwhile, is a good example of one of the women who gained an adult education post because of the unusual circumstance of the war, and the need for organized activities for conscripted and service-occupied people across the country. The writer and academic Margot Heinemann was at Cambridge slightly earlier than the others cited so far, but her subsequent work either for the Communist Party, or externally with Noreen Branson, also a communist, produced such work as *Britain in the Nineteen Thirties*. Noreen Branson has an additional significance in her own right as a historian of the Communist Party. The inclusion of Clifford Collins, and the subsequent film producer Wolf Mankowitz is rather different. Both at Cambridge, in 1946–47 they worked with Raymond Williams on *Politics and Letters*, a short-lived periodical which I review in chapter four.

The emphasis on the Communist Party should not be taken to imply that the sort of political commitment which I claim characterized those cited above, did not exist elsewhere. Rather the Communist Party affords a good example of an institutional means wherein that commitment could gain expression. However, a restrictive uniformity is not imposed. The difference of futures caused by the rift that split the party following the Soviet invasion of Hungary in 1956, is captured in the contrast of views which structures chapter six.

Two people who help compose the last part of the story told in chapter eight reflect this contrast in another form. The historian Raphael Samuel and the cultural theorist Stuart Hall were of a younger generation. The contrasts between them were important, yet they were part of the different structure of feeling which the inter-war generation had to negotiate from the later-nineteen-fifties onwards. At the commencement the subjects are in their late-teens or early-twenties. At the close, by contrast, they are in their forties, thus still a generation of the future, but already established as figures in their own right. It is a claim of the book that growing up in the nineteen-thirties meant that these young people could not but be affected by the course of events in the world around them. In that sense their personal biographies were rather more pressed and limited by the history of the time than has been common for subsequent generations. Of course, the actual effect of growing up at a particular historical moment will have different effects for people dependent on a whole range of factors. At the macro level we may cite class, gender and region as critical. But beyond these will be a whole set of circumstances which will inflect the effects of each and any of these social pressures. To these we may bring the word culture by way of description and analysis. Within the culture that contributes to the formation of an individual, the playing out of historical events and social forces will be arranged in a personal order

3

which the records of the time will not be able to denote. It is to these historical and social influences that I turn in the next section.

2. The Making of a History

Component parts of the culture to which I referred earlier can be traced forward from the middle of the nineteenth century, when the early rigours of the industrial revolution were beginning to be replaced by a world still recognizable today in the form of houses, roads, railways and regional character. By the eighteen-forties Britain was a nation showing a degree of commonality probably impossible at any previous time. Of course, I do not mean that differences of lifestyle were disappearing—the distance between rich and poor was perhaps still of growing proportion—but commonality in the sense that, to a degree never before possible, people were becoming aware of themselves as part of a greater whole: the nation. The railway operating to a standardized national time, and the modern national newspaper, were but two means whereby people who had no personal knowledge of each other could be aware of doing things in common.

With this growing sense of a national identity, developed a new sense of civic society which offered its own means of identity through voluntary engagement. While the forms this took were varied, there may be detected a common emphasis on improvement both personal and collective. There were, it is true, different expressions of voluntary engagement as between social classes, however this variance does not perhaps detract from the common impulse. From the middle of the nineteenth century societies and clubs of many kinds set themselves up in cities, towns and villages throughout Britain. Many were apparently for no more important an activity than the playing of some sport or continuance of a hobby. Yet even in these instances, where records needed to be kept, there arose a need for the learning of necessary skills in literacy and numeracy. However, many clubs and societies were more serious, and directed themselves toward the improvement of their members. Among these were friendly societies, mutual societies and any manner of savings clubs. The warding off of destitution, particularly the feared pauper's funeral, was the keenest pressure in some cases, though in time they too could serve as means toward improving present standards of living. Much more expansive in intent were the co-operative societies, which at one end overlapped with the idea of mutual savings, but centred on the more complex business of purchasing and selling. From these central activities extended those of education and politics leading directly on to adult education and the eventual formation of the Labour Party. Trade union branches, meanwhile, connected home and work place, requiring a degree of organization and thus communication for which learning, both instrumental and liberal, were recognized as necessary. Finally, chapel attendance for the respectable skilled working class brought empowerment, offering a means for co-

4

operative activities ranging from the religious to secular adult learning class, to the production of large-scale cultural events often centred on music or displays of speaking and reading. To a considerable degree these examples were working-class inspired, though in the case of mutual societies, the lower-middle class were to be major benefactors.

More obviously middle-class inspired were the great societies for the improvement of people, more often for the inhabitants of a particular town, though sometimes with aspirations far beyond. The ending of slavery, the improvement in the position of women or the advancement of enlightened education were each very much examples of nineteenth-century campaigns for enhancing the common good. Philanthropy has been the term often used to describe the intention of these societies, though Raymond Williams's description of service is perhaps more useful (1958a 325–330). The feeling stemmed from a duty towards not just individual others but to the place itself. When put in these terms it may reasonably be asked whether the idea of duty can be described as characteristic of one class more than another. Certainly it would be hard to deny the service with which people carried through trade union work often requiring the gaining of respect from a wider community in order to be effective. This last point returns us to the ethic of voluntary engagement. Not bound by legal sanction, moral force was more likely to be the inspiration behind becoming involved, whether because of a belief in the duty to improve the lot of those 'less fortunate', or more commonly a felt duty to enrich the next generation either through something positive such as an education, or the absence of something negative such as funeral expenses which savings in a friendly society could avoid.

The extent of voluntary effort across the social classes to bring education to all required a collaborative cultural effort of a magnitude rarely witnessed before or since. There are still few histories of the development of nineteenth-century education other than those limited to the enacting of state provision for children. The ethos upon which provision, whether of education or other public good, was one of social improvement. Among the impulses giving rise to such effort was a sense of duty. While this drive can be readily recognized as part of the muscular Christianity, much of whose efforts went into sport, the preaching of what came to be called the social gospel and Christian Socialism, the ethos comes also from more secular sources in politics and morality. Writing about workers' education in the first half of the nineteen-twenties, Margaret Hodgen cited the tradition of education which she wrote about as stretching back some seventy-five years. In fact, the length of time can be pushed back further if the Owenite and Chartist efforts of the second quarter of the nineteenth century are included.

According to Hodgen the range of initiatives, while varying regionally, as exemplified by the Co-operative College and the People's Colleges in the central Midlands, the Working Men's College in London, and Mechanic

Institutes in many towns, had a similar feature:

> The characteristic feature of English adult working-class education in the Nineteenth Century was the centralization of administrative control in the hands of upper-class persons and institutions (Hodgen 1925 128).

This was not entirely an accurate claim. Hodgen herself suggests that, in the case of the People's Colleges, working-class students shared control over the content of the teaching. We might add that by the very nature of the movement, the Co-operative College cannot but have been partly working-class controlled. What perhaps makes Hodgen's history more difficult is an insistence on the term 'workers' education', but under which are included many instances of adult education. One consequence is that very different aims and practices between different movements or institutions are not perhaps contrasted as much as they might be.

The work remains, though, an excellent collection of instances of philanthropy, self-help, and social reform blending in different ways to advance the cause of adult education. A detailed study of one of these many cases, the Working Men's College in London, was completed by J. F. C. Harrison in 1954. In the introduction, Harrison provides a summary of the point being made here about the general ethos which inspired the political commitments of the subjects in this work. Having located the college in the adult education movement, Harrison continues:

> The College can be considered secondly as part of that great development of Voluntary Bodies, ranging from, powerful Trade Unions and large Friendly Benefit Societies to local Temperance Societies and humble Mutual Improvement groups, which did so much to mitigate the worst excesses of mid-Victorian industrialism, and which have characterized so distinctly the form of British liberal democracy. The spirit behind this plethora of voluntary associations was a peculiar blend of Samuel Smiles' middle-class doctrine of Self-Help, with the Owenite teaching of the need for the working class to attain independence through their own co-operative efforts (Harrison 1954 xvii–xviii).

What comes across very clearly is the manner in which moral, religious and political impulses combined to bring people from university backgrounds to teaching part of the London working class. The subject matter ranged from public health, to Shakespeare, to law. The scope suggests the principle of extending the best in learning to all, rather than the stratified knowledge which came to be offered in the state schools some years later. The difference has been set out in terms of the 'public educators' versus the 'industrial trainers' (Williams 1961 142). If the ethos detected by Harrison comes closer to the first, the latter approach is caught in a statement from the time:

> To every class we have a school assign'd
> Rules for all ranks and food for every mind
> (Crabbe in Williams 1961 136).

Good biography may serve as good history. Certainly the history of philanthropy, self-improvement and voluntary effort can be detected in the accounts of the subjects of biography. Beatrice Potter-Webb and Sidney Webb were born in 1858 and 1859 respectively. Royden Harrison has recalled that Beatrice Potter-Webb's own upbringing was that of an '... open-minded and cultivated ...' household which had exchanged Anglicanism for Dissent, and the Tories for Radicalism (Levy ed. 1987 46). Certainly, the family was sufficiently wealthy for the progressive ideas about girls' education to be taken full advantage of, and Beatrice Potter-Webb gained greatly from it. Her 'apprenticeship' included working for several years with her cousin Charles Booth on the investigations of East End life, and a number of studies of her own on the conditions of workers' lives in London and elsewhere (Webb 1948 13). In writing of Sidney Webb's upbringing she comments that his father was—

> ... singularly refined in character—modest and unassuming, remarkably public-spirited, always ready to do unpaid work either for public bodies or friends who were in trouble (Webb 1948 2–3).

and of the house where in part he grew up, that—

> The intellectual atmosphere of the home was made up of the Radical politics of his father ... and the broad evangelical religious feeling of his mother, who took the children to one church or chapel after another in search of an eloquent preacher free from sacerdotalism (ibid. 3).

Somewhere between a few years and a generation later came R. H. Tawney 1880, G. D. H. Cole 1889, Margaret Cole 1893, Harold Laski 1893, Victor Gollancz 1895, Kingsley Martin 1897 and Barbara Wootton 1897. The list could, of course, be much lengthened but the point may be made just the same. Tawney's family was Anglo-Indian, Church and trading. His path beyond this took him first to Toynbee Hall and from there to the Children's Country Holiday Fund (Wright 1897 3). Later energies were devoted to the advancement of adult education. G. D. H. Cole and Margaret Cole spent much energy in the causes of guild socialism, the Labour Research Department, the WEA, the London County Council and the *New Statesman*. Harold Laski came from an orthodox Jewish background and was later to devote much time again to adult education, the Left Book Club and party politics. Possibly the most exceptional of all those I cite here was Victor Gollancz. Also born an orthodox Jew, he seemed to have rebelled against any and every, at least English, lower-middle-class expectation. Later he married business with political evangelism most notably in the form of the Left Book Club. The club probably did more to spread socialist arguments than any other comparable organization, before or after. Gollancz proudly identified himself with an enlightenment conception of education which, in line with many early adult educators, he viewed as elementary to the bringing of socialism. Kingsley Martin came from a chapel background, and one whose dissenting character was growing ever more radical. Martin's own direction was set very early on

7

when he enlisted to serve in the Friend's Ambulance Unit during the First World War (Rolph 1973 53). Later, and like so many others, he taught for the Workers' Education Society, and for a short while at the London School of Economics. After this (while the greater part of his active life was devoted to the *New Statesman* in a paid capacity) he engaged in any number of voluntary schemes of his time, both for good causes and more overtly political objectives. Barbara Wootton was brought up by two classical scholars, though her turn toward economics occurred fairly early (Wootton 1967 39). Her own conviction was that it was through economics that a socialist society could be built, and she used the craft for deliberately political ends in much the same way that the Fabian Research Bureau used its output. One outlet for her teaching was through extra-mural classes and once again the WEA.

Together even these few examples cover a considerable range of political and voluntary activity in the first half of this century. A key impulse was a sense of dissatisfaction with prevailing cultural and social behaviour, the norms which governed that behaviour and the social relations which gave rise to both. Politically, the Fabian Society was a vehicle through which that sense of estrangement from the dominant culture could be shared with like-minded persons (Tanner 1993). The frequency with which Fabian summer schools are mentioned in biographical history of left figures in the early years of this century, is one indication. The issues which called for the attention of social reformers were varied, but that of poverty, its causes and consequences, was probably the most consistent. The ethos which carried campaigns for reform of the Poor Law, improvement in maternity care (an aim of particular importance for the Women's Co-operative Guild), or the advancement of education, all assumed that enlightenment and reason were of themselves good, and that the wider their distribution, the greater the good to humankind. The commencement and extension of adult education from so many disparate beginnings should be understood as a practical assertion of just this belief, and is well caught in a description of the principles underlying the foundation of the Working Men's College:

> Not only did it exist to benefit the workers, by bringing within their reach opportunities for development hitherto regarded as the sole privilege of the upper classes, and so train them to take a fuller share in the life of the nation and in the reform of social and industrial conditions: but it desired to influence the wealthier and more fortunate, by giving them the means of coming into personal contact with the lives of those from whom they had been separated by birth and circumstances, and so teach them the responsibility of their position, the joy of service, the value of friendship with the poor, and of sympathy with the aspirations to which ignorance had hitherto kept them strangers (Raven 1968 354).

Such a view was, I assert, not peculiar to one social class but rather held appeal across social divisions and to an extent across political positions. The drift though was firmly from the liberal to the socialist. The generation with which the present work is concerned nearly all held views that would commonly be described as being to the left of their parents. Among the politically conscious working class, the change starts from around the turn of the century and is largely completed by the radicalizing effects of the First World War. The switch from Liberal to Labour was perhaps only the most obvious indication of a change that had more important cultural roots beneath the surface. Michael Foot describes this process at the beginning of his biography of Aneurin Bevan, which I discuss in chapter seven.

The case is of course one from Wales, where the movement from Nonconformity and Liberalism to atheism and socialism was very much more profound than in England. It was also distinctive in being fostered by a geographical movement of people from Mid Wales to South Wales. The older area was to remain Liberal for a further three decades. It was thus the peculiarity of South Wales to which reference must be made in citing the strength of Welsh socialism in the early years of this century, and the advancement of the new creed by the evangelical work of adult educationalists. Elsewhere in parts of England and Scotland the development of working-class socialism was more patchy.

The movement of the politically conscious radical middle class runs slightly behind. This population could, and to a considerable extent did, remain liberal through to the end of the First World War. After this the attraction towards socialist thinking was often through the appeal of planning, as the capitalist world seemed increasingly incapable of providing the levels of employment and social welfare, reformists came to expect. Slowly the ideal of planning as the strategy to adopt for the future gained acceptance in the Labour Party. The Fabians were important in this development, though it would be correct to say that the greater pressure came from the experience of the First World War and a recognition that planning, particularly for production, was a possibility. Pressures towards re-establishing state planning for major industries, particularly coal, advanced during the inter-war period, and were extended toward organizing the provision of health care and welfare. Though it took a further war to see major advances, it would be fair to say that efforts in this direction were gaining ground before the end of the peace in 1939.

The development of adult and socialist education was not left unaffected by this trend toward planning, though in its earlier years this pressure was little advanced and a degree of flexibility in provision and organization was still apparent. The manner of teaching and learning took two forms. On the one side was the formal class: a series of fairly regular meetings, either following a single theme or a series of talks by various speakers. One example of the use of this method was that by the National Council of Adult Schools. Founded in 1899 the National Council's schools worked alongside the many Nonconformist Sunday school and Bible classes. In turn these were augmented by the growing University Extension Movement. Commencing in 1873, the Extension Movement grew as more universities became involved and the range and number of classes increased. While much of the history of this movement has still to be written, there does exist both local and general accounts of its composition, aims, teaching methods and political aspirations (Harrison 1961, Rowley n.d., Rowbotham 1981). Adult schools, church and denominational classes, the University Extension Movement, each represented important parts of a broad adult education movement that was within a few years to lead to the creation of the Workers' Education Movement (WEA). Eve Rowley's local study is actually entitled *A History of the WEA in Longton* and takes the reader on from the activities of working people in the area through the provision of university tutorial classes and eventually to the establishing of more substantial educational provision with the creation of the Workers' Educational Association.

The politics of the WEA have never been of one view or even kind, and in the years before 1950 two main tendencies may be identified. On the one side was a conservative social democratic ethos, largely Fabian in tradition. The emphasis was on a steady advance in the standard of living for the majority of the working class, as part of the progress toward a rationally organized society for which ignorance and cultural poverty were unacceptable and unnecessary failures of human planning, in this instance educational. On the other, was a radical-liberal sentiment which sought to maintain a forum for different views to be exchanged, and a belief that through enlightened learning and disinterested teaching, people in future generations would simply be better.

Before 1939 the WEA was certainly keen to attract manual workers, though the extent to which it aligned itself with the Labour Movement was always more tenuous. It was this tension and, at the opposite end of the chain so to speak, the association with universities, that reinforced the division between the WEA and the National Council of Labour Colleges. The relationship between these two bodies has to date received little attention, though some inroad into this neglected subject is being advanced (Simon ed. 1992, Lewis 1993). There is little evidence that the co-operation realized under the conditions of the Second World War made for any improvement in that particular dispute. Yet in many instances the war had a radicalizing effect, monitored in the unique experiment Mass-Observation, and producing at least one original political party, Common Wealth, whose call for the socializing of production rested almost entirely on moral and ethical grounds. Adult Education could, it was argued, make a positive contribution towards this end, though as Harold Shearman pointed out, its aims should always retain the wider value of enlightenment and human advance:

> It is vital to democracy that government should not become the sole concern of the specialist, whether bureaucrat or statesman. It must be studied and reflected on by ordinary men and women engaged in the affairs of life. It is vital in particular to the labour movement that industry and economics, local administration and international relations, the

social relations of science and the arts should be studied by those whose lives they most directly affect, in an atmosphere of free enquiry and critical discussion (1944 10–11).

Shearman had been appointed Education Officer for the WEA in 1934–35 from whence he had stimulated and encouraged protests against cuts and limitations to adult education imposed by the inter-war Conservative 'National Government'. Partly for this reason, the WEA could attract the support and services of the younger militants growing up between the wars. However, in the earlier history of adult education leading up to the work of the WEA there existed organizations for whom the WEA's aims, even in the radicalized atmosphere of the nineteen-forties, would have been unacceptable. Fundamentally, the difference lay in the very purpose of education. The aim of classes run by the Independent Labour Party (ILP), Co-operative Societies, the Socialist Democratic Federation (SDF), the Socialist Labour Party, the South Wales Miners' Federation, and a number of smaller and lesser known bodies was always overtly socialist. Put another way, while for the WEA teaching and learning should enable people to understand society, and thus judge both its worth and the need for change, for these earlier organizations, the classes themselves were meant to directly contribute to the bringing on of a new social order.

In the main these bodies worked on the basis of classes addressed by speakers, local where possible, but often from further afield. In time these were replaced or augmented by the National Council of Labour Colleges (NCLC), which overlapped with the Central Labour College in London. The progress of the NCLC and the Central College was from the start troubled. Closely associated with the NCLC was the Plebs League. The origins of the Plebs lay in the famous Ruskin College dispute of 1908–9 and the setting up of the Central Labour College. One of the purposes of the league was to produce material for what today we would call distance learning, and through the pages of its newspaper, *Plebs*, considerable quantities of booklets and leaflets were provided. The reading matter was used by people who formed themselves into groups, meetings being held at times and places of mutual convenience. The flexibility this provided could obviously be of great benefit in easing co-operation and even saving money. Unfortunately, the effectiveness of this distance learning material remains to be assessed, there being as yet little detailed study of their production, content, distribution or usage. The very substantial material afforded for research by *Plebs*, which remained in print for many years, makes this lack of research all the more conspicuous, and Richard Lewis's study of adult and workers' education in South Wales, published in 1993, all the more necessary as well as interesting. In Lewis's view, the relations between the two major traditions, the WEA on the one side, and the NCLC on the other, were more complex than has been presented by supporters of one or the other.

There existed also overtly propagandist socialist education which sought intermediate goals short of the complete transformation of society depicted in the booklets, etc., of the SDF, the ILP or the Plebs. Writing in her early biography *Growing up into Revolution,* published in 1949, Margaret Cole refers to this second form of socialist adult education as 'Labour research'. She goes on to warn us though that the term can be used to mean two different types of work, both of which were engaged in by reformists and radicals in the first decades of this century. The first usage refers to, '… research in subjects important to the Labour movement …' (ibid. 148). The second type was of a more clearly partisan nature:

> … research designed to establish conclusions in accordance with the general tenets of the Labour movement … (ibid. 148).

In the work of the Fabians, Cole suggests these two forms of work overlapped,

> … the Fabian belief was that by *proper presentation* of the actual verifiable facts capitalism could be convicted so to speak out of its own mouth, and the necessity of Socialism established (ibid. 149).

The approach bears all the hallmarks of the moral force which radicals and reformers brought to their work, whether educational or propagandist. If this was appropriate for the denouncing of capitalism, then equally could it be so for argument concerning the poor law, or nutrition, or the necessity for co-operation and trade union membership. If these were expounded sufficiently well their rightness would be recognized. The evangelical spirit of the early socialists, whether of the Co-operative Movement, Morris' Socialist League, the SDF, Plebs or Fabians, was by the generation maturing in the inter-war period, taken forward most keenly by the Communist Party of Great Britain (CPGB). The hunger marches organized by the National Unemployed Workers' Movement (NUWM), were a very real means whereby middle- and working-class radicals could join together in both convicting capitalism of its inadequacies and inspiring others to stand up and be counted for the cause.

In the thirties the CPGB became a home for many of the figures of the generation with which this work is concerned. That they then attempted to reinvent the party as the heir to the radical movements of the previous century and more, is perhaps not surprising. The key element in the attempted continuity from a varied and heterogeneous range of socialists to the more dogmatic yet efficient Communist Party was precisely the evangelical belief that moral force and reason would eventually win out. Though people were active in both, educative activity in the Communist Party was in sharp contrast to the approach of the WEA. The aim was to recruit members, but more than that to convince people of the wrongness of capitalism, and the consequent necessity and rightness of socialism. In these respects the party was closer to the Fabian Research Bureau, and the link between the two formed by the passing of people from one to the other, is returned to in later chapters. The means for this educational activity were varied and at their best, highly imaginative. The pamphlet was of course a mainstay, as with most evangelical bodies. But communists produced a most extraordinary volume of written material aimed at different sections of society. The *Daily Worker* was for the factory gate and the surrounding working-class neighbourhoods, while *Modern Quarterly* attracted several members of the Royal Society to its editorial board. But beyond the printed word were a number of visual statements, ranging from Unity Theatre in the pre-war days to the historical pageants celebrating the life of the free-born Englishman. In film too, a number of communists proved themselves to be highly competent in both production and critical analysis. No other political party of comparable size, or even bigger, has managed the sheer range and volume of material which communists were able to create in the years before 1956.

The cultural politics in the years leading up to the Second World War are discussed at greater length in chapter two, and I wish here to only raise the points examined there. So far we have tended to cite liberal education as carried forward by way of immediate class contact, while political education was likely to involve more distanced forms of learning. The Fabian Research Bureau, the Plebs League and the Communist Party were each able to provide propaganda material to suit differing needs within the Labour Movement. Yet in the years leading up to the outbreak of war and beyond, there existed cultural interventions which disturbed any simple division of the liberal and the political. In *Under Siege*, Robert Hewison (1988) offers an account of the literary and artistic scene running right through the forties. Hewison cites a number of experiments in fictional publication. At this time it was still possible for there to exist a considerable number of literary, poetical and cultural reviews, each surviving on small circulations and the goodwill of both writers and readers. Included among these were *Adelphi, Horizon, Now, The Christian Newsletter, Poetry and the People* (later renamed *Our Time*), and *New Writing* which became *Penguin New Writing* after the salvation of the earlier title by Allen Lane. Styles varied as too did their politics, yet their coverage and circulation was of a kind difficult to imagine in the international corporate publishing world of today's magazines. Orwell has provided his distinctive, and typically unfavourable, interpretation of a number of these publications, accusing Catholic and communist alike of undermining literary judgement in favour of political intentions. For many of these small magazines the experience of war had both negative and positive effects. On the one side they were able to partake of the interest in the arts and culture which, as part of efforts to keep up morale, was fostered by the government. Against this though the magazines suffered the dislocations which war brought, both in the form of the movements of people, and in the disruptions to supplies of materials. One small magazine, *Politics and Letters*, published just after the war, is discussed at some length in chapter four, together with the circumstance of its publication, readership and demise.

Penguin New Writing, one of the leading publications, was particularly important in providing a means for a wide range of expressive writing. Even a brief examination of the contributors' details for the war years reveals a surprising range of backgrounds and experiences. While the number with university or similar training still dominated, they did not account for all the writers. The period witnessed a brief though significant flowering of working-class writers representing differing regions and experiences, though sadly women of the same class were almost entirely absent. In the pages of *Penguin New Writing* were included both persons in civilian occupations, coal mining being featured in more than one case, and others serving in the forces. A very early contributor whose writing, particularly *These Poor Hands* published in 1939, has retained at least some public awareness was B. L. Coombes. What perhaps *Penguin New Writing* signifies still is the crossover in this period between the educational and the political through an intervening medium of literary work constituting what only in retrospect came to be called 'cultural politics'.

It may be as well at this point to briefly restate the main themes identified in this section since they will underpin much of what follows. I have suggested that voluntary engagement was an ethos directing people into varied activities which displayed a sense of duty often coupled with a desire for self and collective improvement. To this may be added the values of dissent. The last is clearly taken from a religious context wherein dissenting practices constituted a way of life. The values and more importantly the behaviour of the chapel extended into everyday life, turning respectability into reality through not only Sabbath observance, which meant far more than merely attending chapel, but also teetotalism, manners and ascetic display. However, the influences of dissent were not of one kind, and could equally mean engagement in the public world where social witness against dominant values—commercialism, militarism, monarchy—was a duty, even a calling. Dissent could bring to voluntary engagement a decidedly democratic orientation creating space for ordinary people to effect their will.

However, it was another dimension of voluntary engagement which is noted here. Adult education is important both because many of the figures in the present work were at some time in their lives engaged in teaching classes, and because adult education classes provided both a communications network and a pool of people to fill the ranks of movements ranging from the Left Book Club to the Campaign for Nuclear Disarmament. This connection between learning and politics may be understood as a form of politics expressed through culture, or cultural politics. Neither formulation is ideal, the former because it suggests that culture is in some manner passive, a set of activities through which may be expressed some prior or more fundamental cause. This would be entirely false, since it is from experience of the cultural patterns within which we live that political choices are formulated. Cultural politics on the other hand is a formula which has only become common currency in recent years. To transpose this back therefore to an earlier time is to run the risk of positing a package of meanings, which the term has acquired at one time on to a different period. It should be said that the present work does not resolve this tension between culture and politics, but rather explores specific historical expressions of the problem, of which voluntary engagement, dissent, and adult or workers' education are important examples. The themes of adult education and political culture are pursued in chapters two, three and four, while chapter five takes the discussion forward specifically in an examination of the character and composition of the Communist Party. The remaining chapters, the conclusion excepted, examine the changing circumstance into which this inter-war generation had slowly to move, starting with the partial break-up of the Communist Party, the rise of the first CND and finally the new generation of socialists around *Universities and Left Review*. Before this though it is necessary to situate the book in relation to existing works and to explain more fully the premise upon which it is written.

3. COLLECTIVE BIOGRAPHY AND A CONTEXTUAL HISTORY

This section sets out the approach of the book, in part by contrasting it with a small number of comparable writings. Briefly, there are three elements to this discussion. The years covered, from the mid-thirties to the end of the fifties, do not fit any obvious framework; inter-war, post-war, etc., but rather set down limits which serve to carve out a period peculiar to the work. The next feature is the convention chosen to present the history. Collective biography is not a common means by which to write history, nor even is history commonly given primacy in the writing of biography. Finally, there is an emphasis on the actual people in the story, their lives and what they did rather than their ideas. The last is particularly important to stress in the case of persons who have become known in large part precisely because of their writing and ideas. Taken together these three features mark the work out, while at the same time enabling it to offer an account which builds upon our knowledge and understanding of the period and people making up a remarkable generation.

Beginning with the point of periods, the history of the twentieth century has been marked by out by very precise dating. Thus we have Edwardian histories ending with the outbreak of the First World War, inter-war histories with their clearly defined beginnings and ends, and the post-war histories whose conclusions are dependent on the date of their writing. Alternatively, histories are of the war periods themselves, beginning and ending with the starts and ends of the particular war in which they are set. Overwhelmingly the choice has been one or other of the two world wars. Biography though cannot so easily be separated out into such discrete compartments. The problem is that the lives of individuals while affected by the course of the larger regional or global events around them, will still lead continuities across the breaks these great events may impose. In like manner, the lives of individuals may experience breaks and changes which have no obvious connection to the dates by which the world around them is recorded. Personal loves, losses, joys and sorrows do not neatly coincide with those of populations and nations as recorded by archivist or historian. Finally, though the crossing of what are often taken to be separate periods, is necessitated by the story to be told, there is a deeper importance. The times covered by the book, are clearly different. In charting a single group of people, through them, we can gain some sense of the differences between what were clearly very varied periods. Rather than measuring that variance by judgement of selected features of each period, the book reviews the response of a small number of people to the changes they were experiencing. These responses varied in timing and manner, yet throughout the book glimpses of these shifts are, I hope, perceptible.

A biographical narrative might not unreasonably be expected to wind itself around the chosen figure, though how far it does so has in reality varied. Less often has biography served as history, psychology often being preferred on the grounds that this better provides the reader with an understanding of the work's subject. However, history in the form of biography has many good examples to its credit, the figure in these cases taking form as the history develops them. However, in merging history and biography considerable variation exists, as can be indicated by reference to writings on one figure: Aneurin Bevan. The well-known and widely-sold two-volume biography *Aneurin Bevan* by Michael Foot stays very close to its subject. Indeed, until the renunciation of unilateralism in Brighton in 1957 which forms the third to last chapter of the second volume, Foot is positively enraptured with his hero. The 1993 work by Dai Smith *Aneurin Bevan and the World of South Wales* by contrast almost marginalizes the figure whose name forms the first part of the book's title. The emphasis is firmly on the second part of the title, Bevan being confined to one long chapter in the middle of the book. It is perhaps an extreme example, but Smith offers a case where it is the history which is foregrounded and the person created out of that historical account. The styles of Foot and Smith vary greatly: the one simple, if at times burdened by a tediousness deriving from being too close to the subject, the second presenting the reader with hard intellectual work unravelling the layers of meaning which are laid on by way of the many varied cultural sites which Smith chooses to include. Such a style is not necessary for the task of writing history through biography, witness Will Paynter *My Generation* published in 1972. However, it is likely that complexity in writing will be created where the attempt is to capture real historical complexity. Taken far enough a figure becomes in fact a peg on which to arrange a series of arguments, historical, literary and sociological, as for example in Raymond Williams's Robert Tressell Lecture which appeared in *History Workshop* in 1983.

In common with most of those cited in the preceding two paragraphs, the present work is a political biography. Thus, while details of childhood or adult personal relations are important in achieving a full portrait of a subject, where that is the aim of the biography, the purpose here is both more limited and more extended. As a political biography the work is limited to those dimensions of life wherein a person's political expression is pronounced. It is for this reason that adult education and a range of political associations have been chosen as subjects for the book. Yet the work is more extended in moving back and forth between national, even global, events and the lives of the selected figures so that we gain a sense of the contexts within which people made their decisions, and thus the pressures and limits which served to mould them. This last point moves us beyond conventional biography's concern with a single figure toward creating a collective account.

In moving on to discuss collective biography, I will need at the same time to introduce the third theme which distinguishes the present work: the emphasis on lived experience rather than merely ideas. The latter have tended to be the basis for intellectual biographies, which in turn have tended to concentrate on a single figure. Thus a common format has been for a biographer to rehearse the ideas of their chosen writer or academic. A refreshing difference occurs when a figure has produced an autobiography, a vehicle far more likely to carry detail of the historical experience which produced the ideas than usually appear when the account is the work of another.

It is to describe this concern with experience and the circumstance of peoples' lives that I use the term contextual history. In practice what is meant by the expression is demonstrated throughout by my movement back and forth between the global and the local. However, there exists a theoretical dimension to its use, where political biography requires an approach which sets out the tensions, even dialectics, caught up in the word experience. At one level exists the pressures and limits shaping the circumstance in which political action takes place. However, the terms also denotes the taking into consciousness of that circumstance and therefore the creation of a response which will in turn affect the context within which further political action occurs. A contextual history provides for the continuing circumstance of political action, while a collective political bibliography enables us to see how that context was further shaped by the characters in the book.

There are, however, important exceptions where a biography of a significant thinker has also served to carry an account of the circumstance of those ideas. One example, signified by the writer's choice of title, is Dona Torr's *Tom Mann and his times* published in 1956 which is still worth revisiting forty years after its publication. One year previously, Edward Thompson published his *William Morris*—1955 was also, incidentally, the year before he left the Communist Party. The subtitle *Romantic to Revolutionary* indicates the direction of the book, though the differences between the first and second editions mark shifts in that path. However, the same structure is retained, and it is one which integrates the ideas and actions, most particularly in part four, 'Necessity and Desire'. The earlier parts tend to lead on from 'Romantic' through 'Conflict' to revolutionary,

Morris's ideas being conveyed through each of these in the varied forms of poetry, decorative arts, and finally political tract. In the 1976 postscript, Thompson argues that Morris did not change from Romantic to Marxist but rather reformulated each to create a rupture and a new unity. Indeed 'Necessity and Desire' may be understood as something like a dialectical synthesis in which the earlier forms of thought appear reformed through political engagement, intellectual and practical. It is thereby an unusual biography, not narrow in the usual sense of an intellectual biography yet still giving great space to the subject's ideas, while itself weaving a theoretical web of its own by which that unity of circumstance, life and ideas are joined together.

There exists also the more usual explorations of one or other of the main figures in *History in the Making*, which require brief mention here. Among these are some books of variable quality on Edward Thompson. The first, Bryan Palmer's *The Making of E. P. Thompson*, relies entirely on published material and is intended for a Canadian audience with no immediate experience of Thompson, the person. The second, *E. P. Thompson Critical Perspectives* edited by Harvey Kaye and Keith McClelland, stays close to the ideas on the page, failing even to discuss why the themes of working-class history, humanism, peace, or the Marxist concept of base and superstructure were important for Thompson. Since Edward Thompson's death, Bryan Palmer has returned to his subject. Not a biography, *E. P. Thompson Objections and Oppositions* yet seeks, Palmer writes in the preface, to 'locate Thompson historically'. To do this, Palmer traces Thompson's family back through missionary work and India, before turning to two of the main thrusts of Thompson's energy—peace and internationalism. The net result it is a considerable advance on what has gone before.

The case of Raymond Williams, around whom as I have said, the story is woven, has called forth a growing body of writing on his work and ideas. They can be split into three sorts: the edited collections of Williams's own writings, the collections of essays by others, and the book-length discussion by one or two writers of some part or parts of Williams's writings. The quality, while varied, is generally good and those which include extracts and comment pertaining to the early years particularly deserve wider notice. The coverage of Williams's teaching as well as writing and politics, in the 1940s in *Border Country* edited by John McIlroy and Sallie Westwood, is the best example to date.

The history and the manner in which this went to making the life that was Raymond Williams is now becoming available. Fred Inglis' *Raymond Williams* is the first biography and as such should be welcomed. The detail to be found there no doubt owes much to the numerous interviews which apparently went to make up the material for the book. Unfortunately, for reasons that are hard to be sure of, Inglis indulges in two tendencies which seriously detract from the work. The first is a pretence to have an intimate knowledge of Williams's personal life which is completely untrue, and secondly, an inability to refrain from petty put-downs of Williams which actually say more about the writer than his subject—points cogently made by Raphael Samuel in his review of the work, which he wrote only months before his own death in 1996. We still await from Dai Smith what, given previous examples of his writings on Williams, we might expect to be a more authoritative work.

Departing from a single person format towards collective biography there are two works, the relevance of which to the present study both in subject matter and form is obvious. Gary Werskey's *A Visible College* published in 1988 is a collective biography of a number of socialist and communist scientists, and in its form and the politics of its subjects, is the nearest of any to the present work.

In Werskey's own words,

> The book takes the form of 'collective biography' on the grounds that 'no significant social phenomenon can be understood apart from the motives and aspirations of the persons who shape it.' (ibid. XX).

The sentiment is one shared by the second work, Molly Andrews's *Lifetimes of Commitment*. In contrast to Werskey, Andrews's subject matter was a selected group of interviewees, published sources serving to provide background rather than primary material for the study. In terms of age, both Werskey and Andrews are dealing with earlier figures than the present work. Werskey's five scientists were born between 1889 and 1901, while of Andrews's fifteen respondents, all but one were born between 1899 and the First World War. Thus the figures in both studies tend to have been formed in an earlier period to those in the present work, though in every case they were politically active during the inter-war years.

Andrews includes many of the same themes as the present work; the turmoil of the inter-war period, the radicalizing of young people by the events of the time, the development of political convictions and the self-identity of socialist. However, because of the underlying approach of Andrews's work, the interview is used as the primary source of information. The point is illustrative of the main difference between the two works. The present is firmly a cultural history for which original published sources are the main reference, interviews being a means of providing confirmation and validity to the printed word. Andrews by contrast is writing as a psychologist, specializing in political psychology. The interview is essential in her work as not merely a means for information but as part of a psychological examination.

Like Andrews, Werskey gives considerable space to interviews with his subjects. However, his approach is more firmly set in the historical and sociological, published works are a central source for discussion, and the conditions of the different periods he covers given greater weight. One contrast with Andrews is Werskey's greater concern with his subjects' professional lives. His own background includes scientific training, equipping him with understanding of the five scientists' general concerns. Of course, the fact that Werskey's subjects are scientists makes *The Visible College* a very rare work, the overwhelming majority of studies of socialists intellectuals of this century having concentrated on figures from the arts' side of the cultural divide. It might, for instance, have been interesting if Andrews had selected one or more socialist psychologists among her case studies. As it is the professional or occupational part of her respondents' lives gains little attention.

By contrast, occupation or profession does play a part in the present work, where adult education is taken to be an expression for commitment and belief and a ground upon which more overtly political movements took their lead. From the first, champions for adult education recognized that their demands could not be forwarded or indeed met solely in terms of educational provision for adults or even the public policy necessary to make this possible. Rather, the demands were couched in terms of the wider structures thought to characterize present society. In this manner, social class could not but be a prism through which unequal distribution of power and wealth were understood. In like manner were relations between bosses and workers understood, and thus the interests of adult education to be on one side and against the other. It is perhaps this issue of adult education and its identification as part of a social movement for change that readily distinguishes the present work from most of those mentioned so far. However, there is another work for which adult education is a centre around which the book is organized. Tom Steele's *The Emergence of Cultural Studies 1945–1960: Cultural Politics, Adult Education and the English Question* is a historical correction to the popular belief that cultural studies started in the university during the 1960s. In this he is taking his lead from Raymond Williams. Williams was speaking at a celebration for an Oxford Extra-Mural colleague when, in coming to the question of cultural studies, he continues,

> … if I may tell this as a story—when I moved into internal University Teaching, when at about the same time Richard Hoggart did the same, we started teaching in ways that had been absolutely familiar in Extra-Mural and WEA class, relating history to art and literature, including contemporary culture, and suddenly so strange was this to the Universities that they said 'My God, here is a new subject called Cultural Studies'. Don't believe a word of it (Williams 1989a 162).

Steele's book fills out why the claim that cultural studies started in the lecture hall should not be believed.

History in the Making is supportive of Tom Steele's thesis. Yet, as the start of this section suggested, the book draws on other themes, which make it more firmly a history and a story. How that is set out in the following chapters, is summarized in a short final section.

4. History in the Making: An Outline

This short last section is intended to provide a summary of the subsequent chapters, drawing out the links between them and thus connections which hold the whole work together. Chapter two moves from the general circumstance of the thirties to the specific experience of several of the main protagonists. Spain takes centre place in the first section, as the moral symbol which initially fired these figures. From there the focus narrows as we turn to university and primarily Cambridge, for reasons I have already explained.

The third chapter takes the story forward through the war, the return to Cambridge, particularly of Williams, and the working holiday in Yugoslavia where several figures were involved in building a railway. The contradictory effects of this experience and that country's subsequent expulsion from the Soviet bloc, made her a continuing problem for communists in the after war years. To emphasize this contradiction, chapter three includes discussion of a very different figure, Basil Davidson, who served as a member of the Special Operations Executive in Yugoslavia, and whose account of that experience highlights why the Partisans served to symbolize the hopes and aspirations of several of the lead characters during these years.

Chapter four forms the central spine of the whole work. In it I deal not only with Williams's years in adult education but with his departure from the Communist Party's thinking on culture. *Politics and Letters*, a short lived periodical which Williams co-edited in 1947–48, serves as the vehicle for that break from Party thinking. The subsequent sections go forward from then, tracing Williams's thinking through of post-war culture in the shadow of Eliot, *Scrutiny*, the Leavises, etc., ending with his departure from adult education and turning inwards to the university. On the way I make the point that the retrospective interpretation of Williams as a part of a post-1956 New Left, crucially misses the reality that the thinking through of culture had been carried on for the previous ten years, not within a university but through the adult education class.

Chapter five offers an examination of the Communist Party. There is discussion of the developing circumstance within the Party from the end of the Second World War and through the decade of the cold war, but the greater part of the chapter is devoted to discussing the culture and character of the Party. Where chapter four is looking at an emerging understanding of new cultural patterns, chapter five is concerned with how a culture of secular puritanism with all its attributes of voluntarism and commitment, continued to find expression in this unique political formation.

The remaining three chapters of the story form a unity. Chapter six focuses on an initial critique which found voice in the manner of a dissident communist paper, *The Reasoner*. The three issues are studied as political interventions, contributors responding to other statements which appeared in official organs of the party. Appearing between April and November 1956, *The Reasoner* bears the marks of anguish, frustration and eventual rejection as a party to which lives had been devoted forsook all pretence at moral principle, not just for base political expediency, but because of an inability to understand what was happening around it.

Chapter seven turns south from Hungary to Suez. More exactly, we turn from a protest at resistance to change, toward protest at an attempt to reverse change. Yet the protest against Suez was equally inspired by the revelation of the new power relations which forced the British and French withdrawal. If the United States was the new dictator, then the role of a declining imperial power, was in part the question which inspired, the Campaign for Nuclear Disarmament (CND). In its answer, the campaign encapsulated both moral outrage and moral bewilderment. Yet CND provided a focus whereby people separated by circumstance not always of their own making, met up again to give voice to sentiments learnt twenty years earlier when, behind a flag of 'non-intervention', another British government was also viewed to have shunned moral integrity.

Finally, in chapter eight, the link forward from Williams and *Politics and Letters* is rejoined. *University and Left Review* coincides with the supposed moment of Williams's entry on to a public stage. Yet before discussion of the magazine I review the Socialist Society at Oxford and argue that other links may be discerned. The Socialist Society revolved around the Coles, and I argue that much of what came to be called the New Left took its lead from an earlier guild socialism, and the narrow stream which flowed forwards in opposition to the competing left currents advocating centralized state control. A means for continuance of that alternative socialism was the voluntary adult education class, which in turn provided the constituency of New Left clubs. Yet clearly in other respects the expression had changed. The magazine format of *ULR* and its use of pictures were just one indication of what in the *Uses of Literacy* Richard Hoggart called 'unbending springs'.

In the concluding chapter I review the pressures and limits which sculpted the formation traced in *History in the Making*. My final point is necessarily speculative and dependent on the interpretation drawn from the preceding chapters. My contention is that this generation which matured in the inter-war years came out of a tradition of moral socialism formed during the nineteenth century. I have tried to capture the characteristics of that ethos through the terms; secular puritanism, voluntarism, commitment, etc.; vehicles through which it found expression included adult education, the Communist Party, the people's front and CND. My tentative conclusion is that the moral socialism upon which these bodies depended has been unable to reproduce itself through the changing world of the second half of the twentieth century.

chapter two

FORMATIVE EXPERIENCES

1. THE INTER-WAR YEARS

The left activists who entered into politics and education in the years preceding and following the Second World War have, at the end of the century, come to be recognized as a remarkable generation. Bryan Palmer's *E. P. Thompson Objections and Oppositions*, Harvey Kaye's *The British Marxist Historians* and *The Education of Desire* and the Terry Eagleton-edited collection *Raymond Williams Critical Perspectives*—among several others it must be said—have been of considerable value in exploring their ideas as these have been recorded on paper. However, less has been done by way of investigating the contexts within which those ideas came into being. Arguably for these contexts to be given due weight, a different approach is needed whereby the recorded ideas are viewed as responses to experiences. It is such an approach that I have referred to in chapter one, as a contextual history. As I suggested, where such an approach has been attempted, as in John McIlroy and Sally Westwood's *Border Country* or Tom Steele's *The Emergence of Cultural Studies*, the results have been very worthwhile. While a contextual approach is followed throughout the book, this second chapter in particular follows this method with a discussion of the inter-war world in which the figures on which this work focuses were maturing.

The formation of this generation of socialist intellectuals reaches back to combined events of the First World War and the October Russian revolution. Circumscribed by the pressures of class and culture arising from these events, they matured into the inter-war generation and all that this phrase entailed. Two interwoven conditions seem to have been important in their formation. While evidence is scant, suggestion has been made that the First World War itself had something of a radicalizing effect on many participants. The effect of the war may in turn have contributed to the second condition, that of the decline not just of the Liberal Party but of Liberalism as an expression of progressive social and political thought. Together with the enhanced strength of the trade union movement, itself an effect of the war, these two conditions created a viable alternative to the left. While the Labour Party was the principal beneficiary, forming its first government in 1923, there was also made possible a space for intellectual thinking of alternatives to that of the progressive reformism that had attracted radicals hitherto, and it is to tracing out the effects of these earlier upheavals in another generation that this second chapter is devoted. Divided into two sections, the first addresses the pressures and limits which shaped the lives of those growing up between the wars. The second section examines these events in the lives of a small number of figures, as they passed through university, before graduating into political turmoil and war.

It has become part of the mythology of the First World War to blame it for having disposed of the flower of England. The citation is, of course, class as well as gender specific. It was not to all men that the phrase refers, but to that class for whom the economic inheritance of Edwardian England was to underpin a future cultural power. One consequence of the destruction of so many of that privileged elite was the space created for a different class of students to make at least a tentative entry into the academy. The development was part of a larger process, undermining the certainties of the pre-1914 world. Notably effective in the changing relations of class, inter-war society witnessed the decline of the certainty of obedience and of the exercise of overt domination. The decline in the numbers employed in domestic service may serve as one indicator of such changes. Among the university population it is likely that the major changes of class occurred at some of the newer provincial universities such as Sheffield, Bristol, Leeds, Liverpool and Birmingham. Even so, by the nineteen-thirties the opportunity for the son, and—as Dorothy Thompson describes in her autobiographical 'Introduction' to *Outsiders*—even the daughter, of the lower-middle class to partake of Oxbridge air had moved beyond possibility to become reality.

The point is not without significance for our group of young future radicals. The paucity of left academics before 1936 was more than a little apparent. Of communists there were fewer still. In 1931 Cambridge had but two members of the Communist Party, the molecular biologist J. D. Bernal and the economist Maurice Dobb. Before the mid-nineteen-thirties progression from university to inside the party typified what few intellectual communists there were, and made Dobb and Bernal's decision to continue an academic career almost unique.

From 1936 circumstances began to change considerably. One of the earliest and most pronounced expressions of interest in socialism was on the part of scientists. In *The Good Old Cause* Willie Thompson suggests that the motivation may have come from within their intellectual activity. It would seem to be something of this kind which Gary Werskey rather annoyingly refers to as 'Bernalism'. The term derives from the name of one of the figures in Werskey's *Visible College*, J. D. Bernal. The other four principal characters in Werskey's excellent study are the geneticist, J. B. S. Haldane; Lancelot Hogben, the biologist; the biochemist, Joseph Needham and Hyman Levy, the physicist. The apparent bias, of socialist scientists in favour of the life sciences, is lessened if we spread the net wider. Of the two leading centres of left scientists one was the Dunn Biochemical Institute, but the other was Cavendish Laboratory for Experimental

Physics. If the inspiration toward socialism did come from within scientists' intellectual activity, then any weighting between the different sciences may reflect both its receptiveness to materialist understanding and whether the present state of the science was one of relative stability or experiencing a Kuhnian style revolution. In short, Werskey's argument is that science and socialism were viewed as inherently related, since between them, they have the capacity to meet human need, and presumably answer it. What was being practiced in the Soviet Union seemed to epitomize just such an association; official communism presenting itself as the scientific implementation of socialism.

Left-wing scientists were also driven by the sense that science had a duty toward moral responsibility. The Cambridge Scientists' Anti-War Group which came into existence from 1939, was not merely a late flowering of pacifist tendencies, but made practical contributions to issues such as air raid protection which were shortly to prove so essential. Long before this, the attempts to resurrect the Association of Scientific Workers, and the formation of the Socialist Medical Association, a forerunner to the wider aid for Spain campaigns, were already demonstrating the much felt need to bring science into line with the perceived humanist responsibilities that would characterize a future socialist society. Creation of this future was a utopia that could be realized through practical action that was also rational and scientific. This certainty was one part of the stimulus to growth of socialist sympathies at Cambridge and Oxford, for which the scientists were innovative in providing much of the earliest stimulus. The existence of the Dunn Institute and Cavendish Laboratory was perhaps one reason why, by the end of the nineteen-thirties, Cambridge should witness the creation of a generation of intellectual socialists.

By the end of the thirties, the worst of the unemployment of the inter-war years had declined. While the poverty consequent of enforced long term idleness was still very real for many regions, its effectiveness for political mobilization had receded. In the early thirties, unemployment had inspired a few of the professional classes to adopt left-wing political views and identify themselves with the working classes. From 1936 the heightening international tension altered the emphasis, creating a space for a professional class response in its own right. Schematically, the conditions pressing forward these changes may be set out thus: the declaration of the liberal Spanish Republic in 1931, the Italian invasion of Abyssinia in 1935 and the brutal assault of fascists and royalists on Spain in 1936, made for an altered world. Added to this was the bipartisan 'non intervention' policy towards Spain of Conservative and Labour. Michael Foot recalls how the fighting was presented to a Labour conference in 1936:

The two Spanish delegates had arrived and were at last allowed to speak.'We do not ask your country to change its policy. We do not

25

want to mix in your affairs. But we are fighting with sticks and knives against tanks and aircraft and guns and it revolts the consciousness of the world that that should be true. We must have arms. Help us to buy them somewhere in the world.' Then came Senora Isabel de Palencia, a proud Amazon straight from the Spanish battlefields, ... No one who heard that speech will ever be likely to forget it; it was a marvel of calculated passion (Foot 1966 200).

Foot, though, was at odds with the leadership of the party and the unions and consequently with the majority of delegates, who as in all matters, followed the leadership. The Labour Party never gave more than tokenistic support for the Republic. By contrast the bipartisan non-intervention policy inspired a vigorous campaign of communists and smaller left groups. To this must be added the drives for unity on the left, epitomized in the intellectual appeal of the Left Book Club (LBC). The combined effect was to shift the tone of intellectual life in the closing years of the decade as war became more imminent, fascism more powerful, and the Soviet Union apparently the lone European power prepared to offer a fighting resistance. Interestingly, beyond Europe the Spanish government received aid from Mexico, itself having enjoyed something of a successful revolution some twenty years earlier.

Characteristically, Edward Thompson has caught the pressures of the time in a tone that, while not denying faults, nevertheless throws down a gauntlet to the numerous accusers and detractors that have since passed verdict on the 'red decade'.

It is true that specious apologists and romantic attitudes were to be found among the Left intelligentsia in the thirties. Orwell succeeds in pinpointing those which most irritated him. What he does not do is suggest that any other, more honourable, motivations might have coexisted with the trivia. And in this he falsifies the record. Nor does he tell us anything of the actual choices with which intellectuals of his generation were faced within an objective context of European crisis. Popular Front, Left Book Club and the rest are seen not as a political response within a definite context, but as the projection of neuroses and petty motives of a section of the English middle class (Thompson 1960 163–4).

The link between anti-war and anti-fascist tendencies in the thirties is a difficult one to trace. In part reflecting a change of opinion over time, in part a distinction between moral and political persuasions, the relation between the two was far from static. We can gain some indication of the intrusion of war, or fear of war both from the activities of scientists and from writings of the time. On the practical side, Haldane undertook a study of the effects of air raids during the Spanish war, while also arranging ambulance aid to the republicans. In the popular front publication *Modern*

Quarterly, Lancelot Hogben published 'The modern challenge to freedom of thought'. Published in the October 1938 issue, Hogben ended with an optimistic view of a future of plenty, to the service of which must be brought scientific reason.'This must be the positive minimum of a united front to meet the challenge of Fascism'.

Always *ad hoc* in practice, institutional anti-fascist activities centred on three political parties, the Communist, the Independent Labour Party and the small Socialist Party. Yet many more people attended marches and rallies than took out membership of any party. Reasons for taking the extra step of joining any of these political groupings are of course varied, but the political divisions of the time were a contributory factor. If a very broad sweep of all those who might identify themselves as against fascism, which critically excluded a number of the Conservative Party, were brought to view, the deep divisions would be all too apparent. Arguments about fault for the undermining of any broad left in the thirties have given rise to much writing since.

Opinions range from Ben Pimlott's 1977 book *Labour and the Left in the 1930s*, in which the left were a problem to the advance of any feasible Labour movement, to the more balanced discussion in Mervyn Jones 1987 work *Chances*, where the restrictions within which the opposition to fascism and the national government had to operate are presented; to the extreme attacks on the Labour leadership from within some of the smaller parties, such as that mounted by William Rust in his *The Story of the Daily Worker*, published in 1949. In the sectarian view of Rust the Labour leadership is depicted as remaining firmly wedded to a policy of minimal activity beyond that of parliamentary debate. Trade union action was considered to be only that permitted by a leadership which cared more for crushing any militancy than pursuing the political themes with which unions had been associated before 1926. The style of Labour-union relationship represented by the figures of Arthur Henderson, Walter Citrine, Ernest Bevin, Hugh Dalton and Herbert Morrison, was viewed as one where the primary concern was to create a sufficient degree of respectability behind which to defend the status quo of a centralized and bureaucratic labour movement. Yet if this portrayal is extreme, it is not so different from that in Michael Foot's biography *Aneurin Bevan* in which the Labour leadership sought during annual conferences to prevent any deviation from its own line.

The non-party political groupings were, though, more important in invigorating a new generation of post-war socialists than perhaps the constitutional parties themselves. Together they formed a complex of vehicles through which a generation of socialists could hear and find voice. Recurring time and again in people's memories of their early political action was the presence not only of political parties but of a range of political clubs, societies and circles. Publishing ventures either founded on some such grouping or the progeny of a few unusual talents, were many and varied. *Tribune* was an example of a child of a few talented and resourceful figures. Founded after what Betty Vernon, in her biography of *Ellen Wilkinson*, the post-war Labour Minister of Education, called the 'disastrous Labour Party Conference of 1936', the paper's greatest importance was perhaps less the pulling together of those who wrote and edited the paper, than providing a symbol which could inspire people through the defeats which mounted up before the change of circumstance brought on by the turnabout in the war from 1941. However, this was but one of a number and Margot Heinemann lists a wide range of groupings, each in different ways responses to the felt need to create not merely political unity in the form of agreements between leaders, but rather a popular participatory unity from below. Scientists, artists, writers, musicians and historians are cited by Heinemann as just some of those making up the groups that developed from the middle of the decade.

Active and influential from this time was the Cambridge scientists anti-war group. In 1936 the group was already eighty strong. For members then, opposition to the war rather than fascism formed the key focus. In the late-nineteen-thirties the *Modern Quarterly* served as an important outlet for the work of a number of scientists. Published jointly by the Left Book Club and Lawrence and Wishart between 1938 and 1939, the *Modern Quarterly* was attacked on the one side by *Nature* for its attempts to impose Marxism and Russia as a dogma, and on the other for failing to apply Marxist insights to science. A brief review of its editorial board and contributors disproves the former claim, while the latter was merely the necessary criticism that *Labour Monthly* felt duty bound to make. The status of the *Modern Quarterly* is not difficult to establish. Editors included some members of the Communist Party it is true, but they were never in a majority and all could be said to have held their position on intellectual rather than political grounds. Of the various figures notable in Werskey's study, Haldane, Levy, Bernal and Needham were all on the editorial council. Of these Haldane and Bernal made up two of the five council members who were Fellows of the Royal Society.

A brief review of the journal between the first issue in January 1938 and April 1939 reveals a diversity of articles, some more closely connected with the writers professional area, others responding to perceived political or military threat of the period. Haldane's contribution in April 1939 fell within the first category; his own area of science, genetics. Hyman Levy's 'A chapter in modern scientific history' contained an overview and critique of the marginalization of science and consequent failure to fully harness the potential contribution of scientific workers. The fault was apparently the fetters placed on scientific experiment by capitalistic social relations. The apocalyptic style used by Levy reflects the widely held view of fascism marking the last stage of capitalism and its imminent decline. By contrast, the already noted article by Hogben on challenges to freedom of thought sets its focus on the growing threat of fascism, which it places alongside the church as the suppressor of free expression. The response of scientific application and the growing menace across Europe, is given a more practical focus in an article by F. W. Meredith, a Principal Scientific Officer in the Air Ministry, in an article entitled 'Aerial Warfare'. The article stands out amongst the *Modern Quarterly's* usual diet of Greek Tragedy and Soil Erosion, reflecting not only the actuality of war by 1938, but the very real fear of the effects of bombing. The more alarmist pronouncements predicted entire cities being reduced to rubble and populations wiped out within the first days of bombardment.

Alongside the scientific critique of *Modern Quarterly*, stood the literary criticism of *Left Review*, one of the best known examples of popular front practice. It was put together primarily by writers as a left cultural intervention which, while close to the CPGB, was never under its control. That some connected with *Left Review* belonged to a section of the communist-inspired Writers International, did not prohibit the magazine from carrying a wide diversity of views connected by little more than the then felt 'threat to letters from Fascism and crisis of capitalism' (Clarke et al 1979 67). *Penguin New Writing* had appeared in 1936 thus coinciding with the eruption of Spain into public consciousness. Providing a live means for the transmission of an anti-fascist message, Unity Theatre was able to call on the services of a wider and more professional support than had the earlier, and perhaps more radical, local theatre groups.

Overshadowing yet unifying these efforts, the Left Book Club began from the middle of the decade to provide not just regular publications, but more importantly a network of socialists groups. Based on a small central London office, the club spread information of members and activities through the pages of *The Left Book News*. The first issue was in May 1936, adopting a format of an editorial by Gollancz, 'Topic of the Month' by John Strachey, followed shortly by regular news of local groups by John Lewis. Renamed *The Left News* in December 1936, the monthly paper was made available free to club members and at a charge for non-members. Unfortunately, while regular figures are given for the extraordinary growth of club members, no figures appear for total circulation of the monthly paper. At its height, the club reached seven hundred and thirty local groups with fifty-eight thousand members. Describing this phenomena Pimlott continues,

> The growth of the Club was partly spontaneous, partly a consequence of imaginative organization. From the start, giant rallies were held in large halls all over the country. In attendance and in drama, the Club's biggest meetings outdid anything organized by the Labour Party. People came to a club rally as to a revivalist meeting, to hear the best orators of the far left—Laski, Strachey, Pollitt, Gallacher, Ellen Wilkinson, Pritt, Bevan, Strauss, Cripps, plus the occasional non-socialist, such as the

Liberal, Richard Acland, to provide Popular Front balance (ibid. 156).

Trade union leadership was deeply hostile to any such left grouping. The reasons seem to be a mixture of political substance and form. Certainly the Left Book Club took stands on substantive issues that were considerably more radical than the Trades Union Congress. But the greater source of antagonism was over the form of the club's political activities. Freed from the hindrance of bureaucratic procedures, the Left Book Club required minimal organization beyond that of publishing. Campaigns such as medical aid for Spain relied on voluntary will, while the meetings of local clubs arose from the desire of people to engage in intellectual politics. An active social dimension which included walking, sports and recreations was a further considerable incentive. Members were given notice of activities in their own and other areas together with names of contacts, as part of John Lewis's regular round-up of local club activities in *Left News*.

The organization of the clubs and the campaigns was under the control of Betty Ried and John Lewis. The general pattern was for interested individuals to contact the groups department, who in return would make available propaganda material and the support of guest speakers. Judging from the notices in *Left News* and remarks about regular meetings in local areas, the club was beginning to achieve the semblance of a popular movement. Immediate problems of political campaigning though were never the primary function of the club. Rather,

> The aim of the club, like that of the men of the Enlightenment in the age of Reason, who created the movement of political reform which culminated in the American War of Independence of 1776 and the French Revolution of 1789, was 'by speech and pen to make men enlightened' (Lewis 1970 13).

In line with this aim, the function of the local clubs as reading groups was probably the element of the LBC which left the greater impact for future years. Lewis recalls how, like himself, members of the many reading groups continued their educational activities in the armed forces. Lewis was appointed a Staff Lecturer with the Army Bureau of Current Affairs:

> ... my equipment for the job largely consisted of books issued by the club. I found that keen Education Officers were often former Left Book Club members ... (Lewis 1970 124).

Potential examples of Lewis's education officers might include the then communist and later Oxford Extra-Mural Delegacy Staff Tutor, Tony McLean; the communist and historian, Eric Hobsbawm; and the socialist and historian, J. F. C. Harrison.

The extent to which LBC books served as educational material in the armed forces is unlikely to ever be ascertained. However, the recording here does offer support for the general contention, not only that the club was central to the radicalizing of the forties, but also that the generation on which this book focuses took from the voluntary activities of the thirties the inspiration to advance political education into the forties and beyond.

Attention was called not only to the immediate dangers of war, but also to the alternative means by which society in the future might be organized. Scientists, writers and poets' groups all contributed to a constant flow of information and argument, ranging from developments on the Soviet Union to personal accounts of unemployment. The link into the war and post-war circumstances was supplied, though not only by the many books. As important was the membership of such figures as Richard Acland, the leader of the Common Wealth Party during the war years, and Canon Collins who still later served as one of the central figures in the formation of CND. Given the manner of its influences we cannot measure the club's effects, though it can safely be assumed that its existence was a positive inspiration.

We are faced here with one instance of a more general problem with regard to the influence of the radicalizing years of the nineteen-thirties and the later post-war advances. The Left Book Club was not the only thread by which that influence was carried forward, nor were its effects confined to the communists or any one other single grouping. Running in tandem, if not always in complete political agreement, was Kingsley Martin's *New Statesman*. Serving as the most influential left weekly, the *New Statesman* provided a rare place where diverse opinions could be forwarded and left policy, if policy be the right word, could be worked up. Certainly the *New Statesman*, with its editor Kingsley Martin, was of the most important links between the anti-fascism of the thirties and the creation of CND twenty years later.

Where the *New Statesman* editorial line could be located was not always clear, though reasons for this were more bound up with the dilemmas of the pre-war years than any incapacity of the paper itself. By way of illustration we can turn to a case of considerable present relevance: the war in Spain. On getting—

> ... out of Spain in 1937, [Orwell] telegraphed from France to Kingsley Martin and sold him an article about the course of the civil war (Rolph 1973 226).

The *New Statesman* refused to publish the piece, as it did a review which it had asked Orwell to write by way of replacement. The whole incident was in effect a rehearsal for Gollancz's refusal to accept *Homage to Catalonia* some months later. In both cases the refusal was based not on a blind belief that all was well with the Government forces and that the fault lay entirely with Spanish or foreign anarchists and Trotskyites, but a felt need to maintain support for the Republic as a matter of principle. The *New Statesman* was the only large circulation weekly in Britain not supporting the fascists. Whatever the truth of Orwell's claims, to publicize them could

31

only further the already shrill accusations of the pro-fascist papers.

Alongside and associated with both the Left Book Club and the *New Statesman* were the Coles, and with them the important circles of the Society for Socialist Inquiry and Propaganda (SSIP) and the New Fabian Research Bureau (NFRB). The closeness of these with the LBC was represented through the figure of Victor Gollancz, who acted not only as the publisher for the club's books but served the same function with regard to the output of the NFRB. The link was made all the stronger by the fact that the first publication of the club in 1937, *The Condition of Britain*, was written by the Coles. Gollancz's own history had earlier included guild socialism, and in *My Dear Timothy* he recalls the meetings at which its advocates preached their conviction. The link with the *New Statesman* had been formed over a long period when G. D. H. Cole had acted as an assistant editor. The appointment of Kingsley Martin from outside the paper's staff, created for a while at least, no small amount of friction.

The place of the Coles in the creation of an intellectual left generation during the thirties and beyond cannot be over estimated. Apart from the formal associations like the SSIP and the NFRB there existed the equally important 'Cole Group' at Oxford. We shall have cause to return to what was probably the same thing in chapter seven, and Stuart Hall's recollection of his own political maturation in the Cole Seminar at Oxford twenty years later. Unfortunately for the present chapter, the lack of accounts of socialist university life between the wars prevents us from being sure about the membership of this grouping and whether it included such figures as Bill Moore, Christopher Hill or Rodney Hilton. Such evidence might help illuminate the extent to which a popular front really existed in universities from the mid-thirties.

In her biography of her husband, Margaret Cole expresses a belief that groups such as the SSIP and to a greater extent the NFRB and the Cole group did have a direct bearing on the formation of Labour thinking in the war and post-war period. The NFRB is probably the more obvious, since it was a research and policy formulating body, and we may compare its proposals with what in time came to appear as those of the Labour Party. But it was the voice beyond the confines of Transport House that was perhaps the more important in creating the possibilities for a radical left, and for this the services of Victor Gollancz were required. One insight into the partnership of Gollancz and the Coles is the fact that of all the writers published through the club, G. D. H. Cole, with six, had the highest number of books. His second, *The People's Front*, also published in 1937, was a follow-up to the earlier *Condition of Britain*.

The People's Front was a call to arms rather than merely an academic analysis. Dedicated to Stafford Cripps, a partner in the SSIP, the book outlines the principal features of international and home affairs, before offering a possible programme of action for how a war might be avoided and a socialist advance made. In such manner the book reflects what

Margaret Cole refers to as the 'essence of the efforts' then being made by the left (Cole 1971 209). To extend Cole's point, it would not be unreasonable to say that improving the conditions of the working classes after 1931 and confronting the menace from Europe, were not simply the focus of the left's efforts but the very impulses which created a left at this time.

Returning to the relations between the club and Congress House we can perhaps better appreciate the antagonism if we examine the interests of the two. For the leadership of the Labour Movement there existed a strong self-interest in a continuity of procedures into the future, and therefore a consistency of conditions. By contrast, the felt threat which inspired the existence of the Left Book Club was such that they wanted to eliminate the existing conditions, and to achieve this result as rapidly as possible. Beyond this was the crucial difference of the class identity of the majority of the respective memberships. This did not mean that affiliation to the LBC from among the organized working class was rare. But where it existed the presence of this active and largely young left alongside the more stable trade union way of life continued to create tensions. While there is no reason to suppose that there was not a minority of union members opposed to the apparent defensiveness of Bevin and Henderson, it did not mean that a shared set of concerns across the left was automatic. Recalling his early political formation Raymond Williams continues,

> The traditional politics of locality and the labour movement was seen as part of a boring, narrow world with which we were right out of sympathy. To us international action was much more involving and interesting. This was where the crucial issues were being decided. ... Older people went along with it but I think their sense was of benevolent association rather than of international solidarity (Williams 1979a 32).

The international situation referred to included by then the war in Abyssinia and the revolution in China. The Left Book Club again played an important part, bringing awareness of the latter to people with the 1937 publication of *Red Star Over China* by Edgar Snow. In this way the clubs brought together people and provided them with a depth of appreciation of events probably not available in any other popular publication of the time. The left book clubs were in effect the ideal mechanism through which sustained intellectual politics might have been possible. That they proved not to be was due to the force and speed with which those global events unfolded in the months between Munich and the German–Soviet pact.

It was in the context of this fear for the future that Spain would come to represent the battle between capitalism in its most regressive form and the new socialist social relations of the future. Spain provided an opportunity for 'real' political action, whether by going to Spain to fight, or collecting aid to provide support for the International Brigade and the

Spanish people. Spain had become a symbol for the left, denoting a moment when real sacrifice in the name of socialism was made. When the fascist enemy was confronted and when, against overwhelming odds and the indifference of the capitalist governments of the West, the Left fought to the bitter end. Foot's recollection conveys well that tension of excitement and fear:

> All eyes were on Spain. Would Madrid fall, as Badajoz, Talavera and Toledo had fallen to the Franco offensive? ... In the last week of October, six bombs had dropped in the centre of the city. Moorish troops were only a fourpenny tramride away. The great battle for Madrid had started. No one would have believed that it would still be in Republican hands three years later. The people of Spain and the first contingents of the International Brigade who marched into the beleaguered capital that October made it so (Foot 1975 237).

The imagery of Spain and the later imagery of the Second World War run into each other. Spain, Dunkirk, the Blitz, and the evacuations, all serve to create a complex memory to which perhaps few of us are entirely unattached still. The sound of the air raid siren produces an immediate mix of emotions which are hard to disentangle.

2. LEARNING TO BE RADICAL

I want in this second section to discuss inter-war university life and the entry into this by a number of future socialist intellectuals. The framework for this enquiry may be understood through the contours of class and culture. Few studies exist of socialists in Britain, fewer still of academically trained socialists. Those that do tend, like Kaye's, to concentrate on the intellectual ideas of the person(s) in question. One result of such an approach is for a work to read as something of a history of ideas. This approach has, of course, an important academic contribution to make, but nonetheless suffers from not being able to demonstrate the contextual basis for the ideas under discussion. As such we are somewhat limited in finding suitable precedents for any discussion of our subject matter. In chapter one I cited Tom Steele's *The Emergence of Cultural Studies*, Gary Werskey's *The Visible* College and Molly Andrews's *Lifetimes of Commitment* as three examples. However, here I wish to turn back nearly forty years to a much earlier work: Neal Wood's *Communism and British Intellectuals*, a product of considerable research.

Wood's research was ironically enough carried out between 1955–1957, precisely the moment when Communist parties were experiencing perhaps the severest crisis in their histories prior to 1990. How far that may have affected the outcome of the research can only be speculated on. Whatever the answer to this may be, we should note that Wood gives no indication of any affiliation to communism in any form and indeed opens his account with the comment that it,

> ... can at best be only an intimation never a revelation, for the 'ultimate explanation'of the appeal of communism is forever concealed from rational enquiry in the minds and hearts of many diverse individuals (Wood 1959 9).

Wood's book provides considerable details of the names and background of inter-war socialist intellectuals. In the process he makes the suggestion that a distinction be drawn between those at university in the nineteen-twenties and those studying a decade later. Where the former subsequently worked in the party, a majority of those from the thirties pursued academic careers. Indeed it is this latter trend which renders them eligible for consideration within the category of intellectual politics as opposed to work more directed by party requirements.

Yet even this attempt at creating some greater precision as to the lives of socialist intellectuals quickly fails. Cutting across a pattern of periods and chronology is that of the 'two cultures'. Just as in Snow's commentary there was a divergence of activity in the general lifestyles of figures in the arts and those in the sciences, so too there was a distinction between socialists. The core of Werskey's 'visible college' engaged in minimal political activity before entering university. Hyman Levy was a partial exception here, experiencing as a boy both the Zionism and socialism common among radical Jews of the time. Yet all of them were at university in the period before or during the First, not the Second, World War. While Bernal, Haldane and Levy were all to join the Communist Party, none left the world of academia to become party workers. There is, incidentally, some question as to the accuracy of Hobsbawm's claim that Dobb was the only Communist don at Cambridge in the nineteen-twenties. Werskey, while citing Dobb, attributes that distinction also to Bernal.

My real point though is the fact that these 'reds' stayed in academic work, and the radicalizing effect of their presence on the Dunn and the Cavendish may have had a greater impact on the subsequent generation of Arts' socialists than is often acknowledged. Indeed it is possible that while the remembered socialists of the period were from the Arts, any such generation may not have been possible without the prior leftwards shift of their elders or peers in the Sciences. The difficulty in seeing the exact formation of intellectual socialists in the early thirties may be just because of the continued wall separating the two cultures, and the marginalizing of the socialist scientists.

The culture of university life before 1940 was firmly upper-middle class, as it had increasingly been since the middle of the previous century. As such, entry for persons from 'outside' was a process of negotiation. Before the First World War such a person breaking into the ancient citadel could find her or himself contributing to those later changes, which prior to 1914 remained a structure of feeling:

That society consisted of the upper levels of the professional middle class and county families, interpenetrated to a certain extent by the aristocracy. ...

I was an outsider to this class; because, although I and my father before me belong to the professional middle class, we had only recently struggled up into it from the stratum of Jewish shopkeepers. ...

Socially they assumed things unconsciously which I could never assume either unconsciously or consciously. They lived in a peculiar atmosphere of influence, manners, respectability, and it was so natural to them that they were unaware of it as mammals are unaware of the air and fish of the water in which they lived (Leonard Woolf *Beginning Again* quoted in Williams 1980a 160).

This elite and self-referential culture was not confined to undergraduate days with the academy. Throughout Rolph's biography of Kingsley Martin the reader is invited to, as it were, peer into a small circle of figures for whom access to political and cultural influence was taken for granted. A brief look at the index of Rolph's biography of Kingsley Martin shows regular entries for Richie Calder, Virginia Woolf, the Coles, the Webbs, Keynes, Laski, Strachey and Leonard Woolf. The mantle of the Fabian Society stands over the collection and beside it the ancient citadels of Cambridge and Oxford.

Twenty years later the composition of Cambridge had shifted that bit further, though an outside still very definitely existed.

... over the first week I found out what is now obvious: that I was arriving more or less isolated, within what was generally the arrival of a whole formation, an age-group which already had behind it years of shared acquaintance, and shared training and expectations, from its boarding schools (Williams 1989a 5).

Williams's class background made him unusual even amongst the student left entering Cambridge in the later thirties and indeed since. There was though a greater distinction between this generation of socialists and the dominant character of the institutions than has sometimes been assumed. Given more space, Rodney Hilton might have provided rather more detail, but even so his recollections of pre-war Oxford remains extremely enlightening. Recalling his own position and that of fellow historian Christopher Hill he continues,

I suppose that, although younger than Christopher, I had had some experiences similar to his. Both of us were from the North (he from Yorkshire I from Lancashire) and neither was a product of those exclusive public schools whose pupils were very much in evidence at Oxford. The Communist Party group in Balliol in those days, as I remember it, had a social composition not at all like some writers' reconstruction of the Communist intelligentsia of the late thirties as coming characteristically from upper-middle-class backgrounds. Our members were predominantly from grammar schools and from lower-middle-class families, even with working-class ancestors one or two generations back (Hilton 1978 7).

It should be noted that Hilton's reference to some writers' reconstruction precisely fits that of Wood's, whose claim is the very reverse of Hilton's. For Wood, the socialist students of the thirties tended to come from more not less wealthy families than did those of the previous decade. Christopher Hill entered Balliol in 1931. As such he was considerably ahead of other future comrades. Yet there was, as it were, a convergence of experience; Hill's Marxism developed as did others from the conditions of the time. Between the time of Hill's first entry to Balliol and his re-entry in 1938 the pressures pushing many to the left had intensified. Yet perhaps more significant still was the response. In Kiernan's view those attracted to socialism were amongst the brightest of their generation at Cambridge. The reasons relate both to the intellectual power of Marxism and to the felt isolation of socialists from the class and culture of the old universities. We may perhaps gain an insight into a little of this from the biography of Christopher Hill. Between the two dates of Hill's entries to Oxford he had first become a Marxist, then in 1935 visited the Soviet Union for a year, before returning to take up a temporary post in Cardiff and at about the same time join the CPGB. There is a wonderful illustration of Raphael Samuel's discussion of Communist culture by Gwendolyn Whale, a colleague of Hill when he was at Cardiff:

> He was known to have left-wing ideas, but was careful not to upset anyone in the College. He lived in digs on a housing estate in north Cardiff with the Awberrys, a family closely connected with the Communist Party; but the extent of his commitment to communism was not common knowledge. He addressed meetings of the Left Book Club; and he devoted a lot of time to work for the Basque children who had come to Cardiff as refugees from the Spanish Civil War (Whale 1978 6).

Alongside Hill's sojourn from Oxford and engagement with first Marxism and then the Communist Party, can be placed the entry to universities elsewhere of Hobsbawm, Saville and Kiernan. Saville had entered the London School of Economics in 1934 and immediately joined the Communist Party. Victor Kiernan had gone up to Cambridge in 1934, while Eric Hobsbawm followed in 1936 and was from the outset an active party member. Thus, in each case they had, as Ralph Miliband put it in his 1979 tribute to John Saville, 'escaped the worst rigours of the Third period'. Many years later Eric Hobsbawm later celebrated his political allegiance to a people's front style of politics in an essay 'Fifty years of peoples' fronts'.

We can in similar manner follow several other future young Communists who entered university over the next few years. Edward Thompson and Raymond Williams both went up to Cambridge in 1939. Ralph Miliband and Dorothy Thompson entered university during the war itself in 1941 and 1942 respectively. The link between the two can be seen to be that much the greater if it is remembered that the LSE, to which Miliband went between 1941 and 1943, i.e., during his first period of study, was based at Cambridge. After the end of hostilities some of the figures, including Dorothy and Edward Thompson and Raymond Williams, returned to Cambridge, while yet others including Peter Worsley and Martin Eve went for the first time. Thus the formative intellectual experience of a whole part of a generation of communist and socialist intellectuals was set by the particular conditions of war which extended beyond the obvious military consequences to embrace the very ordering of personal lives. The contradictory political circumstances were caught by Dorothy Thompson when, in an interview with Sheila Rowbotham in 1993, she recalled how the fact that she was a communist had not been seen by her tutor to be a bar against her taking the secretaryship of Girton Labour Club. Despite this, there was obviously a problem and it remained difficult for Thompson to gain the post, reflecting the fact that even in the years of Britain's supposed war-time alliance with the Soviet Union, distrust could still prevent practical co-operation between Labour and Communist.

We can gain another indication of the circumstance of the later thirties if we turn back to the time when Hill first entered Balliol. Then, the decision to remain inside the academy and openly espouse communist views, was certainly not a comfortable position, should the option even arise. Referring to Maurice Dobb and Cambridge, Eric Hobsbawm writes:

> Its rebels were isolated, often even from each other. When the General Strike emptied the lecture-rooms, the young Marxist lecturer was left confronting a scattering of students who refused to go strike-breaking (Hobsbawm 1967 2).

By contrast Hilton's recollection of a few years later carries a rather different tone,

> In those days a Marxist intellectual could but not fail to be involved in politics and the almost inescapable choice in the late 1930s was the Communist Party (Hilton 1978 7).

In the first recollection the implication is that of having to defend a fragile position. The holding of certain principles and pursuing intellectual enquiry was, it seems, viewed as a contradiction. The tension arose less from an adoption of Marxism, which as a body of intellectual thought was little known, than the support for a class assumed completely at odds with those who accepted the cultural privilege of university as a right. In Hilton's recollection though a first striking difference is the identifying of a Marxist intellectual. The inference is not of having to defend but rather of political activity being a necessity almost regardless of the preference of the individual. That this activity should take place in the framework of the Communist Party again recalls the lack of an intellectually credible alternative. This dilemma had been in the making from early on in the nineteen-twenties. The demise of guild socialism as a coherent movement, the annexation of groupings like the Labour Research Department by the communists, had set the trend in motion. When the Independent Labour Party (ILP) ceased to constitute a significant force following its split in 1932, the absence of alternative groupings became acute. In these circumstances a people's front offered a genuine route for political commitment which did not necessitate joining any political party.

The importance of Cambridge as a source of intellectual recruits for the left in the later thirties, while not unique, was still considerable. Of a population in 1938 of some four thousand students, one thousand belonged to the Cambridge University Socialist Society. The occurrence of Cambridge among the figures cited here has been notably frequent. Within that there is a more specific identification of Trinity as one particular college with a left presence that included the historians Victor Kiernan and George Rudé, and the writer Raymond Williams. Kiernan and Williams each provide accounts of university life in this period. Taking Kiernan's commentary first:

> The Left Book Club launched by the publisher Gollancz, was in full swing. Progressive bookshops were sprouting up and down the country; one was started in Cambridge in the mid-thirties, surpassing sales of literature by the Socialist Club (Kiernan 1984 37).

Given that we are talking about, at that time, a very large socialist club, the presence of a successful Left bookshop as well, is all the more remarkable. The character of the Left in Cambridge existed, though not only in bookshops. For Raymond Williams and Eric Hobsbawm films afforded a popular form of cultural expression, and an important part in the life of the socialist club or the university more generally. The choice, in the club at least, was it seems far from that of more popular genres and included a number of continental European and Soviet producers. The point may not be without importance for later periods of their lives. Williams attempted to introduce film as a teaching course when working for the WEA after the war. At the same time he attempted, in collaboration with Michael Orram, to produce a film. The film was never made though a still interesting book was written by the two. Later still in the nineteen-fifties the Communist Party's anti-American strictures coincided with what seemed in the post-war decades a slightly puritanical view of leisure activities. The two together may not have been unconnected with the then triumph of Hollywood over the unsupported film industry in Britain.

We gain an insight into the role of the socialist club in how people organized their lives from a further quote from Raymond Williams,

> … there was a clubroom which served lunches. This became the effective centre of social life; much more so than the college (1989a 6).

We might safely assume that these recollections of the club are set at about the time that Williams collaborated with Eric Hobsbawm in producing a pamphlet for the Communist Party supporting the Soviet side in the conflict with Finland. A perhaps fictionalized account of this is pushed back some three years to 1936 in the opening sequence of the Cambridge act in his novel *Loyalties*. The writing of the pamphlet might well have taken place in the context of the groups into which left-wing students were separated. Williams and Hobsbawm were in the writers' groups. While the image of such groups as highly disciplined cultural cells might be tempting, the recollections of actual or potential members suggests a more spontaneous expression of energy in which academic skills were pressed into the service of immediate political ends. In a collection of interviews published under the title of *Visions of History*, Edward Thompson and Eric Hobsbawm recall the situation in a remarkably similar manner. For Thompson, being at Cambridge during and after the war was to have been present at a very important formative moment. But it is perhaps Eric Hobsbawm who pulls together many of the elements that other people have referred to:

> The university establishment was very hostile to Marxism in those days. Nevertheless, we were all Marxists as students in Cambridge and to some extent in Oxford, and, in fact, at university I would have thought most of us learned a good deal more talking to each other than we learned from all but one or two professors. And there were in fact attempts to co-ordinate the discussions of Marxist historians before the war, though I wasn't involved in them (MARHO 1983 30).

Hobsbawm had first gone to Kings' in 1936, so allowing for the poetic licence of 'we were all', he is clearly echoing the statistical one-in-four ratio of Socialist Society students in 1938. The reference to attempts to initiate an historians group similarly supports Williams's citing of the starting of various groups.

The type of commitment to a belief and a way of living to which the club, the films, the writing, etc., gave expression, was the subject of Raphael Samuel, when in 1980 he wrote of the culture of Marxist historians in Britain. One section of what became a number of *New Left Review* essays on the subject, headed 'Communist Party Protestantism', refers to the sense of marginalization felt by many in the Communist Party from a society increasingly dominated by commercial and instrumental tendencies. Yet the essay also carries the theme of the close link between a culture of puritanism and dedication to a cause carried forward from a religious upbringing into the demands of the party. There are several cases of just such a link, and I will turn to them in a moment. However, first I want to use the Samuel reference to get back to Victor Kiernan, and an important insight into the whole culture, of which the types of activities I have discussed as being characteristic of Cambridge socialism in the later thirties were a part. The passage is worth quoting in full:

> The main point I would like to make here is whether or not the sort of change that I and others were going through was an irreversible final stage in history, the world, or Western Europe, seemed to have reached the point where religion was decaying into something else. Was our political enthusiasm really a kind of liberation of energy from some kind of moral transmutation? If so has this reservoir dried up now that there is no doctrinal left? Therefore, is it possible to recapture the kind of socialist enthusiasm of an organized and disciplined form that we had in those days?

> I have a feeling this kind of process is not repeating itself, that the renewal of political life or social responsibility, or whatever it was, faded with religion, having lost one of its vital taproots. I am rather led to think that this feeling of ours, this approach, that we were committed to the party for life, was an inheritance from our religious background. Obviously, if you belong to a religion and take it seriously, then you are in it for life (Kiernan 1984 26).

There are many questions raised by Kiernan's extract which in turn give rise to problems of our understanding of history. On the one hand the way the connection is made up: political allegiance seeming to follow from previous religious experience. Certainly there are many cases where just such a connection can be readily drawn. Victor Kiernan himself was of a Congregationalist background, the historian Dona Torr's and Tony McLean's fathers were both Anglican ministers, Christopher Hill's and Edward Thompson's families were Methodists, John Saville another Anglican, Raymond Williams's family were split between Chapel and Church, Dorothy Thompson's family were on one side of Huguenot descent, the political theorist Ralph Miliband and Hyman Levy, Eric Hobsbawm and Raphael Samuel were of Jewish background and Lancelot Hogben, Plymouth Brethren.

However, there is also in Kiernan's comments, a suggestion of time, and therefore of context. Arguably it is these which compose the connection between religion and politics. Perhaps the taproot to which Victor Kiernan refers lies in a culture which created the generations between the mid-nineteenth century, if not earlier, and this inter-war generation. The terms or phrases to describe the culture are necessarily partial and even inaccurate. However, among them must lie the ethos of voluntary action, commitment, and a democratic sense of social change born of non-conformity.

They can only point to some part or parts of the whole culture, however, their expression was possible through religious or political practice. If something marked out this generation from those which have followed, then it must surely be the alteration and perhaps demise of this culture. It may not be possible to recreate the generation, the lives of which were depicted in the examples given above, and the reason for that is that the component parts of the culture from which they came no longer hang together in the same manner, and therefore cannot produce the same outcome. These issues are returned to in the final chapter. They appear here because we have been concerned in this chapter with the formation of the generation, and therefore the structure of feeling from which they were formed.

chapter three

WAR

1. INTERRUPTED STUDIES

The unity produced in opposition to the rise of fascism and the 'appeasement' given to it by the British Government in particular, was effectively broken by the signing of the Soviet–Nazi Pact. Previously the potential for a broad alliance beyond the control of the Labour leadership had seemed more possible than at any time since the creation of the Labour Party.

> On the 23rd August, [1939] however, the Russians took a step which staggered friend and foe alike. That day a non-aggression pact with Hitler's Germany was signed. It was not a mutual assistance pact or an 'alliance'. Under it, Germany and Russia undertook to refrain from attacks on one another and, if one of them were to 'become the object of warlike action on the part of a third Power' to refrain from supporting that third Power (Branson 1985 262).

Rightly, Branson stressed that it was not an alliance. Whatever alterations of view towards Nazism may have occurred in the Soviet Union, there was no lessening of anti-communism within Nazi Germany or elsewhere in Europe. In the event, the claim that the pact was, from the Soviet point of view, a matter of gaining safety, is perfectly reasonable. While views are likely to have varied, at least one must have been that, even if temporary, a non-aggression pact would give much needed time for preparations for war to be advanced. In reality, however, the Soviet Union's signature provided her with little material benefit. In contrast, Germany gained access to much needed raw materials, especially oil. Beneath this macro historical record, the non-aggression pact was politically little short of a disaster for the Soviet Union, alienating across the world those who had believed the Soviets to be the foremost anti-fascist state. In Britain, the political repercussions of the Soviet pact with Nazi Germany were uneven. On the one side there was an absolute split between those who remained loyal to the Soviet turnabout, and those,

> ... alienated allies whose friendship and trust had given the party an influence it would never have achieved on its own ... (Jones 1987 42).

The split was played out in the Left Book Club with disastrous consequences, and although there followed a period of popular support for the suffering Soviets later in the war, the club was unable to revive.

From a distance of over half a century it is difficult to appreciate fully the impact of such an agreement. The long, slow road to national self-determination of Communist parties meant that unconditional support for any and every act of the Soviet Union ended several years before the eventual demise of the respective national party. In 1939, acceptance of Moscow's infallibility was an ingrained feature of the party leadership. That similar sentiments were held widely on the left only makes the circumstance even more remote to the present day. Reasons for the attraction have been rehearsed before. My argument though is that it was less the Soviet Union itself creating hopes for the future, than the peculiar combination of conditions in Britain and desire for an organized alternative, that made the Communist Party, and beyond that the Soviet Union, attractive.

These varied political pressures were played out in the writings of numerous essayists and critics, who proffered their opinions through the pages of any number of the small periodicals circulating in the late-thirties. Few, however, caught the ambience better than George Orwell, and fewer still were as influential on the generation of inter-war students, as they defined their political identities in the years after 1945. Robert Hewison's *Under Siege* chronicles the war years from the perspective of literature and culture, and his account can also be of assistance here.

There is much distortion in Orwell's depiction of the war in Spain. In Orwell's account, fascists disappear quickly from the scene. Indeed they no longer seem to exist. The only presence remaining were communists whose only interest was in killing Trotskyites and anarchists. The most detailed account of fighting throughout *Homage to Catalonia* is that between the communists and an independent Marxist party, the POUM, in Barcelona. This distortion is repeated following Orwell's return to Britain, when the only figures of note are communists, one of whose aims was to prevent Orwell from publishing. There are again apparently not only no fascists but at times it seems no Conservative or even Labour Party in the later-nineteen-thirties. In response, of course, it may be fairly argued that he had suffered perhaps the most brutal assault on his beliefs. Orwell was never a theoretical Marxist. Instead he had taken the courageous step of visiting Spain, and assigned himself to one of the groups fighting on the republican side. This said, however, Orwell's whole image of the episode is more than a little distorted.

His anarchistic sympathies are apparent in his writings during the early years of the war. Rather than citing one or other of the organized sections of society as the means for carrying through what for him was a necessary revolution, he fell back on the idea of an essentially patriotic people, who would overthrow their leaders, rather than allow their country to fall into the threatening abyss. His view of socialist intellectuals on the other hand was distinctly negative. Few points made in criticism of what Orwell was apt to refer to as 'blimps' are as violent as those against these writers, critics and thinkers:

> The mentality of the English left-wing intelligentsia can be studied in half a dozen weekly and monthly papers. The most immediately striking thing about all these papers is their generally negative, querulous attitude, their complete lack at all times of any constructive suggestion. There is little in them except the irresponsible carping of people who have never been and never expect to be in a position of power. Another marked characteristic is the emotional shallowness of people who live in a world of ideas and have little contact with physical reality. ... And underlying this is the really important fact about the English intelligentsia—their severance from the common culture of the country (Orwell 1962a 85).

Certainly Orwell saw Churchill and Bevin as a new breed more capable than their predecessors of creating the conditions wherein the war could be fought more effectively and the peace produce real change. In that sense the Blimps were no longer in control to the same degree and therefore less in need of sweeping away. The intellectuals meanwhile had been drawn into society and rather than serving as a virtual 'fifth column' had contributed their talents to the war effort. The conduct of the war had changed. Rationing had brought a degree of equality, and production was geared more to need not profit. Yet for Orwell something has apparently been lost. In 1940–41 there existed a potential for change which found expression in the collection *The Lion and the Unicorn*. It was, it seems, when the threat of any supposed invasion was at its highest that Orwell finds the capacity for attack and call to arms. With the turning of the war by late 1943, Orwell seems to retreat into a resigned acceptance not only that the speed and extent of change might be slow, but even that the need may be less immediate. Britain could retain its place as a great nation without the extent of revolution previously imagined.

At the end of 'The English People' written in 1943–44 Orwell sets out a series of necessary steps for the English as a people and a nation. He concludes:

> If they can do that they can keep their feet in the post-war world, and if they can keep their feet they can give the example that millions of people have been waiting for. The world is sick of chaos and is sick of dictatorship. Of all the people the English are the likeliest to find the way of avoiding both. They have known for forty years, perhaps, something that the Germans and the Japanese have only recently learned, and that the Russians and the Americans have yet to learn: they know that it is not possible for any one nation to rule the earth. (Orwell 1970 3 55).

There were very varied views in the years immediately before and during the war itself and we cannot know how far Orwell was representative of a wider body of opinion. Certainly, his tendency to use the written word to constantly criticize and argue creates an appearance of a slightly eccentric figure. There is also the danger of putting present valuations on to an earlier time, thus the significance that has been placed on the very name 'Orwell' since his death may distort his presence while alive. Certainly, he did not speak for any group, party or sect, though that may partly have been due to his strongly individualistic character. However, he did perhaps stand for a certain bravery which rejected the brutalizing experience of an imperial middle-class upbringing and sought alignment with all those upon whom the privileges of his own class rested. In the circumstances of the thirties this took the most dedicated to Spain, an experience, which in Orwell's case shaped the remainder of life. The criticism of socialist intellectuals, pacifists and the Communist Party were each part of an anger instilled by what Orwell believed to be a falsification of the Spanish war. Where Orwell can be faulty is in the exaggeration of the power of the Communist Party and naïvety in not realizing that to constantly criticize others on your own side would eventually provide a weapon for your opponents.

The account of literary allegiance told in Hewison's *Under Siege* proceeds via a review, 'The strategic retreat of the left', which appeared in *Horizon* in January 1943. From there he traces not only the departure of Auden and Isherwood, but the rise of neo-romanticism and in time the movement. There is, he acknowledges, a contradiction in this trend to the right by literary and artistic classes and the radicalization of much of the population. Where the far more important latter trend built on the realization for the first time of the potentials of planning and collective relief of need, it was precisely this increased role of the state which depressed the cultural producers.

The contradiction is not one easily explained. Hewison seems to rely on the importance of imagination for political activity. He marks out three periods: 1939—dissolution with the defeat in Spain; 1940–43—'myth', a sense of heroic struggle against a barbarian threat; 1944–45—disillusion as the war is won, and the need to create a new reality beyond.

> The experience of community during the Blitz was real, and … it was the lack of a similar myth—part fact, part imaginative projection—which revived the sense of disillusionment of 1939 (Hewison 1988 xiv).

> One way in which life would be lived differently was shown by the sweeping Labour victory, between VE Day and VJ Day, in 1945. Yet, ironically, many writers and artists were out of sympathy with the mood of the times (ibid. xix).

> It is ironic that after all the political struggles and defeats of the Thirties the general election meant very little to the intelligentsia, if anything at all (ibid. 198).

The timing does not fit easily with that of Orwell's, who places greater emphasis on the radical potential of the first period only to slowly retreat as time passed. By the time the two accounts reach 1944 though, they seem to arrive at a common assessment of matters. In E. M. Forster's words that terminal could be described thus: 'To me, the best chance for future society lies through apathy, uninventiveness and inertia.' (ibid. 202).

We can quickly gauge the distance of such a position for Orwell, if we compare this again with his sentiments earlier in the war. In his 1941 essay 'Down the Mine', Orwell expressed an expectation that some shift in the balance of power might come about under the radicalizing influence of war.

> Anyone able to read a map knows we are in deadly danger. I do not mean that we are beaten or need to be beaten. Almost certainly the outcome depends on our own will. But at this moment we are in the soup, full fathom five, and we have been brought there by follies which we are still committing and which will drown us altogether if we do not mend our ways quickly.

> It is only by revolution that the native genius of the English people can be set free. Revolution does not mean red flags and street fighting, it means a fundamental shift of power. Whether it happens with or without bloodshed is largely an accident of time and place. ... What is wanted is a conscious open revolt by ordinary people against inefficiency, class privilege and the rule of the old. ... England has got to resume its real shape. The shape that is only just below the surface. (Orwell 1962a 47 and 58–60).

The extent of any real radicalizing of a population is very obviously difficult to measure. We could for instance point to the very different evidence offered in the aptly titled *Myth of the Blitz*. In this work, far from a radical shift having occurred, Angus Calder suggests much of the population maintained its class distinction, and protested at such inconveniences as the billeting on them of urban working-class women and children as a result of the evacuations.

Yet Orwell should not be simply dismissed. Calder is after all homing-in on just that which can be used to question the image of community and togetherness. Over and above the social antagonisms which inevitably remained, there was a degree of planning which required a common basis of acceptance of the aims of the war. This same requirement made it possible and indeed necessary for not only communists and socialists to work together but for both to be drawn into the war effort. Far from marginal outsider, the Communist Party member could experience a sense of common purpose between not just the Soviets and British, but a shift upwards, as it were, of the popular front into the very command citadels of the war effort itself.

Even from the vantage point of a half century later it is by no means clear how far political antagonisms were overcome and socialists accepted as part of the same side. Perhaps the best that can be said is that the evidence is contradictory. Several, most notably J. D. Bernal, Christopher Hill and John Haldane were able to gain senior positions in the war ministries. Of the scientists, Werskey recalls that—

> … the greatest fear of many radicalized scientific workers was that their skills would not be effectively utilized by the fighting services (Werskey 1988 262).

Such fears were not confirmed. Werskey reports that—

> The specific contributions of the scientific left's adherents to the effort would make an interesting book in their own right (ibid. 265).

Even a few examples would seem to confirm the general conclusion that Britain's socialist scientists had a 'good war'. Bernal continued a concern for the matching of science to social need, working together with the biologist Solly Zuckerman in the Home Office on the effects of air raids. From there he moved via Bomber Command to Combined Operations which could have an effect across the range of strategic planning. J. B. S. Haldane's official work was on submarines for the Navy, but again under the influence of a belief in the social role required of science, he continued to comment on civil defence. Joseph Needham worked in the Biology War Committee before becoming a leading figure in co-operation between British and Chinese scientific work. Lancelot Hogben, meanwhile, gained a position in the War Office where he took a lead part in the co-ordination of Army medical statistics. Only Hyman Levy's skills were not effectively utilized. Unlike Haldane, Levy had publicly pursued the party anti-war line between 1939 and 1941, which may have been an influence in his being retained only as a lecturer at Imperial College throughout the conflict. A more sinister explanation for Levy receiving different treatment to the other scientists which form the kernel of Gary Werskey's book, would be his Jewish origin and the anti-Semitism still endemic in Britain as elsewhere.

Acceptance of socialists and even communists was not confined to the expediencies of war ministries. In 1940 Tom Wintringham produced a stirring 'Penguin Special' evoking the spirit of revolutionary England in the seventeenth century. Previously an International Brigade leader in Spain, and in the early years of the war a senior figure in the organization of the Home Guard, Wintringham's evocation was very much in line with the Left's recollection of the free and democratic struggles of the English people against servitude. In line with these sentiments, Wintringham was one of those who wanted to see the Home Guard organized on radical democratic grounds, including Edith Summerskill's demand for women to serve on equal terms with men. The limits placed on the Home Guard and consequent conservative manner of its organization, contributed to Wintringham's resignation and subsequent criticisms of national government policy as a member of the new formed party, Common Wealth.

Pursuing this theme of recreating the imagery of an English revolution for a moment, we might remember that it was only two years previously that *The Common People* by Cole and Postgate and A. L. Morton's *A People's History of England* had been published, providing a guide for historical research that was to be carried forward after the war. The better known link both to Morton, and between the Second World War and a radical moment of the past, is Christopher Hill's *English Revolution*. Yet there were other works picking up this same connection with more overt political ends. In 1945 in *Why not trust the Tories* Bevan had turned to Thomas Rainborough and the Putney Debates for inspiration. The book was published by Gollancz some few months before the general election. Aneurin Bevan had set up the opposition as being between an old guard that represented poverty, waste and misery, and a new order that would bring justice and equality. But if the substance was focused on the opportunities of 1945, then it was to Rainborough and the English Revolution that Bevan turned for the inspiration.

Returning to the question of war-time service, Christopher Hill's was not without distinction. He had, a little while prior to the beginning of the fighting, spent a year in the Soviet Union. He had also spoken in favour of Aid to Spain for the Left Book Club. Far from these activities being held against him, his command of Russian, presumably learnt during his stay there, took him from Army service in the Intelligence Corps to the Foreign Office.

By contrast, Raymond Williams was commissioned, becoming the officer of a tank unit. Exactly what his qualifications were for such a post remain somewhat uncertain. Williams's own recollection in the extended interview *Politics and Letters* though was that 'All undergraduates at that stage [1941] of the War were being directed into the single corps'. By 1942 he was an officer cadet, and by 1943 a lieutenant in command of four tanks. Eric Hobsbawm's war career was somewhat different. Remaining a sergeant, Hobsbawm was in the Education Corps. Where Williams recalls that life in a fighting unit inhibited the opportunity for political activity, someone in army education, who was already an active member of the Communist Party, might use their station to advantage. Eric Hobsbawm's advantage in time and resources over others enabled him to continue to write a thesis on the Fabians—a choice he seems to have later regretted judging by the comment, not to mention tone, in an essay entitled 'The Fabians Reconsidered'.

Edward Thompson served as a commissioned officer in the army in Italy and France, while Rodney Hilton had also served in the army, but in North Africa and Italy. Others such as Leslie Morton, who joined the Royal Artillery, remained entirely in England throughout the conflict. Indeed Morton's case is the more interesting since unlike the other communists or known socialists mentioned here he was watched with suspicion by the authorities. To be fair, when Morton was eventually brought before a Court Martial for—

> ... disparaging remarks about the then Minister of War ... he was acquitted on the grounds that the Minister of War was only a civilian whose activities army personnel could deprecate with impunity (Cornforth ed. 1978 15).

The publisher Martin Eve was not able to enter Cambridge before fighting began, and had to delay his studies to serve in the Royal Navy. Following a very different route, Ralph Miliband spent three years in the Belgian section of the Royal Navy. A choice likely to have been influenced by his European Jewish origins. He had escaped from the continent with his father and arrived in London. Following a period of study with the LSE at its war-time home at Cambridge, his tutor Harold Laski conspired in gaining Miliband entry into the services despite his being under age. Despite such a history, Miliband too rose in station to that of Chief Petty Officer. Twenty years later, the paths of Martin Eve and Ralph Miliband were to cross again, creating a partnership which produced one of Britain's leading Left publications, *The Socialist Register*.

A figure for whom evidence is available who did not spend time in military service was the historian of the French Revolution George Rudé. Rudé remained in London, where he had moved after finishing at Cambridge. During the war he served in the London Fire Brigade. Working in London provided the opportunity to complete a degree in history, Rudé having taken languages at Trinity. A member of the Communist Party, Rudé was able to exploit his service in the fire brigade to engage in political activity.

Of other figures, one notable common feature was service in India. Among the Communists this included Victor Kiernan, John Saville, Brian Pearce, and Peter Worsley, all except the last of whom later joined the historians' group. Other socialists included Mervyn Jones, who was subsequently to be closely connected with the labour left and *Tribune*. Brian Pearce, incidentally, later left the party, probably in 1956, and in April 1957 produced pamphlet number one on 'The Communist Party and the Labour Left 1925–1929' for the short-lived dissident newspaper, *The Reasoner*.

Separation of 'fact' and fiction is far from easy in the experience of war. Edward Thompson's accounts of Italy, and Raymond Williams's of Normandy are a mixture of recollection and prose informed by biographical experience. One common factor was the experience each shared as a tank commander—a position in the military web that offered contradictory experiences:

> ... in our self-propelled tank guns, you were not a traditional officer commanding thirty people, but one of a crew of five in a tank with

three or four other tanks under your control. You all had technical jobs to do. So the immediate social relations were not so hierarchical (Williams 1979a 55).

How far this arrangement may have affected people's later thinking can only be guessed at. In the case of Thompson, his war-time service had a considerable influence on his future direction. With Williams too there is evidence that military conflict also left an understanding not available to younger generations—an understanding it must be said which would seem to place his generation in a better position to appreciate the events of Hungary in 1956, Prague in 1968, Portugal in 1974 and the many coups and counter-coups of the third world before and since.

However, the absence of more obvious command structures did not absolve the tank commander from taking decisions, including those for other people:

I can recall a momentary chill of indecision. Then I leaned from the turret and signalled my sergeant to lead the advance.

I don't know whether I did this out of deference to the rule-book or because I was afraid. We all knew that the first tank down the road would probably be knocked out. ... I had been placed at a point in the sequence of military decision at which I was momentarily endowed with the powers of life and death: to enhance the chances of life for some (including myself) and to diminish them for others (Thompson 1985 185–6).

The front tank was indeed 'knocked out' and three of the five crew killed. In Thompson's recollection there is a strong sense of the arbitrary in how the outcome might have been. But at the risk of melodrama the rule-book might be said to have intervened to bring us the subsequent history including the account from which this extract is taken.

The loss that occurred under Williams's command by contrast stemmed from being overruled. The degree of collaboration that might be possible between a team interdependent on each other's skills, was replaced by the arbitrary use of seniority from outside.

When we were ordered into the wood I divided the unit into two pairs, my pair going to one end and the other to the other end of the wood— that was the only way to do it. They never came back (Williams 1979a 57).

The experience of Italy was a more protracted campaign. The outcome became only very slowly certain and its realization a very long way off. The geography of Italy allowed space and time to coincide to a remarkable degree, with the campaign stretching forward month after month, matched by an advance mile after mile northwards. Normandy, by contrast, seemed to have no certainty whatsoever. In Williams's account the whole affair is centred in a void where every piece of intelligence was likely to be wrong and where it was not different armies forming up in a line, but a mass of soldiers and guns moving and firing almost wherever they happened to be.

This sense of confusion was not absent from the Mediterranean front. Its presence is well caught in Thompson's 'Overture to Cassino'. The semifictional story begins at 01.59. In this last minute of 'peace' we are offered what seems to be a confusing scene. If interpreted dialectically we could say that Thompson is showing the potential and actual of each element. In one vein, the river can be the source of irrigation for crops. In another it is the defensive barrier that must be bridged. The hills can be the ground upon which the irrigated crops may grow, in another guise they are a sheet of fire that threatens ally and enemy alike. Each element may be found alternative use. That selected will in large part depend on the most pressing need.

The remainder of the story tells of the first one hour and twelve minutes of the fighting that was to become the battle for Cassino. In this, the sense of direction that might have existed in the 'Italian theatre of war' generally, gives way to the utter hopeless confusion that Williams described as Normandy. The first hour had been the artillery's. At 03.00 the advance was to begin:

> One of the guns had been falling short and its shells have been bursting behind the infantry. Now it lifts its range two hundred yards.

> The first shell falls ten yards from the officer. A man cries out. Clods of mud sting their faces.

> The second shell from this gun burst harmlessly, but the third reaches out farther and claws through the centre of the main bridging party. The major in charge of this is known as a madman, brilliant survivor of a hundred operations, confident of success in this. He is killed outright ... (Thompson 1985 212).

The war in Asia was more complex in its politics. For many socialists there was no question of not opposing Japan. The Japanese occupation of Manchuria in 1931, the internal civil strife involving the old feudal rule, the Kuomintang and within this, the fledgling Communist Party, and the continued imperialism of Britain and other European states, made China a symbol of early communist militancy. The problem with the war in Asia was not the absence of a 'bad' side, Japan fully filled that role, but the lack of a 'good' side. The irony of the war in Asia was that fascist Japan could be viewed as the liberator from European colonialism. The Japanese victories in Burma and Indo-China were against French, Portuguese, Dutch and English colonial rulers. The opposition that developed in Indo-China was as much concerned with liberation from external rule of the past as with that presently imposed by Japan.

There are, unfortunately, no accounts among the university socialists we have been following of actual contact with enemy soldiers in Asia. The recollections are rather of what was perhaps the single most common foreign experience of our intellectual socialists, that of India. Experience of India stretched beyond that of the war itself. Victor Kiernan had gone to India in 1938 to take up school-teaching and remained there until 1946. The first-hand contact with the subcontinent enhanced his own understanding of the workings of colonialism. As he later recorded, while imperialism should be deplored there was still a need to understand the motives behind the conquerors as much as it was necessary to understand that of the vanquished. In *The Education of Desire* Harvey Kaye suggests that of all the better known figures of the post-war historians group, Kiernan least subscribed to the 'history from below' ethic. Rather he was committed to a more rounded understanding of historical relations.

Other people's time in India was more restricted. John Saville only went in 1942–3 after service in England and Scotland. It is clear that for Saville his time in India was important. While there, he affirms that his own experience was largely devoid of the more blatant forms of racism, though he does seem to have met with it on occasions. The experience that should be highlighted from Saville's time in India, was the attempt at forming a Forces Parliament, and the strike that occurred at a camp of primarily RAF personnel. The strike was eventually broken and one of the leaders imprisoned. His release followed a campaign in Britain. But it was the popular front style formation of the strike that was perhaps the most important factor, with people of differing political outlooks working together.

A Forces Parliament also features in the account given by Mervyn Jones in his autobiography *Chances*. The first of the Forces Parliament had been in Cairo in 1943. However, Jones's account is situated after the war in Deolali in 1946. Mervyn Jones had been a lieutenant in the Royal Artillery, spent one year a prisoner of the Germans, and was not posted to India until after the war had ended. The authority's reaction seems to have been mixed. While certainly not condoning the abrupt undermining of military discipline, and deeply perturbed at the Parliament's Labour domination, there was a sense that it might be reasonable, given the by then reflection of this arrangement in the London Parliament. At any rate Jones recalls the pleasure he experienced at mixing in a basically egalitarian body, and, like Saville, the atmosphere of co-operation that existed between political parties.

Edward Thompson's contact with India recurred at various points in his life. His parents had served there previously in the ministry, but the aftermath of that experience had been a continued trail of present and would-be nationalists and socialists from India through the Thompson home. Given the later political involvements, we can safely assume that the meeting with Nehru and others had a radicalizing effect on the young

Edward.

India presents us with a difficult problem in understanding the relationship between the history which some of these people were later to write, and their politics. Taking the Communist Party historians separately for a moment, Eric Hobsbawm has commented that—

> The older products of the 1930s were soon joined by a group of students who were slightly junior in professional terms, though after six years of war comparatively mature. ... The minds of several had been broadened by work or war service abroad, notably in India (Kiernan, Saville, Pearce), and this ... safeguarded us against excessive provincialism and concentration on contemporary history (Hobsbawm 1978 24).

Despite Hobsbawm's claim, the presence of international, or simply non-English history in the work of members of the CP History Group was very varied. The beyond the borders excursions of Edward Thompson, John Saville and Christopher Hill were, for most of their lives, few. Yet Edward Thompson's political engagement across many countries, including India, was on-going. By contrast, Eric Hobsbawm and Victor Kiernan, have produced a body of work very varied and thoroughly international. On the other hand. Kiernan, as already noted, was very far from subscribing to the history from below approach, for which Hill and Thompson have been inspirational. There is not the space to pursue these comparisons further here, nonetheless, given the war experience and in particularly that of India, the question of the relationship between the politics and the historical writing of even the few figures I have just cited would bear more rigorous investigation than it has hitherto received.

Though accounts of war experience are few, they are sufficient to draw at least a few tentative conclusions. It is noticeable that in the recollections and accounts noted here there has been comparatively little talk or writing of actual fighting. There may in this lie something of the doubt regarding violence which has so bedevilled socialist thinking over the years. Certainly for Raymond Williams, coming from a working-class background, the issue of violence remained problematic irrespective of war service.

> You must remember that I had very strong pacifist background from the thirties: both from Wales, where there was a very close connection between socialism and a brave constructive pacifism, and from that ethos so strong in working-class families—the very strong sense that the way to conduct a strike was to be extremely orderly, on the good working-class grounds that if you gave the enemy the slightest excuse to act violently against you, you're weakening your own position, so that discipline must be exercised to avoid any disorder which distracts from the main purpose of the action (Williams 1979a 409).

However, there was also the genuine difficulty of speaking about experiences that ex-service people may have felt would not be understood by those who had not shared them. The silence was held against public expression, and in this there existed a contrast with the First World War. After 1918 there were erected in countless towns and villages memorials listing the names of the dead. Yet after 1945 very few such stones were set. Instead the names of those killed in this second great war were simply added on to those who had fallen in the first. The difference was a mark of the contrast with which the two wars were remembered. At the end of the Second World War, whatever the horrors, it was possible to believe that there had been a purpose. The fighting had had to be done, and now it was over, a person could put it behind them. No such assurance existed at the end of the First World War. The erected monuments were perhaps physical expression of the different sentiment. It is, however, hard to imagine that the response to the war in 1945 was not deeply circumscribed by that in 1918.

The accounts discussed above express a degree of political comradeship born on by the war-time people's front, whether inside or outside of the military. Perhaps one instance where this unity was more directly available than in many others was in action with the partisan groups that existed in many European countries. It is with the account of the experience of that movement given by the writer and one-time liaison officer with the Special Operations Executive, Basil Davidson, that I shall end the present section. It is today little remembered or realized that, far from alone, Germany and Italy had allies across Europe, including the armies of Hungary and Bulgaria. Both states joined the occupation of Yugoslavia, and became thus engaged in the long bloody conflict with the partisan movements there. While the effectiveness of partisans was variable their potential to hinder the smooth running of the Reich and its supporters was always present. Nowhere was this more true than in the future Yugoslavia, where Slav, Serb and Croat combined to create a partisan movement of sufficient strength to make Yugoslavia a front comparable with that in the Soviet Union and North Africa. Davidson was first flown in from North Africa to join the partisans in the autumn of 1943. At the time the number of liaison missions into Europe was minimal. Two reasons may be suggested; first, the sheer lack of active resistance to fascist forces with which to work, and second, the uncertainty of what someone dropped into the Continent would actually *do*. Many of those who had entered before Davidson had simply not been heard of again.

The territories making up the future Yugoslavia were poor. The majority of the population were rural peasants. Peace equalled grinding poverty, war meant the belt was tightened yet one more notch. The majority of the people, however they felt, were in no position to take any active part either in support for fascism or against it. Of those that did there were two groups. The first, the Chetniks, were fighting in support of a leadership who attempted to create sufficient support to give co-operation with the occupying armies respectability. The peculiar divisions, Croat and Serb, meant that these leaders were effectively sectional in their appeal. In London, a government-in-exile had been constituted from supporters of the Royal family of Yugoslavia. With Foreign Office help, the group maintained a constant barrage of encouragement for the Chetniks and the new pro-fascist leaders and condemnation of the partisans. It was eventually only military expediency that finally overruled the Foreign Office and insisted that support be switched to the anti-fascist forces.

The composition of the partisans was varied. But Davidson suggests that many of the earliest fighters were one-time International Brigaders. Some verification for this claim might be deduced from Hugh Thomas' figure of 1,200 Yugoslavs as having been members of International Brigades in Spain (Thomas 1961 637). Communists, Davidson insists, were never the dominant force in the movement. Rather the partisans were genuinely a popular front, both in the sense that they enjoyed the support of the majority of the population, the peasantry, and in the sense that they held within their ranks a range of ethnic and political differences. A partisan army, like the international brigades before them, differed from either conventional regular or conscript armies in several respects. First, was the basically democratic ethos that pervaded the whole force. Of course, co-ordination had to be achieved if objectives were to be met, and that necessitated the taking of decisions and passing-on of commands. Partisan democracy lived in the voluntary participation of the soldiers. Second, was the basic reliance of partisans on the people among which they moved. Upon the people depended not only the security and safety of partisan soldiers but their need for shelter, clothing and food. In the contexts of Yugoslavia, however, this absence of separation between soldiers and civilians did not mean any lessening in the barbarity when fighting took place.

2. THE CLASS OF 45

There were in effect not one but several ends to the war. Italy surrendered in September 1943. The states of Eastern Europe, Hungary, Bulgaria, Romania, etc., had ceased to fight earlier in 1945 as the Soviet army advanced westwards. The final defeat of Germany was a long process taking the better part of a year from the landings in Normandy in June 1944. That it took so long may at first seem surprising, given the apparently overwhelming combined forces of the Soviet Union and the United States advancing toward each other. The reason, in part, lies with the recklessness with which the SS and some other sections of the German army fought. However, what is often left out of account is that there existed an international force on each side. Hungarians and Bulgarians were active in Yugoslavia, while Hungary, Romania, Finland and many 'volunteers' from several European countries fought on the Eastern front. In the chaos of Normandy, Williams recalls how after advancing and taking many prisoners, they were discovered to be 'Ukrainians and a whole mixture of other nationalities—there was hardly a German amongst them' (Williams 1979a 56). The existence of this large axis allied army cannot but have played a significant part in the events toward the end of the war and in the immediate aftermath.

It was only after the final defeat of Germany that the full horror of the death camps began to be realized by a significant number of people. With the discovery, came the signs of victory against Japan. The arguments for the dropping of the bombs on Hiroshima and Nagasaki have been long rehearsed, and cannot be simply pushed aside. It was in part because of the almost certain greater loss of life that would have occurred had the war continued by conventional means, that criticism of the bombs remained muted. One immediate practical effect, however, was for soldiers awaiting posting to Burma or elsewhere, to be released:

> They decided in the demobilization programme that students whose courses had been interrupted would get what was called Class B release, which meant that you went ahead of your turn in the queue. That happened when I was still expecting to be sent to Burma (Williams 1979a 60).

It is banal to say that the return to Cambridge from the army involved a readjustment. Yet perhaps the obvious does need stressing or it can be almost forgotten in the analysis of an event. The war had coincided with early adulthood for several of the figures followed here. In 1940 Martin Eve was aged only fifteen, Edward Thompson and Ralph Miliband were only sixteen, Mervyn Jones was eighteen, Raymond Williams nineteen, Eric Hobsbawm twenty-three, John Saville and Rodney Hilton were twenty-four, Victor Kiernan twenty-seven, Christopher Hill twenty-eight, and George Rudé thirty. The differences of age may have been in part responsible for the differences of experience. Only George Rudé, the eldest of those listed, did not experience military service, while Christopher Hill, the second eldest, was first in military intelligence and then in a war ministry, and Victor Kiernan was already in India when war commenced. By contrast, all the younger figures gained service experience of one form or another, and several in frontline fighting units.

Military experience, for all the political intellectuals who are our subjects, was an interruption of their lives which none had planned for. They were all war-time conscripts for whom the British military was an institution which they could not but have viewed with distrust. The 1930s had seen the intensifying of anti-imperial activity in India and elsewhere, and its forcible repression by soldiers from Britain. Given the views of the Imperial Government should there have been any real threat to British interests from either liberation fronts or foreign insurgents, the military would very likely have been instructed to use all force necessary. Ironically, service in an historically imperial army may well have provided the war conscripts with a depth of understanding of the potential and practice of socialist and counter-socialist conflict denied later generations. Rather the experience and their response were far closer to that of the preceding generation.

In Europe, such was the manner in which British interests were aligned, there was every reason to imagine that its army would side with any ally to prevent a Bolshevik threat. While Spain was the most obvious example of this potential alliance, the war between Finland and the Soviet Union had seen British assistance being given against the communist power. We gain an insight into the view of the war between Finland and the Soviet Union among conservative interests in 1940 from Winston Churchill, who had previously been a dissident voice warning others in his party of the need for preparation against Hitler:

> Only Finland—superb, nay, sublime—in the jaws of peril Finland shows what free men can do. The service rendered by Finland to mankind is magnificent. They have exposed for all the world to see, the military incapacity of the Red Army and of the Red Air Force. Many illusions about the Soviet Union have been dispelled in these few fierce weeks of fighting in the Arctic Circle. Everyone can now see how communism rots the soul of a nation; how it makes it abject and hungry in peace, and proves it base and abominable in war (Churchill n.d. 137).

On the opposite side, Williams and Hobsbawm had, only months before Britain finally entered the Second World War, written a booklet in support of the Russian case. The war years for many of these conscripts would have been spent in a body with which politically they would have had little sympathy.

In addition, the internal organization of military life depended on a hierarchy deemed to be beyond question. Relations of superiority and inferiority were simply the natural order by which life in the military was led, and as such beyond conscious recognition. Of course, this has often been mocked, and indeed it was an important sign of the popular pressures during the war that public mockery of the military leaders was made possible. As in so much else, Orwell, writing in 1941, catches the mood in biting fashion:

> Since the fifties every war in which England has engaged has started off with a series of disasters, after which the situation has been saved by people comparatively low in the social scale. The higher commanders drawn from the aristocracy, could never prepare for modern war, because to do so they would have to admit to themselves that the world was changing. They have always clung to obsolete methods and weapons, because they inevitably saw each war as a repetition of the last. Before the Boer War they were prepared for the Zulu War, before 1914 for the Boer War, and before the present war for 1914. Even at this moment hundreds of thousands of men in England are being trained with the bayonet, a weapon entirely useless except for opening tins

(Orwell 1962a 80–81).

Military hierarchy in large part reflected class power. As such, this same hierarchy matched the place of Cambridge in the social order. In these environs too, relations of power, and the expression of privilege might also be taken for granted. Prior to the war, socialist intellectuals and students had to negotiate the experience of university with their politics. As officers or significant figures in the defence ministries, parallel social relations were again experienced, albeit that class might have been overlain by more conspicuous adornments of rank. The enlightened activity of the Education Corp went on because of the circumstance of prolonged inactivity for thousands of ordinary soldiers, and despite the inflexible hierarchy which rank might impose.

The circumstances at war-time Cambridge took on their own peculiar shape. One dimension was the difference the requirements of war placed upon the arts and sciences. Students of the former could be considered as part of the general population and thus liable for military or other war-time service. The scientists by contrast could quite reasonably be classified as reserved occupations. Whether that was the actual description of university science is less important. Of more significance was the recognition by parts of the establishment that science could be an invaluable weapon. A lesson no doubt learnt once more from the bitter experience of the First World War.

In 1941 the London School of Economics had been moved to Cambridge from its location in central London. The number of students during the war had also been maintained by an increase in the number of women. Each in their own ways had insulated the impact of war on intellectual life, making continuance of teaching, and all the administrative trimmings that surround this activity, possible. The sciences had less need for assistance of this kind. Its students could enter the war effort inside the Cambridge walls—or more accurately, the walls of the Dunn, Cavendish and other laboratories. We noted earlier that the socialist scientists 'had a good war'. In part the reasons were precisely because the emphasis was placed on the functional contribution their work could make, rather than any political justification the scientists might place on what they did.

With the end of the war, the LSE returned home and the proportion, though not necessarily the total number, of women students fell. Numbers now were made up of a skewed generation of students, made mature by comparison with some new entrants by the years of fighting. The circumstance was not peculiar to service personnel, many women students left temporarily to work in essential industries—Dorothy Thompson recalls in the Introduction to *Outsiders*, that she deferred her studies to train as a draftswoman for an office in central London. The arrangements made for the returning students included a reorganized tripos, judged to be more suitable to the peculiar circumstance of their learning. A decision was made allowing students to be awarded their degree on the basis of their first- or first two-year's work. This arrangement could be highly advantageous, allowing students to specialize in an area to a greater degree than would normally have been possible as an undergraduate. As we shall see in the next chapter, for Raymond Williams this was to prove of considerable advantage.

Before moving on to the political culture of post-war university we should note the changes of class and culture which forced themselves on higher education after 1945. Speaking of the time immediately following the cessation of fighting, Hewison writes,

> ... within ten years university education changed from being an almost entirely private to a public responsibility. The Butler Education Act of 1944 meant that education was no longer the privilege of the wealthy, for by 1949, 68 percent of the student population were receiving financial help from government or local authority grants. At the same time the pre-war university population of 50,000 had increased to 83,000. London was still the largest single university but Oxford had increased its numbers by 50 percent and Cambridge by 17 percent, and these remained after London, the biggest universities by far, retaining their cultural dominance (Hewison 1981 39–40).

But the change was qualitative as well as quantitative. The students of 1946 were mature not simply in age but in experience and expectations. They were also coming increasingly from social classes outside those traditionally dominant at university. We have already noted Rodney Hilton's recollection of a lower-middle-class presence among socialists at Oxford at the end of the thirties. From 1945 this presence was considerably enlarged, drawing the cry that standards would be lowered, and that this new generation was disrespectful of tradition and the cultural rules by which the ancient institutions were governed.

Such a circumstance was likely to emphasize the distance between the teaching population of the universities and the new student population. The difference of experience over the previous few years, the increased numbers of students and the expansion of lower-middle-class students in particular, created a gulf of expectations. For those students with a political conscience, a wish to extend the democratic zeal initiated by the war was more likely to lead them away from the cloisters toward the potential offered by adult education. Of course, the dominant culture of the old universities was not noticeably diluted. Indeed a characteristic feature of the Labour Government from 1945 was to preserve the status quo in higher education as far as possible. The scientists had proved their worth to the state during the war. In peace there was no reason for that service not to continue and for private capital to be the beneficiary. Beyond that, the public school system was left intact to ensure that an adequate supply of suitable candidates for Oxbridge was still to be found. The effectiveness with which these institutions maintained their control over the two universities' populations may be judged from the fact that—

> In 1957 it was calculated that 45 percent of Oxford undergraduates and 55 percent of Cambridge undergraduates came from public schools. No previous figures are available, but the change since before the war is not (at Cambridge, at least) very striking: and in fact (because of the expansion of places) more public schoolboys are now going to Oxbridge than in the 'thirties (Sampson 1962 199).

The politics of post-war Cambridge have been differently described. Hobsbawm suggests that a significant element of the popular front unity across the left continued, and that indeed university life retained a left sympathy. Williams, by contrast, reports that the whole atmosphere had changed. The pre-war causes had given way, in Williams's view, to religion. More than this the pre-war culture of the socialists' club does not seem to have retained its dynamism, nor its appeal. Supporting Williams's assessment, Martin Eve recalls that where in 1941 the Socialist Society had some one thousand members, by the time he arrived at Cambridge in 1946, this had declined to three hundred. Of these there were a hard core of some forty-five Communist Party members. There needs to be some caution regarding this apparent decline, since the figures for the later date reflect only undergraduates, postgraduates forming a separate grouping. The same distinction may not apply to the figures immediately before or during the war.

The situation was exacerbated by the failure of attempts to amalgamate the Socialist Society with the Labour Club. A similar split had occurred toward the end of 1934. Then the rift was quickly mended under the auspices of a shared club. The post-war Socialist Society was not, though, in any sense moribund. Links were formed with a number of Majolas, colonial Arabic students, and several successful meetings held. Speakers include John Horner, Konni Zilliacus and a then well-known Bantu poet, Peter Abrahams. Communist members of the Society scored their own success when one of their number, Sajjad Zaheer, a Singhalese student, gained the Presidency of the Students' Union.

Having recorded the continuation of a socialist society after the war, it has to be admitted that the all important social life necessary to a student body was much diminished. Where Williams recalls the thriving club with its notice boards, on to which his own first public written contributions were pinned, and regular films, Martin Eve recalls the place as having become somewhat less attractive. Of course, personal views vary according to experience. Hobsbawm like Eve remained within the party, while Williams dropped out of political life. Hobsbawm would certainly have continued to find a circle in which a socialist culture was created, which perhaps Williams may not have noticed from the outside. It is with this question of continuity and the influence of war within Cambridge and elsewhere that the most difficult questions of understanding our generation of socialist intellectuals may lie. Werskey has noted how for the socialist scientists of his own study, much of what in the nineteen-thirties they had campaigned for, moved toward realization in the post-war world. Certainly the optimism about science's ability to improve conditions of life, and the respect afforded in return, were important aspirations for Bernal, Levy and the rest.

For a generation of socialist students now returned from the war, the potential must also have seemed bright. The election of the Labour Government occurred in the July, midway between the end of the war in Europe and the end in Asia. In the *Politics and Letters* interviews Williams expresses the view, that the mood of the intelligentsia, in complete opposition to what occurred more generally among the population, had moved to the right. However, Margaret Cole in the biography of G. D. H. took the far more cautious view that it was not so much a conscious movement but rather that 'the Oxford graduate vote played safe'. Yet we might remember that a similar contradiction had previously been noted by Hewison with regard to literary writers. Of course, we could simply say that these were just another part of the 'intelligentsia', though the Soho writers of Hewison's *Under Siege,* do not resemble the same class as the retiring yet cold-hearted dons of Williams's essay on F. R. Leavis, 'Seeing a Man Running'.

Hewison suggests that for writers the war had gone on two years too long. The romantic days of 1940–41 when they could celebrate the myth of England standing alone, had given way to the long tedious war of attrition which the enemy could never win, but could neither be easily defeated. Hewison endorses the general view that hope died because of the length of the hardships and horror. Unfortunately, there is no comparable account for the political inclinations of the university intellectuals. However, if we accept Hewison's argument of a general movement to the right among intellectuals, we might then say that the work of socialist and Communist students in the previous decade, which during the war found fertile ground through an array of channels from the Army Bureau of Current Affairs (ABCA) to the state-provided nurseries, subsequently radicalized a wider public. The Left Book Club and ABCA have both received their share of 'blame' for the result of 1945.

Citing such a process could run the risk of noting the branches and missing the trunk. It might fairly be argued that the most important influence to shift the general political view leftwards was the actual necessity for planning and state leadership during the war. However, the problem with relying on this latter explanation alone is its ignoring of the activity necessary for experience to be interpreted in a particular manner. The actual political education effected by the work of a considerable number of young socialists in the potentially favourable circumstance of national crisis, by contrast, could be considerable. It might also make more reasonable the possibility that a reaction against progressive views should appear first, where their propagators had vacated, the cloisters of the universities. Employment for many young socialists after the war was not inside the institutions but rather in the very different atmosphere of adult education (Fieldhouse 1985a). Fieldhouse continues,

> It was natural process for people to progress from the popular front, student broad left of the thirties, often via army education during the war, to adult education in the immediate post-war years when popular front fraternity was still widespread on the left. There was no sharp division between Communist Party members and others, especially among the younger generation (Fieldhouse 1985a 11).

Williams, as we noted earlier, returned to Trinity while awaiting a posting to Burma. His transition would appear to have been fairly rapid, since he recalls that 'the first term of my third student year had already begun' (Williams 1989a 3). Eric Hobsbawm, who had met Williams in Normandy, would seem to have followed a similar path again in 1945, since he and Williams met almost immediately on their return to Trinity. Completion of studies for these services' students was rearranged from that required of conventional undergraduates. In the case of Edward Thompson, for instance, this consisted of independent research in Elizabethan history and literature, his actual degree being granted on the first part of his tripos. However, it is with another part of Thompson's life at this time that I want to stay at the moment.

3. EUROPE AGAIN

In Yugoslavia, the partisans finally cleared the combined invaders from their territory by the middle of 1945. The Italians had surrendered some months earlier, but the Hungarians and Bulgarians fought on with the Germans until the bitter end. The Hungarian elite corps are cited by Basil Davidson in *Partisan Pictures* (a book I draw on liberally in this section) as having earned particular contempt from the partisans and peasants. Ironically, while Hungarian and Bulgarian armies were still occupying parts of Yugoslavia, their own countries were being put out of the war by the advancing Soviet forces. It is, of course, part of the rewriting of the war that this fighting in Eastern Europe against the combined fascist forces marshalled there has been deliberately left out of the account. The manner in which power was taken or distributed in the months after the end of the war was a direct response to the divisions between peoples throughout the course of the war. In the case of Yugoslavia, Basil Davidson suggests this took the shape of a rural peasantry against an urban middle class. Partisans are neither, as we have already noted, regular soldiers nor conscripts. They were a volunteer army ultimately held together by a common enemy. From well before the end of the war itself the work of reconstruction and indeed new construction of Yugoslavia was already in preparation. The twin processes of winning the immediate war and of building a new state should not, according to Basil Davidson, be separated, if the actions of the partisans were to be understood. When decisions concerning the fighting were made they had also to incorporate the civilian activities anticipated to start as soon as the fighting in that area ceased. Similarly, future economic and social planning could only be advanced as the fighting allowed. In Yugoslavia the situation was made the more complex by the disparate areas and competing authorities each seeking allegiance from a population to their own leadership. A partisan government had to ensure that its authority should be accepted not as discrete pieces each ruling its own enclave, but rather as a national government where as yet there was no nation.

Yugoslavia held a special place in the consciousness of socialists in the middle-nineteen-forties, much as Spain had had a decade earlier. The reasons are not difficult to recognize, and comparison of the partisan's tactics with those of the Republicans, is valid, especially given that several hundred Yugoslavs had been present in Spain. However, it was the symbolic value of the two which perhaps held the greatest importance. Yugoslavia represented perhaps more clearly than anywhere else a continuance of an anti-fascist struggle simultaneous with a revolutionary campaign against its old order. For the left the political fight lost in Spain was being won at the other end of the Mediterranean.

The events recounted in this section demonstrate this symbolic value. While most of his experience was actually during the war, Basil Davidson, was not alone in his association with the partisans. With the war's close, Raymond Williams briefly visited the country, while James Klugmann was there formally 'attached to the British Military Mission to the Yugoslav partisans' (Klugmann 1979 13). There were it seems a number of foreign, including British, observers at the events leading to the formation of the national government led by Tito, and there is a strong probability that Davidson and Klugmann would have met in the first months of peace. Yugoslavia presented to socialists elsewhere perhaps the best example of a popular struggle organized and carried through by the people. It was a struggle designed not merely to liberate territory from foreign occupation, but to rid themselves of the corrupt pre-war rulers, and the social organization which they had maintained. Yugoslavia epitomized the post-war hopes for the creation of a new society and a new people from the ashes of war. But it was during the fighting that the conditions for that new beginning had been laid:

> It is too early to draw sweeping conclusions about the future of Yugoslavia, but certain points seem to be fairly clear. From the very beginning the partisans have been consistent in the working out and application of their political ideas and policies, ... (Davidson 1946 325).

The practice of partisan fighting, with its apparent commitment to democracy and earned loyalty, served in effect as a political movement. Their policies and political ideas were part of the evolving project to build Yugoslavia. It is to this same end that the construction of a railway line between Samac and Sarajevo was undertaken, and it is to this that we must now turn.

Shortly after the war, there returned an international force to Yugoslavia very different from that which had invaded a few years previously. The object was to participate in the building of a railway line from Samac to Sarajevo. The story of the line and of the experience of the British Brigade is retold in *The Railway*, published in 1948, on the brigade's return to Britain. While the benefit of the railway in material terms went to Yugoslavia, an intellectual and moral benefit was derived by the participants who contributed to its building, regardless of where they lived. The use of the term 'brigade' for the railway workers carries obvious connections with the partisan movement of two years earlier, and with the organization of international soldiers in Spain before then. Indeed a number of the figures, not just the Yugoslavs, had been partisans. Transferring the voluntary commitment created by participation in an international military brigade to a peaceful campaign was obviously sensible. Of course, circumstance and measures vary between the work of driving out an occupying army, and driving a way through mountainous landscape in order to lay railway track. Yet the aims were of a similar nature. In each case the intention was to make a contribution to the development of a new country and a new social order. The feeling was not restricted to the Yugoslav workers only. In Martin Eve's recollection of the experience, there is a strong sense that the Samac to Sarajevo railway forged commitments not easily dislodged.

The purpose of the line was to transport coal, iron and machinery from Bosnia to the growing city of Sarajevo. As such, it was to form part of the infrastructure of a new industrial economy. The intention mirrored that of much elsewhere in Europe where the attempt was being made to build an industrial base upon which could be developed an economy adequate to the demands now made after years of suffering and hardship. Volunteers to build the railway were in that respect acting in line with widely held expectations. Where this force of navvies and builders differed was in the belief that this desire for renewal could be pushed forward on a universal basis which paid little regard to national boundary or political system. The railway line was built in the summer of 1947. Its completion was it seems something of a remarkable piece of work discipline. The account in *The Railway* is probably romanticized in parts; however, there is a strong sense that the unpaid labourers collective efforts were more effective than scientific management techniques. It was the responsibility of a particular brigade to complete a certain section of work. Ultimately, the line was completed in less than the estimated period—something not readily achieved by large-scale privately-financed engineering projects.

The brigades were based largely on nationality. However, there were no representation from either the Soviet Union or the United States, their absence being perhaps something of a portent. *The Railway* being published in 1948 by the 'The British-Yugoslav Association', will have been one of the last acts of the association, coinciding so nearly as it does with the break in relations between that country's government and Moscow. A strong flavour of the style of the book is contained in its subtitle: *An Adventure in Construction*. Certainly, there is more than a little boy scout enthusiasm in the telling, though with something of the soldier's taste of wit:

> Every day parties marched up to work (five minutes late and in an untidy blob formation) under the Union Jack (Thompson ed. 1948 ix).

The presence of a large international force of young workers along the railway track typified the symbolic status of the new Yugoslavia. However, the manner of recruitment or even inspiration behind their presence was not to be entirely innocent. Recruitment was carried on by Communist parties, though many volunteers came independently. The actual planning of the building though carried on by youth, had the full support of the Yugoslav government. Yet this should not lead us to jump to conclusions. Basil Davidson records that of the seventeen members of the National Liberation Committee and the provisional government only four or five were members of the Communist Party. Perhaps though the suspicions surrounding the railway project were held more by its detractors than those who actually took part. In the book edited by Edward Thompson, after the brigade's return to Britain there is a clear effort made to gain acceptance for the trip to have been made out of genuine good feeling for the Yugoslavs and the possibility of a peaceful and co-operating Europe. This huge undertaking is reduced to a more human scale in *The Railway* with recollection of the camp-fires that started up after each day's work.

> The students, of course, were more 'sophisticated' in other ways, gaining something in humour and tolerance but losing in spontaneity. The Greeks on our section ... had made up for this by setting a terrific pace at the evening bonfires where we all met together. ... But our good friends the Belgrade mining students stood a little aloof from this their bonfires were tranquil and informal affairs, and they seemed to regard the antics of British and Greek alike with good-humoured tolerance (Thompson 1948 20).

A great deal of *The Railway* is given over to the impressions members of the British brigade gained of the new Yugoslavia. One perhaps naïve emphasis is the extent to which the country was united. A common agreement that the only worthwhile good is that in which all can share seems to abound among all those the British brigade met. Yet the more experienced eye and ear of Basil Davidson had cast doubt on whether there could be such unanimity. The partisan movement had operated primarily among the rural population. The towns had remained always in German–Ustashe–Italian control'. In Davidson's view this urban versus rural division could be understood in class terms. Those that had remained in the towns, the middle class, had in large part done so out of choice. In Davidson's view it was going to be a very considerable task for the victorious peasant army of partisans, and the discredited middle-class collaborators to find a means of communicating. In the account of the Samac to Sarajevo railway, the only hint of any political divisions is in reference to a few people who may have sought to redeem their past betrayal in contributing to the new.

The last part of *Partisan Picture* is given to the social order which could emerge after the war. The key phrase cited is 'peaceful change'. This, Davidson continues,

> … means one thing and one thing only. If our world is moving towards political and economic unity, then 'peaceful change' can mean nothing more or less than the process whereby this historical trend is made in peace (Davidson 1946 357).

The emphasis was in response to the growing threat of hostility between the Soviet Union and the United States. In Davidson's view the collaboration between the Yugoslav regime in exile and the Foreign Office, forced the partisans to look to the Soviet Union for an ally. Yet stronger still than this, he argues, was the will to remain independent. That desire for independence is strongly present in the story of *The Railway*. The tragic irony was that in a short period of only a few months after its publication, that same Yugoslav independence was turned into isolation by the decree of Moscow.

chapter four

PARTING OF THE WAYS

1. Post-war Cambridge Continuity and Change

I want in this fourth chapter to turn to a singular departure at this time. In the years 1946 to 1956, Raymond Williams sought to develop a politics and a theoretical framework which pointed forward to what, after 1956 came to be called the New Left, but which developed in a very different environment. Beginning with a discussion of Cambridge, I focus on the manner of Williams's response to his experience through an intense piece of work on the dramatist Henrik Ibsen. The second section focuses on Williams's time in adult education, concentrating on the historical importance of adult education work for radicals and the special nature of voluntary association which Williams recognized as crucial to the continuance of a tradition for which the Workers' Education Association had become the leading representative. The third section is a discussion of *Politics and Letters,* which I regard as having been a formative experience for Williams's intellectual politics. The remainder of the chapter is concerned with the project which Williams perceived needed to be carried forward following the failure of *Politics and Letters.* From my discussion of these years I conclude by arguing that the major works *Culture and Society* and *Long Revolution* were written not to inspire a New Left , as Lin Chun in the *British New Left* and others have presented them, but rather were part of the same project which Williams had pursued from 1948.

For Cambridge the end of the war brought its own set of changes. At the institutional level the cease-fire meant the return of the London School of Economics to its home in Houghton Street. The student profile, however, continued to look like something quite out of character with that before 1939. Where during the war it had been the increased proportion of female students, in 1945 it was the sudden arrival of probably the first, and perhaps still today the largest, cohort of mature students.

According to Raymond Williams, among the student body at Cambridge in 1945–6 there was a religious conservatism in sharp contradiction to its socialist leaning before the war, though such a change was not necessarily surprising after a war. Of a more precise nature was a desire to embrace a new departure in literary work. The most pronounced expression was practical criticism, taken forward by its disciples, which in time included Williams, with something of an evangelical fervour. With this went a gathering of a group around Leavis. Equally important for Williams was a new interest then being expressed in D. H. Lawrence, though it was many years before a more sustained engagement was published, when he and Joy Williams edited a collection of pieces on the theme of education (Williams, J. and Williams, R. (eds) 1973). More immediately were to be first discussion of Lawrence in the pages of *Politics and Letters*, and then the preparation for teaching him to WEA students.

Before 1940 Williams had been acutely aware of the contradictions between the seeming enormity and inevitability of the coming war, and the consequent irrelevance of much that was being spoken by those to whom students might otherwise look for guidance. Certainly, for a few months at least, Williams had identified himself with the student radicalism of the time. In a very real sense the circumstances in 1945 were different. For one thing he and his generation were older. He had married Joy Dalling in 1942 and they already had one child. But the experience of war itself also had effects, even if their full repercussions were for Williams to be delayed some two to three years.

A change in the regulations, allowing studies to be completed by way of a thesis rather than the standard examinations, was a special departure for this peculiar war generation. The opportunity was used by Williams to carry through work on the dramatist Henrik Ibsen, which was to serve as a basis for the experimental enquiries into drama over the next few years. The reasons why an individual chooses a particular set of options are always beyond full explanation. Certainly Williams deliberately chose not to align with any organized political activity or to adopt an explicit political allegiance in 1945. In answer to the *New Left Review* interviewers, he states that during the war and indeed after, he retained broad agreement with the Communist Party's interpretation of events (1979a 54). However, this claim is tempered by an increasing distance from a cultural theory which the party transferred *en bloc* direct from Moscow to the British Isles. Yet his political views were secondary to the more immediate tasks he set himself of entering into his academic work, and in particular an intense engagement with Ibsen. In reality, Ibsen was in 1946 more than an academic subject for Williams. In one of those rare moments when Williams acknowledges the personal emotions which he kept so well channelled he says,

> I got totally and (in academic terms) quite unreasonably preoccupied with him. It was a very long involvement. The interpretation of Ibsen which I developed during that year I still in part hold today. The chapter on Ibsen in *Drama from Ibsen to Brecht* is that work. The reason for the intense significance that Ibsen possessed for me then was that he was the author who spoke nearest to my sense of my own condition at the time. Hence the particular emphasis I gave to the motif of coming 'to a tight place where you stick fast. There is no going forward or backward' [Williams 1964a 107] that was exactly my sensation. The theme of my analysis of Ibsen is that although everybody is defeated in his work, the defeat never cancels the validity of the impulse that moved him; yet

that the defeat has occurred is also crucial. The specific blockage does not involve—this was my dispute with other interpretations—renunciation of the original impulse. I think this was how I saw the impulse of the late thirties—an impulse that was not just personal but general. It had been right but it had been defeated; yet the defeat did not cancel it (1979a 62–63).

The line 'a place where you stick fast, you cannot go forward or backward' comes from Ibsen's play, *When We Dead Awaken,* and appears at least three times. The theme of the essay was an argument that Ibsen's plays needed to be read as a single unity. The alternative, which Williams states had been otherwise practised, was a division of the plays into supposedly distinct periods of Ibsen's career. A central theme running through the plays is the absolute necessity to strive forward despite the certainty of failure in the face of the equally absolute barriers which could not be avoided. Williams singles out on various occasions, points in the plays where this theme of the absolute imperative to go forward is matched by the equal certainty of failure. It should be noted, incidentally, that Fred Inglis misinterprets Williams here and writes—

> ... what marks the Tripos essay with Williams's own features is the combination of complete intellectual self-confidence ... with his absolute allegiance to hopefulness even in the teeth of certain defeat. ... Defeat is not failure' (1995 105).

Williams, quite contrarily at this time, viewed failure as inevitable, a place where you stick fast, you cannot go forward or backward.

For Williams there was in Ibsen a 'radical lack of belief in the liberal project of liberation' (1979a 198 & 1979b 100–102). By this he means the act of individual liberation. While he wishes to uphold that real advance is possible for an individual, he insists that this was not the case for Ibsen. The individual may walk away, but be left unsure as to what they are liberated into. I think the same dilemma occurs in Williams's fiction. Perhaps the obvious case is Kate in *Second Generation.* The escape for Kate is through a sexual relationship. She attempts to step beyond the limits which hold her, which are as much about place and time as they are about personal relationships, through an affair. Instead those larger constraints refuse to alter. She must still face the blockage, the defeat of those aspirations which her generation had held to after the war. What I think comes through though is that defeat does not mean that the original word or action was wrong. The theme is present again in *Fight for Manod* and more strongly still in *Loyalties.* The loyalty expressed in deed more than in word, was not invalidated by the acts of betrayal or by their direct defeat by an enemy.

This same idea is offered again when Williams is speaking of actual history. The occasion was a conference organized by Llafur, the reference, to the events of the general strike:

What remains of decisive importance from the events of 1926 is the achievement of that consciousness (1989b 107).

Williams's need to enter into close communion with Ibsen in 1946 has also to be understood in the context of the changed atmosphere at Cambridge to which reference has already been made. The Leavisites, despite Cambridge, were having increasing influence over the direction of English literature, and it has long been assumed to relate Williams to them. Views on the relationship have varied, but nonetheless it is not inaccurate of John McIlroy to write,

> It is usual—partly because of his centrality and power, partly as shorthand—to point to Leavis as the prime intellectual ancestor (McIlroy and Westwood (eds) 1993 7).

The chief culprit for this tendency to line up Leavis followed by Williams and Hoggart, has been cultural studies. Attempting to establish an intellectual heritage from which to take their identity, the early exponents of the then newly capitalized Cultural Studies, Stuart Hall, Francis Mulhern, Richard Johnson, and rather differently, Terry Eagleton, each invented a plausible yet ahistorical intellectual legacy. Even McIlroy is apt to too easily fit the one name after the other. The reality is that although Leavis was officially Williams's tutor, the latter only once heard him teaching. Indeed far from following in his coat-tails, Williams seems to regret not having had more contact with Leavis in 1946. The real influence was *Scrutiny*, which Williams points out was greater than just this one person. By way of recognition of this fact, McIlroy lists several names which Williams acknowledged to be influences at this time (McIlroy and Westwood (eds) 1993 7).

Practical criticism was much to the fore in Williams's thinking and teaching, and while it is not possible to explain an individual's choices in the manner of an exact science, I would suggest that Williams became a jealous advocate of the new practice in a reaction to his experience of war. I think it is something of this sort that Thompson is suggesting when he writes,

> His [Williams's] problems were set, and his tone has been conditioned by, a particular social context (Thompson 1961 27).

The validity of my or Thompson's proposals is not amenable to precise verification. However, Williams has himself suggested that after the war he underwent considerable change. In these circumstances forms of intellectual expression might not have been among the most important:

> I think that it was from that time that a quite different personality emerged, very unlike my earlier self. I became much more qualifying and anxious and careful, always stressing complexities and difficulties— all the characteristics of which people were later to complain. They were the absolute reverse of what I was in 1940 (1979a 63).

71

This is no doubt true, however, I would also argue that the years immediately following the war more than usually enabled Williams to harness his intellectual capacity to a political project to which he committed the rest of his life.

2. Adult Education

While Williams's personal decision to enter adult education was in part pragmatic, he was at the same time joining a path being trodden by a number of his generation. The reasons for the trend were varied and Fieldhouse's account, *Adult Education and the Cold War,* raises interesting issues of political commitment and its expression. Summarily we can recognize two dimensions. On the one side was the historical attraction of the Workers' Education Association (WEA) especially to advocates for social change; on the other the radicalizing effects of the war and a determination to turn the suffering toward a common good.

The institutional place of adult education and in particular university extra-mural provision and the Workers' Education Association was far from simple or certain. There were many varied local arrangements by which these two worked together, but a substantial part of the pre-war provision had been in the form of a three-year tutorial class. This was intended to be of an equivalent standard to a university degree. At a time when the total full-time student population was less than fifty thousand, and when there were but a very small number of bursaries, the tutorial class was in reality the only opportunity for extended education available to the great majority of the population.

It was this blockage to participation in university education for the vast majority of people that gave the WEA its founding ethos: the provision of a higher, and especially liberal education for the working classes. Moreover, as demonstrated in the 1908 report *Oxford and Working Class Education,* it was to be an education not entirely at the discretion of the universities. It was this last feature which had led to the criticisms of the university extension movement, to which in part the WEA was a reaction. It was the association's founding ethos that made it so attractive to reformers and radicals from the beginning of the century and the story of how interested persons and small bodies came together to initiate first the university extension movement and later the WEA, has been memorably recorded, first in 1961 by John Harrison in *Learning and Living,* and in 1974 by Brian Simon in his *Education and the Labour Movement 1870–1920.*

A brief look at *The Highway,* the journal of the Workers' Education Association for several decades, may give an indication of the importance of the journal as a platform for radical ideas and political debates. Although the practice of the association was directed toward adult education, it had from the start been concerned with advancing universal education for all ages. Contributions to this theme included R. H. Tawney's 'The School Leaving Age Bill' in the issue for February 1930. Two contributions raising issues of the nature and practice of education appeared in the October and December issues for 1933, respectively by Aldous Huxley and A. S. Neill. The theme of the papers was the question of discipline and each suggested changing attitudes both in theory and method. Finally, Lady Simon contributed a stinging attack on the education cuts proposed by the government in the issue for January 1933. Political issues discussed in *The Highway* included 'The Women's Movement' by Ray Strachey in October 1933, 'The [American] New Deal at the Cross Roads' by Barbara Wootton February 1935, Sylvia Pankhurst examined 'The Threat of War' in March 1935, and finally, in February 1936, Margaret Cole commented on a WEA edition of *Soviet Communism* by Beatrice and Sidney Webb. Few as these examples are, they give an indication of the ability of the WEA and *The Highway* during the thirties to attract a wide range of discussions and contributions from persons who were or became significant political and cultural radicals. Adult education was integral to the culture of the generation with which this book has been concerned, providing a common experience and informing a manner of response which few other projects built upon an ethos of voluntarism and social improvement could have afforded.

What in addition made the generation of Williams move toward the Association was the radicalizing experience of the war years and the determination that some greater good would be made from the horror:

> There were many people who had been involved in the left-wing student politics of the 1930s seeking jobs after the war. The more left wing they were the more they looked toward adult education as a worthwhile job to do—a politically useful job (Fieldhouse 1985a 33).

The provision of adult education had greatly altered and even expanded during the war years, though that provided by and for civil populations had struggled to maintain classes and institutions. The reasons were a combination of movements of people from civilian occupations to those devised specifically for the war effort, and the stringencies imposed from fear of enemy action. William Devereux, in his *Adult Education in Inner London*, has graphically described the measures caused by the extreme fears of bombing at the beginning of the war:

> High expectations for the session 1939–40 were dashed. The opening of evening classes was postponed and heads of institutes were asked to survey their areas and get advice from the Chief Air-Raid Warden on suitable buildings in which to hold classes. ... From the scanty notes in log-books it is clear that air-raid wardens were not anxious to have more safety and security hazards in the shape of students in evening classes (Devereux 1982 148–149).

This situation was not to last. Within a year, fears of bombing lessened and civil adult education restored itself to a surprising degree.

Any decline in existing adult education provision was, however, more than made up for by that provided for those engaged in war-time occupations. The primary reason was the unique circumstance by which a large proportion of the population was under some form of hierarchical discipline. Apart from the obvious case of military personnel there were the large numbers of land army, civilian defence forces, air raid wardens, fire fighters and several armies of troop support personal from canteen assistants to aircraft mechanics. Though the truth of this would vary between different war duties, with army soldiers at or near the top, a very great deal of the time during these years would have been spent waiting around for something to happen. There was therefore a need for time to be structured. It was this need that W. E. Williams capitalized on, in pushing through the programme of classes and reading generally known by the name *British Way and Purpose*. A course which must have left many in the usually conservative military hierarchy bemused. The overseeing body was the Central Council for Adult Education in HM Forces. In the military the work was carried forward by the Army Education Corps and more famously the Army Bureau of Current Affairs (ABCA). In discussing the transition from these arrangements towards a peace time civilian provision of adult education, the point has been made

> That men and women will probably undergo a revulsion of feeling against anything that recalls the highly organized, regimented life they lead in war-time is extremely probable (Shearman 1944 49).

For the generations of radicals maturing in the atmosphere of the people's front, the victory over fascism (Portugal and Spain were forgotten at this moment) and the victory over the Conservatives fulfilled the promise of the war years. The need for substantial redistribution of capital in all its forms, was overwhelming, and adult education presented an obvious means through which that change, now in harness, could be carried forward.

However, the manner of those changes was far from agreed, and for many years there continued a dispute between the WEA and the National Council of Labour Colleges (NCLC). While the former must receive the greater attention, the latter requires brief discussion, not least because of its influence on the identity of the WEA. The NCLC came to dominate a diverse and largely non-sectarian independent working-class education (sometimes shortened to IWCE) movement which could trace its routes back through the nineteenth century. In the present century it included a number of local Labour Colleges, responsible for their own curriculum, resources and recruitment. The NCLC, and in particular, its controllers J. P. M. and Christine Miller, sought to bring these disparate bodies into one organization, intervention and direction emanating from the centre into each of these areas of work. The eventual demise of IWCE and its disappearance from working-class life was no doubt in part the result of the authoritarian and sectarian tendencies of the Millers. The WEA was able to not only attract but also keep a much higher quality of teaching staff, while the NCLC lost many of its tutors through internal politics and strained relations with its directors. Perhaps the fundamental reason for the success of the WEA and the failure of this rival was that the association was politically a broad church, making it possible for people of very different persuasions to become members and supporters.

The point is supported by the example of South Wales. With its social and political complexion, it would be reasonable to have expected the NCLC to have succeeded here at the expense of the WEA. Yet the reality was that, while far more successful than anywhere in England, the NCLC even in South Wales was never able to equal the WEA, and eventually succumbed as it did everywhere else. In Richard Lewis's account of the tempestuous late-nineteen-thirties, *Leaders and Teachers*, the WEA is recorded as being able to attract from a militant background, the South Wales Miners' Federation (SWMF) in which was supposed to be the basis for IWCE, while still receiving support from the 'settlement' movement, which had arrived in missionary style to serve and save the unemployed in the coalmining valleys. Unlike the membership in many places in England, where the lower-middle class was already in the ascendancy, the composition of the WEA in South Wales was overwhelmingly manual working class, primarily miners. In other words, even where the social composition, political tendency and intellectual tradition best favoured IWCE, the 'responsible body' as the WEA was designated, was able to attract potentially militant activists. Thus from the middle of the thirties people inspired by the apparent disregard of the national government, whether for the poor which populated the distressed areas, or for the actions of the fascist powers in Spain, could be politically effective through the WEA, thereby robbing the NCLC of just those resources it most needed to remain alive. There is, for instance, no evidence that in 1946 Raymond Williams considered and then rejected the idea of working for the NCLC. However, that perhaps is just the point.

Having completed the work on Ibsen, Williams forsook the option of a fellowship at Cambridge for the post of Staff Tutor for the Oxford Extra-Mural Delegacy. In fact he had started to write a novel, but financial pressures required more regular income. It was with these immediate pressures in mind that the family moved to Seaford in East Sussex. In practice the post required working jointly with the University Delegacy and the WEA. The first year's classes included International Relations, though these rapidly altered to English and Literature, a change which years later Williams was to come back to in a lecture given to WEA tutors past and present,

> I know in my own case ... the first four tutorial classes I had were all in International Relations, and in some curious way in the next year they had all become classes in Literature. The process by which this happened has never been satisfactorily explained (Williams 1983b).

In fact, though the particular example is given somewhat tongue in cheek, the episode was not uncommon among classes during these years, with the consequence that classes in Literature increased disproportionately.

Such a tendency was one of the changes that overtook adult education from the late-nineteen-forties to the late-fifties. Coincident with the shift in curriculum was the altering composition of classes. The number of students earning a living from their hands declined, to be replaced by either 'white-collar' workers or married women not in employment. The change was marked in WEA circles by heated discussion of whether the name of the organization should be changed, and, more seriously, what the function of the association should be. Attempts were made to redefine the term worker so as to include new groups, thereby enabling the WEA to keep to the purposes for which it was founded. Yet there could be no denying that tutorial and other classes were changing and that these changes were part of a wider adjustment of the population. Culture was the prism through which first Williams, and then the New Left attempted to form an assessment of this process, and it was to the extending of the word toward a whole way of life, and at the same time transforming the content of that way of life away from that offered in T. S. Eliot's 1948 thesis *Notes Toward the Definition of Culture*, that the earlier essays of Williams and the pages of *Universities and Left Review* were devoted.

That culture and politics should become intricately interwoven in the course of these enquires should be of little surprise. The circumstance, particularly of the earlier Williams essays was one where attitudes were hardening. The period is now labelled by the blanket expression 'cold war', yet in living through these years it was perhaps the day to day tensions which drew one person toward another and in opposition to a third. The charges against the delegacy that it served to bolster a Communist cell have been discussed elsewhere (Fieldhouse 1985a). In Fieldhouse's account the eye of the storm centred on the Wedgwood Memorial College at Barlaston where it was alleged there existed a core of Communist or sympathetic tutors. A review of the *Annual Reports* for the college for the three years in question, 1947–49, reveals perhaps a relatively high number of names of tutors who might fall into one of these categories, though by no means were they in the majority. In the event, the warden of the college, John Vickers, was replaced, while in a quite independent move at least one of the suspected tutors went to teach in another region of the country.

An as yet little researched manifestation of the cold war in adult education was a debate as to the possibility of objectivity in teaching for people with a political commitment. Again the real concern was with people holding what were perceived as Marxist sympathies, equally strongly held views which fitted in with the Labour Party were rarely if ever questioned. The debate was carried on through the pages of *Highway*, under the theme of 'objectivity and ideology'. Contributors included Sidney

Raybould, Thomas Hodgkin and Henry Collins. We can quickly gain a sense of the tension in which the debate was caught from the following extracts taken from issues of *Highway* for the opening months of 1951:

> Does one in practice find that a very large proportion of Conservative, Liberal and Fabian tutors are able to expand sympathetically the theories of Marx, and that a very small proportion of Marxist tutors are able to expound sympathetically the theories of Burke, Mill and the Webbs? I doubt it. Hence, I think that the tendency, not uncommon nowadays, to take for granted that the minds of Marxists are necessarily rigid and closed, while the minds of non-Marxists are necessarily flexible and open, is foolish and harmful (Hodgkin 1951 80).

The following month Sidney Raybould replied that 'Mr Hodgkin has done us all a great service'. However, the apparent gratitude was no more than that. Raybould proceeded to draw a distinction between tutors who may be sympathetic to the ideas of Marx, and those who couple this with membership of the Communist Party:

> If any teacher, or would-be teacher, has entered into a commitment which is not compatible with the requirements of objective teaching as set out so unambiguously by Mr Hodgkin, it is no violation of freedom of conscience to refuse him employment as a teacher. On the contrary, it would be a violation of the freedom of conscience of students to put them in the charge of a tutor who was committed to trying to gain their acceptance for views which he or his party (or church) happened to believe to be true and important (Raybould 1951 103).

His role as a staff representative meant that Williams could not avoid the conflicts of the later-forties, yet at the time he demonstrated no formal alignment either within the WEA or beyond. Such absence of political affiliation made it possible for Williams to maintain cordial relations with both Hodgkin and Frank Pickstock, the social democratic Assistant Secretary and then Secretary to the Tutorial Classes Committee at Oxford. It was this same disengagement from party politics that made for the unusual circumstance whereby Communists were able to confide in him and in some cases form friendships with the Williams family, while at the same time Williams could still retain the acquaintance of Labour Party stalwarts.

Williams's teaching during the nineteen-forties has been extensively discussed by Roger Fieldhouse and John McIlroy. The result of the influences of practical criticism, a continued socialist commitment and the struggle to establish such new areas as film as viable subjects for adult education classes, compounded to create something of a contradiction in Williams's methods. On the one side was a commitment to the purity of the text and a practice of close reading. On the other was a desire to experiment with the technique of critical practice by adopting it for media other than literature. Crudely, if the first thrust can be said to have produced *Reading and Criticism* in 1950, then the second became manifest in 1952 in *Drama from Ibsen to Eliot:* the chronological closeness with which the two books were written demonstrating the tensions all the more.

Claim has been made that this tension might be understood as one between Williams's allegiance to both Leavisism and socialism and the attempt to bring them together. I would suggest that this may be a little too brash. First, as I noted earlier, Williams's relationship with F. R. Leavis was tenuous and it is not certain as to the extent of any direct influence of the one upon the other. Second, Williams openly rejected the elitist conclusions of the Leavisites' argument. Third, Williams had already begun his own long questioning of socialism.

It is perhaps in the nature of academic publishing that these tensions and contradictions have come through to later generations as a problem with the meaning of culture. The texts are there as evidence, and upon these the histories have come to be written (Johnson 1978, 1979). Yet to understand the history simply in terms of what can be read, is to miss out so much of why it was these books and essays and not others, which came to be written. Real changes in a way of life, in experience, were happening as the hardship of the thirties and forties slipped into history, to be replaced by a vibrant capitalism in consumerist clothing. Culture became the site of the struggle because, on the one side, a way of life *was* changing. Hoggart's brilliant encapsulation of working-class life in the *Uses of Literacy* was born both of a fear that that way of life was being eroded and of a pride made all the more fierce as the threat grew stronger. Williams's arguments lacked the vividness of Hoggart's picture, and were, in any case, very different both in their manner and conclusion. In part, this difference was because of the other side of the equation, the accumulation of the Cambridge tradition plus Eliot, Leavis and *Scrutiny*, and beyond these the reactionary turn in post-war thinking. To argue with this power required a theoretical working through which, in the absence of an adequate existing body of work, necessitated Williams to develop a new field and a new practice.

In the adult education classroom these pressures came through in the contradictions. The attempts to apply critical reading to forms of communication other than literary texts, in order to make a way forward for study of ways of life not valued within the walls of the academic citadel, ran up against the changing composition of the classes. There, he was trying to prepare a mode of analysis which could be of use for the study of working-class life, only to find that post-war change was effecting a relative decline in the attendance of precisely that social group. Eventually, the big books may have gained a reputation for having confronted Cambridge and the tradition. The steady shift in the constituency of his classes eventually confronted Williams. The essays of the earlier-fifties, such as *The Idea of Culture*, published in 1953, were wrought out of these pressures as they were lived in the classroom, in the politics beyond, and in the research which the developing of arguments around the meaning of culture required.

We get a better grasp of this work if we fill in some of the empirical detail. The years immediately following the end of the war seem to have been extraordinarily full for Williams. He completed his degree in June 1946 and directly began teaching a WEA class in the Fens. The unsuccessful move to North Devon to start a novel had followed. He had, though, already applied for the post of full-time staff tutor, and this he took up in September, which meant moving to Seaford at the same time. In 1947 the pace of work increased considerably. Apart from the many duties of a staff tutor, Williams began his first novel, *Brynllwyd* which some three versions later was eventually published as *Border Country* in 1960. At the same time he began work on *Drama from Ibsen to Eliot*, which, though completed in 1948, was not published until 1952. Nineteen-forty-seven to forty-eight was also, of course, the period of *Politics and Letters* and *The Critic* for which, aside from his editorial work, Williams wrote nine contributions in the form of essays and reviews.

In addition to all these activities, Williams began work on a film for Paul Rotha. The topic was to be agricultural and industrial revolutions. Though never finished, due to the intransigence of the officials with whom they were to negotiate financial support, Williams did complete the film script. Later, in 1953, his partnership with Michael Orram, with whom he had been in the Socialist Society before the war, produced the book *Preface to Film*. However, once again a planned film remained just that. Finally, again in 1948 Williams completed a radio script which, being rejected, he turned into a novel, though one that was never published. An extraordinary output has of course since followed, but nonetheless the circumstance of this early work, the instability and redefining of self that had to be worked through after the experience of fighting, makes these early years especially remarkable. Referring to the work, Williams recalls the years in his own terms,

> These seemed much more exciting projects than doing a thesis. The shape of the immediate years was that one would take WEA classes to support oneself through them (Williams 1979a 64).

The expectations of the war and the immediate aftermath were not fulfilled, and the failure formed what I consider to be a pivotal experience for Williams. I want to pursue that feeling of failure and blockage, and the need to understand the changing cultural patterns of post-war Britain through examining Williams's reflections on adult education and his eventual physical, though not spiritual, movement away. Williams is quite clear about the part adult education played in the loss of forward momentum suffered by the Labour Government and the relative ease with which a new conformity was established following the war years (1979a 73–74). It is a view which others have since come to share. He argues that the failure of the Labour Government to continue to support popular educational provision for people after 1945 left the conventional pressures in newspapers and elsewhere an easier propaganda task than might otherwise have been the case.

Unfortunately, the *New Left Review* interviewers do not pursue Williams's generalized statement toward any empirical example. However, the suggestion finds an echo in Corfield's 1969 book *Epoch in Workers Education*. In it Corfield discusses the funding of the WEA. In brief, the problem was that while the regions were awarded additional money for their work, the central office was left in poverty and thus unable to provide the role of co-ordination and innovation that it might otherwise have done.

However, *Epoch in Workers Education* contains a more sensitive argument which integrates the fortunes of adult education with a deeper and more profound change in English society after 1945:

> In common with all voluntary organizations they [the WEA] faced the special problem of the age: the increase of professionalism, of the scope and power of government and the pull of big organizations, commercial as well as public. In this situation they acknowledged that some of the spurs to individual participation in voluntary movements were weakened (Corfield 1969 176).

The point is perhaps another way of describing the change which, in chapter one and elsewhere, I have referred to as religious behaviour or commitment. In Corfield's eyes it was a spirit of voluntary involvement that had declined, thereby undermining the very basis upon which the WEA and bodies like it rested. The voluntary ethos reaches back into the nineteenth century, and the varied bodies who took responsibility for the social and moral improvement of one section or another of the population. Yet the ethos was not merely that those who received should benefit, but that those who gave should also be improved. The various societies for the poor, the university settlements and educational bodies, recognized that those who contributed could gain a sense of social consciousness and of their part in a greater whole (Harrison 1961). We are here at the cross-roads of collectivist Liberalism, Spencian sociology and the rise of modern socialism in the form of the Labour, Trade Union and Co-operative Movement. Adult education was founded at this intersection, pulling together Christian Socialists, university staff and members of the Labour Movement. It would of course be purely romantic to suggest that this earnest amalgam was better than the professionalism which superseded it. That is not the point. Rather it is that the mutation weakened the inspiration upon which voluntary movements for change—charitable, educational and even political—depended.

The trend in the provision of adult education, already in place before the war, and intensified after 1945, was for the universities to make direct provision through their own extra-mural departments. On the other side the Local Education Authorities (LEA) were given greater charge to provide technical education. The traditional focus for the WEA was liberal education, thus the latter development was less threatening. That posed by the professional staff of extra-mural departments, however, was crucial. Williams was of course himself just such a new style professional, if a critical one.

Yet the rise of professionalism was not the only pressure detracting from the voluntary ethos:

> Some of the vitality of local voluntary action seemed to be declining with the decay of the older industrial areas (Corfield 1969 177).

In calculating how much the decline of older industrial areas detracted from voluntary involvement, regional variation must be taken into account. In South Wales the effect on educational culture of the decline of an industrial base has been all but terminal. Elsewhere the change may have been less dramatic. Yet the two, the rise of large organizations and professionalism, and the decline of the nineteenth-century industrial centres, overlapped. The point at which they met was that where the autodidact came into contact with the itinerant preacher or teacher. There is a serious danger here of romanticizing the past. However, it is also true that an exceptional amount of learning did take place through contacts between skilled and even unskilled workers and tutors, who were themselves often not from college cloisters but had absorbed all they could from learning and now sought to encourage others to follow (Harrison 1961). The voluntary effort worked on both sides; while the autodidacts clearly gave up their time to seeking knowledge, teachers, while they were paid, nevertheless were both ambassadors and evangelists of the philanthropic desire for the betterment of society and the individual. Yet two world wars had been fought since the establishment of adult education on a national basis. They had each demanded a degree of organization and management never witnessed before. In such circumstances the call for professionals to administer resources, including people, inevitably grew stronger.

Turning to Williams's own decision to move on from adult education, certain of these pressures repeat themselves. The WEA had been driven by the trade union movement toward provision of instruction immediately applicable to the work context. With this went the pressure from LEAs toward rationalization, and accreditation of learning. Certain skills had to be demonstrated as capable of being learned from a particular activity, and measurement brought to bear on how 'successful' the trainee or student was in acquiring them. For Williams, the last straw was the establishing of a residential centre for the teaching of future business managers.

In fact Williams's departure from adult education was not an altogether straightforward affair. Three elements conspired to complicate matters; first, the timing, second, the manner in which Williams gained a new post, and last, his own contradictory response. Over and above any one of these was the sheer extraordinariness of his moving from external adult education, to which one might have thought he was entirely suited, to an internal post, for which he might have been thought entirely unsuited. That the move was extraordinary for this very reason has not perhaps been fully appreciated.

The timing was remarkable because only one year earlier the Williamses had moved from Seaford to Oxford where Raymond took up a new appointment as Resident Tutor. When a year later he received the appointment at Cambridge, the surprise was all the greater since he did not know of the post and had therefore not applied. Perhaps as a result of the factors I have already mentioned, Williams's response to the appointment was contradictory. He did not wish to leave adult education yet recognized that its nature was changed. I have already mentioned the setting up of a centre for management training with which Williams was supposed to be associated. At the same time the opportunity of a Cambridge post would clearly leave him more time to write, especially compared to the new post of Resident Tutor at Oxford. Either way, the move was made without undue delay.

I will conclude this section with a brief review of Williams's *An Open Letter to WEA Tutors*, first published in 1961 by the WEA and reprinted in the collection edited by McIlroy and Westwood (1993 222–225). The letter was written at the time of Williams's move from Oxford, and from outside the institution to the very central place of the Cambridge English Department. In it, Williams recites the founding principles upon which the WEA was established, and refutes that '… the WEA's historic mission is over.' (ibid. 223). The charge resided in the belief that with extended and improved schooling, the 'ladder' of opportunity was available to children of poor families as well as rich. Williams's answer is short and to the point: the WEA's purpose was the betterment of all through the changing of society. Yet Williams is aware that this response alone is not sufficient reason for the continuance of the association. The idea of a more equitable society had been claimed to have been, if not fully realized, then at least sufficiently achieved since 1945. It was this same endorsement of welfare capitalism, that *New Left Review* and its forerunners—essays in the 1958 collection *Convictions*, edited by Norman Mackenzie, *Out of Apathy*, edited by Edward Thompson two years later, and, parallel to these, Williams's own *Long Revolution*—had also been arguing against. Placed in this context, the contention in the *Open Letter* that the social and democratic reforms since 1945 were necessary but not sufficient gains greater weight.

Yet the *Open Letter* is citing not only the inadequacy of the reforms, but also a further point specific to the nature of the WEA. At first sight the argument seems be that of Corfield's; however, its development moves it in a different direction. The people who make up the association, are part of '… one of the best and deepest traditions in Britain: that of voluntary, independent serious work.' (ibid. 223). Looking at that tradition in the present and the future he continues,

> Its historic mission is as urgent and central today as it was in the 1900s, because its basic challenge stands out much more clearly, and is no longer propped up by simple missionary feeling, that the fortunate should help the unfortunate, or by simple class feelings, that the odd pearl should be picked out of the swine heap (ibid. 223).

Further on, he offers three specific examples for where future progressive work might advance; trade unions, women's organizations and young people. Unfortunately, the first of these continued ever further in the direction of technical skills and away from liberal education, as Williams had already noted.

Though this is not the manner in which it has been discussed by John McIlroy and Sallie Westwood, the *Open Letter* may be read as evidence of how Williams's work during the years of the New Left issued not from the departures of 1956, but ran back further toward the war, and the project as it was set by the conditions of the post-war years. Williams's move into the institution marked a change in place from whence in future, the arguments contained in this passing salvo, would stem.

3. POLITICS AND LETTERS

With the exception of the interviews published under the title *Politics and Letters*, neither *Politics and Letters* nor the *Critic* have to date been the subject of anything more than a passing mention. While the total material represented by the two periodicals may not be great, their pivotal importance in the life of Raymond Williams makes the lack of attention somewhat surprising. Produced by characteristic voluntary hard work the editors were, with Williams, Clifford Collins and Wolf Mankowitz. Mankowitz was in addition the sole editor of the *Critic*. The two journals were centred on a small London office in Noel Street. A quick check of the geography will reveal how very close, a few minutes walk, the 1947–8 office in Noel Street was from the 1958 home in Carlisle Street of *Universities and Left Review*, and, from 1960, *New Left Review*. However, in the circumstance of 1947, it is less clear why the editors felt the need to establish what would have been a more expensive central London editorial address when there had since the mid-nineteen-thirties been a rich literary output away from the capital (Croft 1990). *Politics and Letters* was the senior publication to the *Critic*, which it eventually absorbed, and it is to the former that I shall give greater attention.

Politics and Letters has been described as an attempt to 'unite Leavisian "criticism" and left politics' (Mulhern 1979 230). Of the three editors, Williams had the least connection with either the Leavisites or *Scrutiny*, thus while the claim may well be accurate for the journal, Williams's own project was different. The *Critic* was intended to carry through the activity of practical criticism not dissimilar from that which appeared in *Scrutiny*, and Mankowitz himself published in the latter. By contrast *Politics and Letters* was intended to explore the links between the literary and the social, an activity which was certainly not necessarily Marxist though could, when convenient, be condemned as such (Wilson 1932).

There is always a danger of viewing the past from the perspective of today, and it is very easy to understand the opening editorial 'For Continuity in Change' through Williams's subsequent writing. Viewed in this way, that the first line of a journal of which Raymond Williams was an editor should run, 'If a formal position were implied in the phrase "Politics and Letters" it would, necessarily, be a complex one' (ibid. 3) would only appear characteristic. But that of course is to read history backwards, the earlier in terms of the later. Yet, as a description of the editorial which followed, the line was thoroughly accurate. The aim of the journal was to explore the relationship between politics and letters. The two words signify two levels of experience. Politics denoted the objective, the impersonal, planned government. The first two terms come from the thirties when they were among the watchwords of progressive writing. They referred to the inevitable destructiveness of capitalism, both of human life and of itself. Capitalism had turned into totalitarian fascism across Europe, and it was the function of intellectuals to turn their skills to the revealing of this fact. Planned government on the other hand was the experience of a younger generation both during the war and on into the post-war years. Letters, by contrast, related to the individual, the subjective and the personal. In the post-war years, and I recall here Williams's claim for a conservative turn among academics and students, this side of the equation had come to capture the ground of values, standards and even morals. These qualities, it was in turn proposed, were to be best found in literature.

The job of *Politics and Letters*, and the job of the editorial to explain to readers, was to find a means for unifying these two sides in such a manner that morals and values could again be brought to the side of progress. The earlier part of the editorial clearly agrees with the case for literary works to embody the standards by which society should be judged:

> The case which those whose concern is for morals might have made, and which the Marxists throughout the thirties tried to find room for, seems to us to rest upon experience of literature and the arts. … What is valid, and in our opinion supremely important, is that the structure of society, its institutions and directions, should be constantly assessed by standards resting on certain immediate qualities of living, qualities which social history scarcely records, but which 'for continuity' our cultural tradition embodies (ibid. 3–4).

However, the thrust of the article is for those qualities, individuality, etc., to remain impotent, unless harnessed to the progressive movement of society. The function of the journal must be to identify and plot the means by which the standards of 'our cultural tradition' can inform the active planning of social relationships and institutions. The first step toward this must be to explore and disclose the real nature of the division between the two poles. From this, the 'criteria of literary criticism must be brought to bear on social art forms' including cinema. The third step referred to a continuing of standards in education. The editorial's final measure, arising from the rather vague proposition that it was not possible to 'directly ... relate' the experience of a work of art to 'more general qualities of living in the society', was the need to plot 'the social and intellectual background of the present time'. The sentence is best quoted in its entirety:

> And to this end, the most satisfactory means (failing the direct relation of literature and social events) would seem to be the enlistment of specialists to assess evidence provided by their own fields of enquiry, and to revalue the conclusions arrived at by other disciplines (ibid. 4).

These steps amount, I suggest, to little short of an early statement of Williams's own project as it developed over the decade after the collapse of *Politics and Letters*, and indeed beyond. There were, of course, important changes. The nature of the relationship between orders of experience as between art and society altered so that by the time of *Culture and Society* we read,

> An essential hypothesis in the development of the idea of culture is that the art of a particular period is closely and necessarily related to the general prevalent 'way of life', and further that, in consequence, aesthetic, moral and social judgements are closely related (1958a 130).

Yet clearly even in this change, the line of continuity is apparent in the manner in which the problem is formulated and remains the relationship between different orders of experience.

This was not the only argument for how moral value may be rejoined with the political, and a series of contributions on the theme were published under the heading 'Critic and Leviathan'. While these crossed the different editions of the journal, they are here discussed together. Writing in the first number, Christopher Hill proposed that a reunion of morality, value and the political could best be made through the offices of the Communist Party. Apparently crude, Hill's argument held apparent weight. The basis was that the traditional values upon which criticism was founded were implicated in social anarchy and destruction, imperialist war, the poverty and social division of the twenties and thirties, and then the ascendance of fascism and war again. As such a new set of values had to be forged. For this to happen a new social order was required, and for this a force clear in its aspiration and judgement was needed. The Communist Party was just such an agent, indeed *the* agent, since it alone had the intellectual and organizational basis upon which what would be fully human values could be created.

Hill was, in fact, responding to an article by Raymond Winkler which appeared in the same issue. Likewise writing under the heading 'Critic and Leviathan', Winkler is critical of contemporary society, judging the development of mechanized industrial production to be inimical to the maintenance of the traditional values which sustain literature and art (*Politics and Letters* 1 1947 32–9). Hill's response is to declare that this is a 'false antithesis' (ibid. 40). Instead Hill enlarges the problem from that of the presence of machines, to the social relationships between people, in the context of which machines are worked, and which is usually referred to as capitalism. That Hill should move rapidly to this point (line six to be precise) is not of itself a cause for complaint. The cause lies nearer the conclusion. In arriving at his own conclusion Winkler argued that whereas in the thirties it was the

> ... bearing of political beliefs on literary taste and practice that usually occupied the arena of discussion. Here it is the converse—the bearing of values implied by literature on political practice—that is being considered (ibid. 38).

Thus the literary person should not abdicate responsibility for the material world in which they live. Rather they should bring to bear on social and political matters, those values which literature can offer. Where, it was claimed, in the thirties the call to political commitment might also require the abandonment of literary and critical investigation, now the critic and writer must hold anchor in their literary experience, and only then venture on to speak of issues in the social and political spheres. Judgement must always rest on the sure values found in the former (ibid. 38–9). Interestingly, Winkler qualifies this argument with the recognition that the great absence which divides the literary and the social is the lack of the generalist. It has been the tendency toward specialization that has undermined the ability of people to speak generally. The literary critic with an understanding of economics or politics has, mourns Winkler, become a scarce being. That this should appear in a periodical edited by Raymond Williams is wonderfully ironic. Indeed the title 'Politics and Letters' and the range of material it was intended to carry made it precisely an agent of the type that Winkler assumed to have fallen away.

Returning to Hill's article, the cause of complaint is in its complacency and potential arrogance. In the last paragraph Hill leaves aside any questions about means and specific ends, instead citing membership of the Communist Party to be the one necessary step toward not only founding a set of values by which the literary and the political may be judged, but the very means by which the intellectuals may find their place in society. Ten years later at the special congress of the party in 1957, Hill was to be one of those hounded out, not least because his place as an intellectual had apparently caused him to adopt bourgeois values and drawn him away from the class who alone could provide him with the measure by which to judge the world and his experience within it.

The heading of 'Critic and Leviathan' is continued in the combined issues two and three of *Politics and Letters*. The contributors this time are F. R. Leavis and Lionel Elvin. I want for the moment to leave aside Leavis' contribution, not least because the other is more interesting. We can quickly get a flavour. Elvin is weighing up between Winkler and Hill:

> The Labour Party believes in collective economic planning, though in my opinion (and here at last Mr Hill and I will agree) it will have to plan our economy a great deal more seriously and comprehensively than it has yet (*Politics and Letters* 2 & 3 1947–8 64).

The aside in parentheses provides an important clue. The problem is that Hill viewed the Communist Party alone as the vehicle for change. This Elvin retorts is 'arrogant: does he really believe that no other party but the Communists has as its aim the destruction of the barriers of capitalism'? (ibid. 64). In other words, Elvin will not accept, just as the editors of *Politics and Letters* will not accept, that membership of the Communist Party was the only option available to those for whom the present order must be replaced.

For what might be called the more standard position adopted for the critic, Elvin has little time. The creation of a 'Literary Critics Party' will, he states bluntly, not be sufficient (ibid. 61). Indeed from Elvin's point of view, such a stance is all the more dangerous precisely because it legitimates the Communists' charge. The necessary changes required in society demands organizations adequate to the effort needed. What is clearly feared is the imposition of correctness, that was even then taking place in the Soviet Union, and which Communists were defending.

The specific problem of the Communists and the literary and artistic situation in the Soviet Union had already been addressed by Williams in the first issue of *Politics and Letters* in his article 'The Soviet Literary Controversy'. Working on a much larger canvas, Williams rejects both a recent case of Soviet central state intervention in a literary magazine, and the manner of its condemnation by both newspapers and periodicals in Britain. The response of the former was unsurprising, though 1947 was early for such hysteria. The latter, Williams comments, approached the issue from the question of the relationship between the 'modern, centralized state' and literature (*Politics and Letters* 1 1947 21). In Williams's view the problem should not, as *Horizon* tended, be viewed as a problem peculiar to the USSR, but recognized to exist, if in different forms, in Britain and similar societies. In these it was the market which, in perhaps more subtle manner, defined the conditions within which literature was produced, a theme to which he subsequently returned more than once (Williams 1961, 1971).

The article, supplied by F. R. Leavis, under the heading 'Critic and Leviathan' raises again the point of what purpose *Politics and Letters* is to serve. Leavis repeats Winkler's assertion of the need for the non-specialist, able to bring to the harder sciences those values of the critic. As to the present circumstance, Leavis is not sanguine:

'… how long can they [the editors] go on finding approaches to political and sociological questions that can profitably be made by people of literary training' (*Politics and Letters* 2 & 3 1947–8 60).

Not unreasonably he assesses *Politics and Letters* in terms of his own project for the creation of an English School which he had set out some four years earlier in *Education and the University*. In so far as the present periodical pursues that end he wishes it every success. Whether such a project might be placed under the heading of a 'Literary Critics' Party', may be a matter of disagreement, it is, though, hard to imagine that such could be an end towards which the all editors of *Politics and Letters* might feel themselves disposed.

The last contribution from the series 'Critic and Leviathan', was penned by George Orwell, and again raises questions of the relationship of literature and state. Writing in 1948, Orwell's preoccupations remain those he held in the later thirties. The paranoia took the form of an all powerful Communist Party, indeed in Orwell's imagination it was the only existing political formation. In this fantasy the one aim of the party was to stop George Orwell writing and publishing. Characteristically, Orwell's theme is the threat to the writer presented by an overbearing state. Not surprisingly the source of this danger is posed by the Communist press and party. Yet the party and press were guilty not only of bringing on a supposedly all-powerful state, but in the process of undermining literary values. This last was achieved by passing judgement according to whether the 'book is on my side' (*Politics and Letters* 4 36). As to which or what side this might be, we learn a page further on; 'Obviously, for about fifteen years past, the dominant orthodoxy, especially amongst the young, has been "left".' (ibid. 37). The truth of this last claim is dubious. What makes the statement objectionable is the manner in which Orwell cites an assertion as an absolute.

Orwell's though is an appeal. It is an appeal for and to artists. It is a plea to artists to maintain their integrity. He does not say that they should not engage in politics. '… no thinking person can or does genuinely keep out of politics, in an age like the present.' (ibid. 39), rather they should split themselves so that their political activity is kept quite separate from their writing. It is an appeal for writers, such that they should not be required to give their writing to a party or group:

Group loyalties are necessary, and yet they are poisonous to literature, so long as literature is the product of individuals (ibid. 39).

There may be time and circumstance when Orwell's contentions are valid, even necessary. However, Orwell seeks to bolster his argument on the grounds that writers are a special breed, that writing is unlike other activities. For others, Orwell contests, there is no need to establish this split since their occupations already engendered a division between people's work and political life—a claim which is at best dubious. The splitting of work from politics is a difficult choice that many are required to make, and writing and writers do not make for special pleading.

Leavis's point about *Politics and Letters* needing to attract contributors who did not stem from a literary origin was entirely justified, and while the range of other disciplines represented was not wide, the journal nevertheless contained some formidable contributors. In political history and the social sciences, the list included G. D. H. Cole on 'Politics and Sociology in the twentieth century', Henry Collins on Karl Popper's 'Open Society and its Enemies' and Morris Ginsberg on 'Psychoanalysis and Sociology'. Henry Collins' article, while ostensibly a review of Popper's then very recent major work, may be read as an argument in its own right. While he provides a substantial rebuff of Popper's treatment of Plato, the article really warms as he approaches Marx via Hegel. Perhaps the worst indictment of which he finds Popper guilty is a failure to have read Marx, or at least to have read Marx in a manner sufficient for the accusations Popper came to make. The flavour of Collins' repulse may be gained from the following lines,

> Tendencies to sloppiness, to distortion and to a somewhat slapdash acquaintance with his subject, more than perceptible in Popper's treatment of Hegel, simply overwhelm the chapters on Marx (*Politics and Letters* 1 1947 53).

In the reference signalled in this passage, Collins gives an example of this 'slapdash acquaintance' in respect of Hegel.

Of course, much more of Marx's writing was yet to come to light, and judgements of the master have been revised by disciples of many shades since. However, Collins' charge that Popper's criticism of Marx and quite blistering attack of Marxism, was in no small part founded on insufficient reading, remains serious. Unfortunately, while Collins justifies his argument against Popper, it is hard not to get the feeling that the particular examples are either rather technical, or suggestive of a first-rate party intellectual.

Cole's article announces itself to have a more limited intent than the title might suggest. While the term politics, may appear in the title, this is not a reference to the political activities, institutions, etc., of a society, but to politics as an academic subject. Cole's is a 'plea for ... a new shape to the study of the theory of society' and a search for 'an institutional type Social Economics.' (ibid. 84). However, Cole in reality pursues the circumstance of the social and political world through discussion of attempts at its theorization. In doing so he relates the development of a theory to the historical conditions of a society. Thus, his argument that the problem with political theory and economics is their specialization, is placed against the practice of unregulated laissez-faire. The latter allowed economists to discuss rational 'economic man', and political theorists to talk of a state that apparently had no connection with society beyond itself. Interestingly, Cole's argument mirrors that of Winkler in its criticism of a tendency towards over specialization. For Cole the need can arise where newly created subjects not supported by the expertise of a tutor in a traditional discipline, may nonetheless have to struggle forward until such competence is gained (ibid. 92), a view expressive of the situation often encountered in adult education.

Ultimately, Cole's is a plea for nothing less than 'the general study of society as a whole' (ibid. 91). As such it may be read as a reply to the literary-cultural expression of Leavis. An agreement as to the need, if a divergence as to the manner. With the closure of *Politics and Letters* Williams's aim became in effect to advance the substance of culture from the point at which Leavis would seem to leave it, to incorporate the theoretical and political insight of Cole.

Morris Ginsberg's 'Psychoanalysis and Sociology', which appeared in the combined second and third issue of the journal, attempts a genuinely academic act, examining the usefulness of Freud's propositions for social-psychology and the understanding of social groups. Reasons for Ginsberg's enquiry include a claim that

> ... now there is hardly a branch of sociological inquiry which has remained unaffected by Freud's teaching of the part played by unconscious factors in the growth of the mind (ibid. 74).

Unfortunately, I am unable to judge the truth or otherwise of this claim, though note that in *Politics and Letters* 1 there appeared a discussion of different schools of psychoanalysis and their validity for the study of society and political activity. The verdict there was not encouraging. Ginsberg's article coincided with the publication of *Reason and Unreason in Society*, the second volume of his *Essays in Sociology and Social Philosophy*. The volume was reviewed in the last number of *Politics and Letters*, the verdict being that while it tends toward abstraction with little immediate correlation to everyday experience, it was a major improvement on the then tendency to publish records of social facts with little or no theorizing as to their meaning. If this last circumstance was true, then we need to be rather careful in accepting Ginsberg's claim of the pervasiveness of psychoanalysis in sociology, instead suspecting this to be more accurately a statement of what ought to have been the case rather than the situation as it actually was.

Among other features of the journal was a 'Commentary' section which provided space for essays on contemporary issues affecting education, or literary and cultural values. An interesting example of these commentaries occurred in the second edition, and reviewed the child of ABCA, the Bureau of Current Affairs. Established directly at the end of the war, the bureau sought to extend the work started with service personnel into peace-time conditions. The review concentrates on the methods of teaching advocated by the bureau and concludes that, while not wholly wrong, they were probably insufficient. The bureau is acknowledged to be concerned,

> … not with the small selective minority for which formal adult education caters, but rather those who up to the present have remained outside its work (*Politics and Letters* 2 & 3 1947–48 98).

The method of teaching was that of the discussion group, intended to elicit from participants their understanding of a subject, which the method assumed they were already capable of possessing. It was the justification of this faith in the capacity of people that the writer doubted. The doubt, however, rested upon the most familiar of grounds, and ones which the political thrust of the editors sought to rebuff. The problem turned on the question of values, and, it would seem, a felt loss of respect for the profession of teacher. The writer concludes,

> Thus today the greatest danger is not the lack of general understanding as to the specific conditions in Italy or the USSR, or the legal or local government set-up in this country, but the general acceptance of a smug mediocrity of aesthetic and spiritual values and a general degradation of taste. By its basic approach the BAC encourages a democratic philistinism, and emphatically is not fitted to deal with this aspect of adult education (ibid. 100).

There can be no doubting the tone. It is an example of the traditional conservative defence of values and taste. Though not cited here, it was just such a battle that the Leavisites fought through the medium of literature, where these attributes were meant to exist in their best form. Leaving aside the issue of taste, which the present writer has never been able to understand as anything more than a personal preference, the question of values was at the very centre of *Politics and Letters*. For the reviewer of the Bureau of Current Affairs the danger lay in a supposed 'democratic philistinism'. The reverse side of this claim was the presupposition of a cultured elite among whom the capacity to appreciate that which was of value, and presumably define what was of value, already existed. The apparent support for the work of the WEA and the university classes, suggests that for the writer acquisition of these abilities was possible, but only after the correct learning process had taken place. The rebuttal of the discussion group method favoured by the bureau and the preference for a suitably qualified leader in the learning process, can be seen to correspond to this view of values and the need for their protection. The editorial direction of *Politics and Letters* was a brave attempt to cut through this knot, denying both the incapacity of people to have values, and at the same time rejecting the standards of commercial enterprise which for old liberals was synonymous with 'the masses'.

Politics and Letters carried a range of reviews, not only of fiction and academic books, but theatre, radio plays, and from Lyn Byrtles, its only regular woman writer, visual arts. The otherwise near-complete absence of women writing in *Politics and Letters* should make us a little surprised, given the time. The numbers of women in universities had increased, while many more than previously had spent the war years in a public role. The situation might have been different had the editors made any effort to attract female writers, for which there is, unhappily, no evidence.

I want to conclude the present section with the article, 'Notes on town planning, architecture and community' from the last issue of *Politics and Letters*. Surprisingly, and perhaps reflecting a genuine limitation of expertise among the journals contributors, this is the only piece on this obviously topical and highly appropriate subject for *Politics and Letters*. The piece has a further importance here in offering an opportunity for direct comparison with the later *Universities and Left Review*. At the end of the fifties the concern with living space and town development, and the effect of these on senses of community, resurfaced. By then, sociologists and others were expressing theories to account for a supposed decline of working-class solidarity. I will review some of these speculations, and the perhaps less rose-tinted historical image offered by Raymond Williams and others later. For the moment I want to catch the sense of this post-war review and its place in *Politics and Letters*.

The review contains a number of arguments each in one way or another expressive of the time. There is no hesitation as to the need for planning and equally the dismissal of 'nineteenth-century laissez-faire' building principles (ibid. 49). These, the author argues, provide only an illusion of choice, since the vast majority of the population did not have the economic power to exercise control over their type of living environment. However, acceptance of the need for planning would seem to open up a whole series of further questions. For J. R. Armstrong, the author of the article, these seemed to revolve around a number of variables. His proposition was that,

> ... the final aim in planning is presumably the creation of an integrated, organic, and yet democratic community (ibid. 59).

In arriving at this there are some very interesting suggestions as to size, character and architecture of communities. Far from any of these having been achieved, fifty years on the pressures have been in the reverse direction, underpinning the joke about Milton Keynes being the first purpose-built slum. Armstrong's call for cultural and social needs being met on a small scale would seem equally as utopian as his assumption that people would soon be working a drastically shorter working week.

His image for the organic community seems to be a little imprecise. At times Medieval, there are moments when it comes forward to Tudor times, and yet others when it seems only to have disappeared some two hundred years earlier (ibid. 55–56). Many years later Raymond Williams was to write an amusing and pointed criticism of supposed golden ages, complete with their respective organic community of people living close to the earth and the natural rhythms of the seasons (1985b 9–12).

The three variables through which creation of an optimum community of the future must be negotiated were: democratic mediocrity, an enlightened minority and a paternalist welfare state. The first and third Armstrong points out, were potentially in conflict. The last is by its nature a top down approach to social planning, which in the case of house building and design of environment, rural as well as urban, left little room for the views of those directly effected by the plan. Democratic mediocrity on the other hand came to be feared with a

> … realization that values of the majority have become degraded and that the majority has neither the capacity or the will to decide what, in the long run, it wants (ibid. 49).

From a comment made near the beginning of the article I would surmise that Armstrong had been a tutor in the armed forces, and it may be upon that experience that such a judgement is made. Whatever the case, the alternative would seem to be an enlightened minority, which in the face of paternalist planning, however, seems, in Armstrong's picture, to be unable to exert any real effect. As such, the piece wonderfully elicits the perils felt by some at the end of the war, when, while supporting the efforts of Labour to reform and eliminate the worst excesses of free market capitalism, they were horrified at the prospect of ill-informed people creating a society where a shallow mediocrity would become the norm.

Unfortunately, Armstrong's was the only article to be included in *Politics and Letters* on the subject of town planning. However, it would still be interesting to compare this with those appearing in *Universities and Left Review* a decade later. There were a range of pieces on subjects concerned not only with town planning, particularly that of such new towns as Croydon, but also with what was perceived, all too readily by some, as the poverty of old inner-city slums (*ULR* 1 1957, *ULR* 5 1958). I discuss some of these issues in detail in chapter eight.

One difference between the tendency of some of the *ULR* articles and Armstrong's, was the strong sociological tendency of the former. The perception even in the left-wing *ULR* was of a people incapable of doing anything for themselves and existing at the mercy of developers both private and public. The language is closer to that of victim, rather than Armstrong's unenlightened masses whose sense of worth had been degraded by capitalist industrialization. The consequence, though, does not seem to be substantially different.

However, this is not the only presentation in *ULR*. An interesting article on a recent architects' conference published in *ULR* 1, picks up on a number of points in Armstrong's piece, arguing that further developments should be within existing city areas rather than by the building on virgin land. In design though, these developments should form 'towns within cities' (ibid. 43). These would have their own centres of employment, education, recreation, etc. Admittedly on a larger scale than Armstrong thought necessary, this *ULR* article nonetheless contained the same principle, that planning was itself a process of building communities. Alas, this case put forward a decade later has, like Armstrong's, been largely ignored.

Armstrong's concern for the creation of community is most strongly present in some of *ULR*'s early ethnographic work. Centred on two new towns the conclusions of one study, in part carried on by members of a New Left club, are worth quoting at some length for the likeness of concerns retained from a decade earlier:

> Where communal organizations spring up like fungi, there is no true community spirit; where youth is supposedly well educated and provided for, young people are vaguely dissatisfied, aimless, disintegrated. Where class consciousness is theoretically denied, working-class people are consciously trying to elevate themselves, lulled into a belief in the dream land of status through possessions; where the concept of a true community is advanced as a motivating factor for the New Towns' inauguration, no true community in the senses indicated elsewhere in this issue of *ULR* seems to exist (*ULR* 5 1958 23).

The pointed, and as usual accurate, response to this theme by Edward Thompson is discussed in chapter eight. Here I merely note that there exists within this conclusion a negative nostalgia very similar to that in Armstrong's. Embodying a reference to an organic community living at some past time, and against which judgement of the present may be made, there is certainly a dismissal of present people for not living up to the ideal these New Left club researchers envisaged for them. The pattern has become all too familiar. Socialist sociological theorists create a working class which empirical research fails to uncover. In despair at discovering their theoretical figures to be just that, they heap disgust on the actual people they find.

There was, as I have said, sadly only one contribution on the issues of architecture, town planning and ideas of community in *Politics and Letters*, yet comparing it with *ULR* a decade later has highlighted continuing concerns of the post-war years. These were the years of reconstruction and new building so that the engagement by progressive people should not be at all surprising. The disregard of those arguing for the regeneration of old cities through the creation of new and localized centres, is a tragedy for which we continue to pay. However, the dismissal of ordinary people which continued from the earlier to the later periodical, as either an unenlightened mass or worse still 'aimless and disintegrated', was weak thinking on the part of writers and researchers. Not absent from this tone is a new form of moral rescue.

Turning to Williams's work, one distinctive element was a refusal to indulge in an imaginary working class, and therefore the cry of 'foul' when the illusion was blown, or in the paternalism of the outside voyeur. It was a difference born of coming from the people Armstrong and the *ULR* researchers viewed as objects. In *Culture is Ordinary* (1958b) Williams offers various ways of understanding the term through discussion of his own life and experience. Eventually he recalls a recent occasion with his family; a shopgirl, fitter, signal man and domestic help (ibid. 85). The argument that follows denies that a simple line can be drawn between those who possess a good culture and those a bad. Similarly rejected is the simplistic idea that bad culture is driving out good. With these is the denial, though not here phrased in these words, that there existed masses. The last, a characteristic of that way of viewing those with whom we have no direct contact, yet who seem continuously to pass us by moving in one direction or another. In place of these Williams asserts,

> ... we live in an expanding culture, and all the elements in this culture are themselves expanding. If we start from this, we can then ask real questions: about relative rates of expansion; about the social and economic problems raised by these; about the social and economic answers (ibid. 87).

Viewed this way it is no longer possible to imagine the masses whose critical sensibility has been dimmed by industrialization or mass production. Neither does it remain possible to imagine a people who can be simply monitored and levels of class consciousness, or communal spirit measured.

In the next section I review Williams's own circumstance during these early post-war years. In concluding the present, it may be as well to offer a balance sheet of the successes and failings of *Politics and Letters*. Of course, in the obvious sense that the journal folded in less than two years it has to be regarded as a failure. Indeed Williams, in the interview with the *NLR* people, suggests little else than that it was a failure, and one which affected him terribly. However, the circumstance of the period and the writers made publication far from easy,

> ... there was always a slightly asymmetrical relation in that they would come for a weekend and plan the magazine and write things together, while I would get to the office less often (1979a 68).

Paper rationing restricted the volume of material which could be published. More importantly it interrupted the regularity with which the printing could take place, preventing the sort of confidence which certainty could inspire in readers. Indeed, reading *Politics and Letters* it is striking how much the editors seem to rely on people somehow being in the know in order to obtain their copy of the next issue. The use of initials and at times the vaguest of referencing suggests further a close familiarity between writers and readers. Certainly this was much more likely than in the nineteen-nineties, when the professionalization of publishing has led to the most tedious bureaucracy over every detail of an article, and when the expansion of education, albeit under ever more restrictive and authoritarian state regulation, has put a far greater distance between writer and reader.

We can shed further light on the readership which may mitigate the apparent difficulties of receiving a copy. According to Williams's recollections in the interviews with the *NLR* people, the journal was aimed at staff and students in adult education (1979a 69). Each of the three editors was connected with adult education, so that it was likely that news of the next issue could be passed on through tutors' networks. I have not seen any advertisements for *Politics and Letters* in WEA or tutors' publications, and it is likely that paper rationing would have limited such inclusion. However, the editors aimed to sell 1,500–2,000 copies (ibid. 68) and such a number suggests that some printed notification of an issue was likely. The number and range of contributions were not meagre, again suggesting that knowledge of its existence must have been reasonably widespread. As to the periodical's influence, the details of sales, readership and contributions would imply that this too was not insignificant.

On balance then, we may wish to if not reverse the earlier label of failure, then at least make amendment. The after-war years while presenting practical difficulties, would have provided considerable stimulus to writing and publishing. If inside the academy there had been a conservative turn, adult education offered an apparently natural attraction for progressives. Yet because of this, the damaging effects of the cold war were soon to make their presence felt especially hard (Fieldhouse 1985a). Against this wider political circumstance, *Politics and Letters* was at least evens in the balance of success and failure.

However, it was not the political or even cultural conditions that eventually defeated the journal. Williams recalls that,

> There were serious practical difficulties. We had hardly any working capital and there was the usual problem of late book shop payments. But in [the] last year there were increasing personal strains between the editors. It's hard to talk about that, after thirty years, but as I remember it we had no quarrels about editorial policy. The decisive and concluding disagreement was in fact on a business matter. ... There must, under all this, have been deeper problems of project and alignment, but if so it's interesting that they surfaced in these ways, and not as explicit difficulties about policy (1979a 74).

Clearly there is much being held back here which will never be available for full recovery. Eventually Williams left the threesome, Collins and

Mankowitz attempting without success to continue the project without him. In these circumstances we can only conclude that the nurture of *Politics and Letters* for the two years of its life may have been no small success. Its real accomplishment was in the direction it gave to Williams's life and with that the future of what eventually became a 'New' Left, and socialists' nearest realization of the non-alignment which *Politics and Letters* had sought.

4. THE NEXT TEN YEARS

The years 1946–1956 have in recent accounts of the Left been relegated to something of an anonymous, sombre period eclipsed by the big bang of 1956 (Chun 1993). However, that, as this last section will attempt to show, somewhat falsifies the history. The previous sections have discussed Williams's involvement in *Politics and Letters* and the crisis which followed its collapse. In this last section I want to fill in the history up to the middle-fifties arguing that much of what has been presented as the product of the New Left , was in fact a project set in particular conditions and worked out over the coming ten years.

Nineteen-forty-eight saw the publication of T. S. Eliot's *Notes Toward the Definition of Culture*, while *Scrutiny* served as a conduit for post-war cultural conservatism. At first glance it appears as if culture had become the means through which political battle was pursued. Yet a closer look reveals that it was culture itself which after 1945 was being struggled over. That one vehicle, published in 1953, through which Williams carried forward his project was called *The Idea of Culture* should not surprise us. Looking back from the end of this period, Edward Thompson has summed up the circumstance thus;

> Ten years takes us back to the aftermath of Zhdanovism: the onset of the cold war: the enfeeblement of energies which had brought Labour to power in 1945: the rapid dispersal of the Leftist intellectual climate of the war years, and the equally rapid assertion over a wide field of the authority of Mr Eliot (Thompson 1961a 27).

At one level *The Idea of Culture* was a response to Eliot. Yet it had also to be a response beyond that to the whole tradition, Williams's own description for what he had experienced at Cambridge. It had to go back, to take hold of the term 'culture' and to begin the long tracing forward to the present; the only means by which the reworking could be possible. In Williams's view, completion of *The Idea of Culture*—

> ... should then provide the grounds for the subsequent analysis of more developed systems of ideas in this field (Williams 1953 246).

Culture and Society published in 1958 and *The Long Revolution* in 1961 are the two obvious continuances of that subsequent analysis. In the introduction to *The Long Revolution* Williams also includes *Border Country*, the eventual title of his first novel published in 1960, as the other work of this period of the project. The dates of publication should not deceive anyone. *Border Country* had begun to be written in 1946 as *Brynllwyd,* and represents the most immediate means by which Williams pursued his own passage through these years. *Culture and Society,* the more public statement of that project, had begun to be written in 1950.

The *Idea of Culture* was a marker of the progress Williams had made at that point. In the foreword we get a clear indication of the sources of the book. *Politics and Letters* is clearly stated, but with it are a series of names, who were all, or nearly all, connected by the world of adult education and its institutional link into the universities. *Culture and Society* was aimed at tutors and students, and although its nearest place was clearly in English studies, the work attempted to carry on the historical social science not fulfilled in the pages of *Politics and Letters.*

The holding together of the literary critical with the historically informed social science had been the failed intention of one publication after another. Though there were differences of emphases and politics, *Left Review, Scrutiny, Politics and Letters, Arena* and eventually *Universities and Left Review,* each carried forward this attempt at drawing historians and social scientists to the literary people. *Scrutiny* was of a different order, and *ULR* too late for present consideration. The remaining trio did not survive.

One publication, open to the Left, attempting some kind of drawing together of intellectual trajectories, and which did struggle through the fifties was *Essays in Criticism.* Edited by Freddy Bateson, who invited Williams to join the editorial board, *Essays in Criticism* was something of a competitor to *Scrutiny.* Looking back, Williams, observes of the period,

> Bateson personally was a socialist and a genuine one. That was important. His project was also an open review—you see how the same structure kept repeating itself (1979a 84).

Even more than was the case with *Politics and Letters,* Williams was at a distance from the heart of *Essays in Criticism.* Control, rightly, lay with Bateson. But it is the reference to the same structure repeating itself, that points to the potential difficulty. Like the editors of *Politics and Letters,* Bateson deliberately invited contributions from a range of viewpoints, while allowing a number of people to influence the content of an issue. In this manner *Essays in Criticism* was not unlike *Politics and Letters,* so the ingredient which enabled it to survive where the other failed, may have been less to do with the published outcome than the working arrangements by which it was produced. Either way each publication represented important attempts to carve out a politics that was difficult to sustain, while providing an opportunity for its exploration.

The Idea of Culture was an important marker in the development of Williams's project. Written and published in 1953, the essay coincided with Williams's final complete rejection of the Communist Party for what could now only appear sycophantic defence of the Soviet Union. The event that brought him to this conclusion was the uprising in East Berlin. More exactly it was the 'intervention of the Russian troops [which] shocked me very badly' (1979a 88). The account of his response in the *NLR* interviews suggests the strained relationship he obviously felt was shared by historians within the party, leading him to question how they could possibly stay in such a body. In fact, Williams's questioning began to be repeated by the historians, sooner than any one in 1953 perhaps imagined. The Berlin uprising followed only shortly after Stalin's death, and the relative liberalization which followed, in part provided the conditions in which disquiet within the Communist Party membership became increasingly difficult to suppress.

In the following year Williams began the major work which contained the intent of the project more fully than anything published hitherto. At the end of the foreword Williams states that,

> Parts of the book have previously appeared, in other forms, in *Essays in Criticism* and *Universities and Left Review* (Williams 1958a viii).

What he does not say in the foreword is that he had met editors of *ULR* at Oxford where they discussed problems of culture and socialism, and when he had given them two of the early written chapters of the book. These they read over the summer while hearing the strains of the mounting crisis that was to result in the Suez invasion. It is these coincidences which contributed to the overtly political intervention of the New Left being expressed through issues of culture. In chapter eight I discuss the magazine in some detail, together with some of the themes in *The Long Revolution* which Williams was preparing over several years. These earlier meetings probably owed much to the inspiration of G. D. H. Cole. On the one hand Cole's delegacy work would have made for contact with tutors such as John Vickers and Raymond Williams during the summer schools and other times during the teaching year. On the other, inside Oxford, Cole was the political mentor to the Socialist Society, from which *ULR* was born. The writing of *Culture and Society* was thus carried on against a background of adult education, whether among classes and a close group of tutors with whom Williams was in touch from Seaford, or summer schools at Oxford. Where this can be lost is if one part of the political context is looked at in isolation when the apparent quiescence of the earlier-fifties quickly gives way to the turbulence of the left and the enthusiasm of the new peace campaign. Nonetheless, if the book is viewed from the perspective of a forward-moving chronology, rather than a retrospective view of history, then *Culture and Society* can be seen to be part of the project as this emerged from the period immediately after the war.

Trying to place Williams politically during these years is difficult, and the description of 'maverick' has been cited before. There is reference in the chronology to *Politics and Letters* to Williams having worked for the

Labour Party in the 1955 general election, though we are not told which of the local constituencies this was in. Unfortunately, this is not mentioned in the text itself, and rather surprisingly John McIlroy and Sallie Westwood (1993) fail to even include the Labour Party in the index to *Border Country*. The same omission from Fred Inglis' work is less surprising being accompanied by those of the Communist Party, the Campaign for Nuclear Disarmament, Plaid Cymru, but perhaps I should not go on. My point is that if the citation is correct Williams had clearly undergone something of a change of view from seven years earlier. That he would have wished for a Labour victory simply reflected the fact, as he stated many times, that there was an absence of an alternative. Indeed he fills out this last point at some length. The Communist Party mode of operation, which Williams described in terms of 'manipulation and centralism', were features for which he held nothing but 'contempt' (1979a 91). Perhaps more important though was that if the party's subservience to the Soviet Union were left aside, then its domestic policy when looked at in detail was very little different from that of many Labour activists. Put together, the picture suggests that while Williams was working through an alternative project he could not find any grouping with which to work in an extensive manner. The existence of a quite possibly left-wing constituency party in a strong Conservative area, not an unknown situation, could well have attracted his support during an election campaign, though he did not become a member of the Labour Party before 1961. Other than this allegiance for a quite specific purpose, the very nature of his intentions at this time make it unlikely that Williams could have found a body with whom to work. As Mervyn Jones has commented,

> The social landscape of the mid-fifties was far from inspiring. We had said farewell to the cheerful egalitarianism, the simplicities, and the brave aspirations of the forties, as well as to the belief in a long era of Labour government. The tide had gone out again, revealing an England that had changed much less than we had imagined (1987 133).

Returning finally then to the claim of writing alone, for the next ten years, I want to alter the emphasis. John McIlroy is right to suggest that Williams was in close communication with a number of tutors who helped him with his writing. The individual pieces or publications all involved a number of people, and Williams owed several debts for ideas and inspiration. McIlroy though is equally right to say that there was no particular influence on Williams. Indeed he goes further, arguing that Williams was original in a very real sense that his ideas came from nowhere. Williams's own description of his writing is of a physical aloneness yet a strong sense of a presence of people. In a broadcast following Williams's death, Eagleton commented how for him as a student it was remarkable to hear a voice in that place (Cambridge) speaking out for those who were quite deliberately excluded from its ancient walls (*Raymond Williams—A*

Tribute 1988). I do not in any way wish to contradict these images. Rather I want to say that the particular manner in which the writing came out was the product of the specific political and intellectual formation that first shaped the Williams who went to war in 1940, and then remade him after he returned. The war, the failure of *Politics and Letters*, adult education, determined the working relationships and the form the aloneness had to take in thinking through the idea of culture. Perhaps it might be fitting to end with Edward Thompson's description of the history, written in *New Left Review*, and what Williams's achievement really meant.

The occasion was an extended review article written in response to Williams's *The Long Revolution*. Throughout, Thompson characteristically stated his disagreements with Williams, the most remembered being his substitution of Williams's 'way of life' with 'way of struggle' (1961a 33). Here though I want to return to Thompson's historical situating of Williams. The section is headed `Conditioned by Context' and I have already quoted from it. Discussing the years after the war Thompson does not hide the scale of the defeat, or the corrosion of 'even the vocabulary of socialism'.

> By the end of the decade the intellectual left was in evident rout: 'progress', 'liberalism', 'humanism' and (unless in the ritual armoury of cold war) 'democracy' became suspect terms: and all those old banners which the Thirties had too easily assumed to be stowed away in ancestral trunks were raised in the wind again.
>
> Looking back I can see the point at which I simply disengaged from the contest: and I can recall friends who were actually broken ... by the experience of the period.

Written against this context, Thompson's description of Williams's achievement is, not surprisingly, euphoric:

> Raymond Williams stayed in the field. ... He held the roads open for the young, and now they are moving down them once again. And when, in '56, he saw some of his socialist contemporaries coming back to his side, his smile must have had a very wry edge (ibid. 27).

chapter five

KEEPING THE FAITH

1. Secular Puritans and Respectable Communists

The Communist Party of Great Britain has had to wait for its death before receiving the attention it so desired during its life. Like a scorpion, once dead, the party is unlikely to sting. A little prodding and probing therefore will not expose the examiner to the risk of being poisoned. In the case of the British Communist Party the poison, unlike that of either a scorpion or the Communist Party of the Soviet Union, would not have been harmful to physical life, but might have damaged one's political or intellectual standing. The reasons for this are of course complex. However, some of the details in the following pages will provide a partial answer. The focus will be on the culture of the party. It might reasonably be claimed that such a topic cannot be adequately addressed without a longer history explaining at least some part of the party's structure; external relations, both international and with the Labour Party; place in the trade unions; leading figures; and a host of other very necessary information, little of which will appear in the account given here. The following is obviously deeply indebted to existing writings, however, rather than either replicating them or attempting some synthesis which reveals a new interpretation, I will concentrate on the culture of the party. In this first section it is the image of respectability that is placed to the fore. For sections two and three I depart from the main story of *History in the Making* to discuss two important influences in the membership of the party. The first is that of the Welsh, who were not only numerically significant, but were important, at times, for the priorities of the party. The second departure is the hitherto little researched presence of Cypriots amongst London Communists. The final section looks forward to the next chapter by way of an examination of the intended theme of the 1956 party congress, 'Unity', which I discuss in terms of the party's history and character, and thus the cultural influences cited in the three previous sections. This in turns allows for a contrast to be may with the renewed libertarian tradition examined in the next chapter.

The formation of the Communist Party in 1920 did not mark the beginning of revolutionary expectations in Britain, but rather was an effect of them. The formation of a 'Party of a New Type' was expected to coordinate those pressures in a more effective manner. In 1947 a young Christopher Hill acknowledged some of the difficulties that entailed:

Lenin's idea of party organization was so different from anything which had hitherto been normal in Western Europe that it is worth recalling that he was developing the Russian revolutionary tradition. In order to control a rebellious and evasive peasantry all over the vast Russian spaces an absolute, highly centralized and bureaucratic government had to come into existence (Hill 1971 54).

Even by the estimates of an, at that time, devoted party member, the Communists were, Hill admits, an organization starkly at odds with that found under liberal Western democracy. The establishing of the new party meant a transferring of the practice of central control beyond the new Soviet Union, so that rather than a number of affiliated national parties, there were established a number of satellites, each moving in accord with the needs and wishes of the hub. The member was closely affiliated to a disciplined body which looked upwards, and in doing so, outwards. The branch meeting was part of a world struggle.

In the majority of histories of the Left in Britain the tendency has been to discuss political and economic struggles, leaving the culture within which these occurred as at best a secondary consideration. One result has arguably been to leave unexamined influences that might otherwise have offered pointers as to why economic and political activities were conducted in the manner they were. More than that, examination of the cultural ethos within which a large section of the left lived, might help explain some of the more exasperating schisms and self-mutilation which has so characterized its history. In this connection one of the first problems encountered in writing any history of the left is the diversity of terms and their meanings. In the context of Britain at least, it would be a mistake to view the terms Marxism and communism as identical. The former has always included many who did not subscribe to communism in the form of a movement, while the latter has always been wider than any one theoretical school. It is possible that mapping the histories of the terms Marxism and communism would reveal a slow shifting in imagery from Christian socialists to socialist humanism. What is perhaps surprising is the extent to which writing of the left has marginalized this heritage quite so systematically. In discussing the characteristics of the Communist Party membership and the effects on its political status, the continued influence of puritan thinking will need to be given rather more prominence.

The image of the communist as a respectable citizen is one that seems to lie implicit in accounts of the movement. Whether it was on street marches or in the manner you kept your home, the necessity to maintain civility was always present. Reasons for such an atmosphere are complex, but for the inter-war period they would need to include the attempt to maintain a sense of self-respect during the long periods of unemployment suffered in so much of the country. At certain times during the nineteen-thirties nearly half of all the members of the CPGB were unemployed. The Communist Party, far from being subversive and undermining values of decency, were re-enforcing them all the stronger. Raphael Samuel suggests that there existed a decorum among communists which reflected itself in conduct at branch meetings and elsewhere. In part a necessity, there is also the suggestion in Samuel's image of the need to keep unity and the name of the party in the face of aggressors:

> Branch meetings were not places to 'thrash out' differences, ... They were concerned rather with 'checking up' on decisions, and involving the membership in party work. If difficulties were raised members were only too anxious to search for common ground, to 'build' on points of agreement, to offer 'constructive' criticism. The authoritative person who closed the proceedings would want to end on a positive note ... if the party was lagging behind the masses—a favourite self-lacerating complaint which always went down well—there were thousands waiting to hear our 'message' (Samuel 1986 65).

But we can perhaps detect reasons for at least some of this respectability in word and deed in the origins of many communists. The chapel and particularly the meeting house of some of the more marginal sects were places where a strict moral code and the values of unity were maintained. Again, of necessity at times, the believers needed to fortify themselves for the fight in a world where all around were apparently lost to the lure of transient pleasures. The good communist like the good believer stood a little apart from the more mortal of their compatriots:

> At open-air pitches we preached our message, like the Salvation Army of old, with words of blood and fire (Samuel 1985 43).

Perhaps this connection is best captured through the concept of the elect. The notion has two rather different parts to it. In the first there was that of satisfaction at being simply better than those around you. You were after all chosen to lead a higher life, to which you gave witness in your manner and speech. But this leads on to the second dimension where to give witness could also entail giving leadership, of showing to others the folly of their ways through example, and scolding them should they fall short. Where a sense of the elect was mixed with the felt need to change not just individuals but society itself, as it was in the Communist Party, then the two could place considerable strain on the incumbent of such an office. In this Samuel's suggestion that civility should extend to the home becomes understandable:

> The idea of the 'good Communist home' although never articulated in the manner of the 'good Jewish home' or the 'good Catholic' one, enjoyed some currency: the home where there was always a cup of tea on the table, always a spare bed for delegates, the welcoming home that would give other comrades strength (Samuel 1988 68–9).

Of course, it would be foolish to suggest that the conduct of communists was directly attributable to the ethics of the steadfast chapel-goer. As though I argued in chapter one, it is perhaps possible to understand such conduct as born of similar origins, that are perhaps best captured in the idea of working-class respectability. Two very different examples of the closeness of political or religious commitment are Will Paynter and Rodney Hilton. Will Paynter was a South Wales miner's activist:

> I went to chapel three times on Sunday, and a band of hope prayer meeting and young people's guild on three nights a week. It was accepted as a duty and on more than one occasion my brother and I were called away from cricket or football to attend such week-night religious occasions. In fact, a group of us young lads and girls became members of the chapel when we were sixteen years old (Paynter 1972 27).

In the autobiography *My Generation*, from which this extract is taken, Will Paynter dismisses this chapel experience as having had a negative influence on his life, yet there is little mistaking the similarity of his later political discipline to this earlier religious temperament. In 1937 Paynter was selected to go to Spain to represent the interests of International Brigade members:

> I accepted, but I must confess, without any great enthusiasm as I had got married only a few weeks before. However, once the decision was taken I proceeded to London where I was more fully briefed on the situation of the battalion and from there embarked to Spain (ibid. 65).

Referring to the very different circumstance of an Oxford college Rodney Hilton records the time when he had first graduated and was beginning research as 'a young student of history':

> The Communist Party group in Balliol in those days ... was predominantly from grammar school and lower-middle-class families, even with working-class ancestors one or two generations back. I think that many had Nonconformist upbringing, or (at least in my case) deliberately irreligious, though with all the cultural attributes of Non-conformity. In fact, it was not difficult for people of this sort to become Communists (Hilton 1978 7).

This reference to the 'cultural attributes' of Nonconformity, is not the same language as that used by Will Paynter, yet the sentiment is the same. The chapel was necessary, even to those who did not enter the building, because it was part of a set of local, concrete, institutions: the co-operative society, the savings' club, the ILP branch, the Clarion Cycling Club, the trade union branch, which at one time or another, nurtured a very particular way of life. These various involvements will often have required reading, and through that, change can have occurred. Stuart Macintyre perhaps puts it rather abstractly, but the sentiment is the same:

> The crucial means of self-improvement was study. ... many were prompted to take up books by a sense of religious doubt or more imprecise curiosity of an existential or social character (Macintyre 1980 38).

In discussing the formation of the Communist Party he points out that,

> ... it is clear that the actual formation of the party sprang from this process of self-education (ibid. 26).

The route presented here is interesting. Religious or philosophical doubt leads to reading, which in turn provides the conditions out of which party membership might develop. We can rearrange this same sequence in terms which may even be familiar to communists, in which the false world experienced in religious beliefs is overcome through diligence and thought. Continued here is the puritan ethic of hard work, as befits the difficulty to enter into the language codes in which party literature was apt to be written.

We find the lineage of this diligent scholar time and again in writings of party members. The steady prose of the corresponding societies, the eager reader of the radical press, the furtive scribbling of the autodidact, pride of place is given to she or he who would forsake rest and even food that they might afford some sustenance of the mind. The pilgrim image is strong in this radical history, and the party member is encouraged to struggle with some of the more obscure formulas of Marxist theory in the promise that mastery will bring with it new light by which to see their way forward. Being a communist was a serious calling.

Self-education, the chapel, the co-operative branch, the political party were not exclusive. They were if not always available together, at least carried on in close proximity to each other. The chapel and the school-room could physically live side by side. Often it was on the initiative of a well-meaning preacher that the adult education class would start. The trade union would be in an interdependent tension with such a class; members while attending outside of work time were likely to test out the union's words and deeds in the light of their new found knowledge. To this scene the Labour Party was a late arrival. Its stance was likely to be parasitic, reaping the benefits of puritan dedication but offering no intellectual advancement to what was already in place. Yet its holding of local political office could make it a vehicle by which the potential of other routes could be advanced.

These institutions were the hallmarks of a serious, respectable working-class culture. In this the Communist Party, far from being in any manner a threat to social order or community, presented a way of life which sought to strengthen what was best in them to a point where eventually they would oust the impoverished culture that was capitalist society's best offer. In the meantime, the party would support a self-nurtured respectability.

2. THE CELTIC CENTRALITY

The use of this obvious reversal of the normal description is intended to acknowledge the actual balance between the Celtic countries and England in the socialist movement. There is neither the space nor the competence for a discussion of socialists in the three countries of Ireland, Wales and Scotland, and I shall in the main confine what I have to say to Wales. Wales has been the least written about, in English at least, of the three Celtic countries. Its history has tended to be more readily subsumed under the heading of Britain and even England, than has been the case for either Scotland or Ireland. Referred to by the English establishment as a Principality, Wales continues to be treated as a rather tiresome colony, while its history as a separate entity remains little known in England. The emergence, especially since 1945, of a radical intelligentsia prepared to take on the role of public political figures—Raymond Williams, Gwyn Williams, Dai Smith, John Osmond—has advanced a progressive agenda in Wales in a manner that has proved quite impossible in its English neighbour.

The presence of socialists in Wales and Scotland has, in comparison to the total population, been very much more obvious than in England. The strength of trade-union activity in areas such as South Wales or the Clyde has long been noted as for instance in *The Fed: A history of the South Wales miners in the twentieth century* by Hywel Frances and David Smith. Where in other parts of Britain that activity might be confined to representation of members interests in the work place, for South Wales and the Clyde trade unionism was very much more a part of the community. Not the least aspect of this presence has been the long traditions of education both formal and personal. Yet socialism was still only a minority conviction, and very much less in volume than the relatively passive activity of supporting the Labour Party at elections. Proof of the strength of the party's support in the inter-war period was delivered when, 'In the 1931 election, Labour was almost wiped out in England; in Wales it lost only one seat.' (Osmond 1988 126). While the Labour Party has been the electoral face of Welsh voting, the politics of community and culture has been carried forward by other less institutionalized bodies. The advance of a Welsh socialist party, Plaid Cymru, in recent years has worked to maintain a cultural politics beyond the electoral machinery of the Labour Party.

The decline of an earlier nonconformist liberalism across Wales had not been even. In central areas a Liberal dominance was maintained by the presence of Lloyd George and his family. In time they became a rump not only in Wales, but also in the parliament for the whole of Britain at Westminster. From the high point of 1906 when the Liberals held thirty-three of the thirty-four seats in Wales decline was, if not without reversals, virtually total. In 1931 it was Labour who held their own in Wales, while they were virtually wiped off the political map in England and Scotland.

The result is worth pondering over for a moment since it provides an incontrovertible statistic for the political culture of the country. Of the total of fifty-two Labour MPs in Westminster, sixteen were elected from Wales. Many of these Welsh seats were among the safest of all Labour seats. Indeed the party managed to actually increase its share of the total vote in Wales from forty-four to forty-five percent in this, the most shattering year in the history of the party. As such the Welsh presence in the Labour Party of the early-thirties was central. In such circumstance Welsh Labour could have demanded and gained assurance of almost anything short of complete independence. The delivery of such assurances in 1945 would have meant the history of Wales and therefore England could have been very different from what it has been this past half century. Yet the extraordinary fact is that not only did the Labour leadership, including its Welsh component, not make any such offer, neither did the party in Wales make any strong demand. It was left to the Communist Party following its Seventh Congress of the Communist International in 1935 to begin to rethink the relationship between the Celtic lands and their English neighbour. By 1938 the CPGB was moving toward a policy of self determination for Wales and Scotland. In Birmingham that year congress heard that:

> During the past year the central committee has given careful attention to the problems raised by the growth of nationalist movements in Scotland and Wales. For many years the party has underestimated the importance of the Scottish Nationalist Movement and the Welsh Nationalists, and also the fact that their influence is much greater than their numbers.
>
> It has been clear that our party stands for a policy that preserves the best traditions of the Scottish people and the Welsh people, resists every attempt to encroach upon their national rights, and demands the fullest opportunities and the development of self-government.
>
> Before the end of the year it is expected that a popular pamphlet giving the Communist attitude on this problem will be published in Scotland, and also one in Wales (CPGB 1938 43–44).

The importance of a Welsh presence in the Communist Party is hard to overstress. If confirmation were needed a quick glance at statistics for membership and numbers of branches would be sufficient. In 1927, just four years before Wales saved the Labour Party, and immediately following the general strike, nearly a third of total party membership was in South Wales. While this level was not to be sustained, Wales continued to represent a substantial percentage of the party membership till beyond the Second World War. In Scotland though to a less significant degree, the number of communists was also impressive. Only London could ever maintain similar membership levels, and in this the presence of continental European migrants, most especially Jews and Cypriots, and a small number of revolutionaries from across the Empire were crucial. Yet we should also remember that there were considerable migrations, particularly from South Wales, towards the South-east of England during the inter-war years. As such, the high figure for the London region may too have been in part inflated by the arrival of Celtic migrants.

Reasons for the Welsh and Scottish dominance are usually attributed to the presence of major industries in the regions. Mining and to a lesser degree steel-working in South Wales were the major providers of communists, while the same was enhanced by shipbuilding in the Clyde area of Scotland. In trying to explain this phenomena Macintyre presents an argument long rehearsed by social historians;

> ... it seems that this independent working-class consciousness emerged with particular strength and clarity in those areas where distinct working-class communities existed and were united in a few large-scale industries (Macintyre 1980b 9).

The idea is not original but it fits well with the picture of miners, steel-workers and shipbuilders as the basis of communist and other left-wing support. Unfortunately, little if any research exists as to whether people in other employment and particularly women, were members of the party in any numbers in these areas, but hidden by the general picture. Such research would probably have to be done village by village.

Yet we should not assume that the presence of the necessary social basis for the development of socialist thinking could of itself be sufficient. Returning to the theme of the previous section, examination of the connections between Presbyterianism and Scottish communism would be of considerable value for better appreciating the manner in which political and cultural thinking can establish itself. We might in similar vein add that it was not coincidental that communism should come to South Wales following the religious revival there at the beginning of this century. The opening paragraph of Michael Foot's biography of Aneurin Bevan recalls the close association between Nonconformity and socialism. The move from one to the other, parallels that from a progressive, radical liberalism toward the Labour movement. Encouraging this departure was a growing sense of collective responsibility and action that characterized social as well as political life in late-nineteenth-century Britain. In this a religion such as Protestantism, with its emphasis on individual salvation and achievement of grace, was likely to loose some of its appeal as a fruitful means through which the world could be understood.

The shift away from liberalism in South Wales gained momentum from the beginning of this century. This earlier liberalism had in part been a continuance of traditions established in central Wales, which had migrated with people. This was a dissenting culture, whose material existence could be seen in the network of chapels. Through this network migrants were able to maintain the community of which they were a part. A particular chapel in the new area to which they had moved would have links to that from where they came. In this manner chapels acted as centres of information and support, providing contacts through which accommodation and work could be found.

Yet this talk of chapels should in no part be taken to mean that the basis of political and cultural life in South Wales was necessarily parochial. The picture presented by Neal Wood in his 1959 *Communism and British Intellectuals* is that visions beyond the immediate issues of wages and conditions were the preserve of the intellectuals. Other accounts, such as that of Stuart Macintyre's demonstrate that the title of *Little Moscows* for some of the villages in the Rhondda was not without meaning. Not only did miners make up a large percentage of those who were to attend the Central Labour College, but it was normal for a selected number to visit Moscow to witness the socialist future in action. In addition to the miners, the National Union of Railwaymen provided financial support to the Labour College. Through the activists of the Independent Labour Party, the National Council of Labour Colleges were able to organize classes, many of them in Marxist dialectics and history, throughout the coal and steel areas of South Wales. Alongside these existed a multiplicity of socialist societies attended by not only ILPers but communist and Labour members as well. The institutional bases for much of this activity were the workers institutes, which during the later 1930s, have been estimated to number 109 with a total book stock of 750,000 (Williams 1985a 279). Maintained as they were by local contributions rather than the state, the institutes were a remarkable testimony to working-class community action.

The issue of marginality has been approached elsewhere in terms of class and culture, but primarily within the context of England. In terms of Wales and Scotland there is also the issue of periphery and centre in geographical and political senses. The English domination of the other regions of the British Isles has, of course, a long history. But the concentration of power in not just England but in its South-eastern quarter in the twentieth century has had the effect of drawing from these regions a continual movement of peoples. Arguably, colonial marginalization and working-class subordination combine in such manner as to create a clearer sense of the dominant classes than is perhaps available to an English working class brought up to believe in its own superiority. Raymond Williams was perhaps giving voice to such sentiments when he spoke of, 'the grammar schools (being) implanted in the towns of Wales for the purposes of Anglicization'. (Williams 1979a 25).

The Communist Party was in reality neither able to rebel against what some regarded as an English colonialism in Wales, nor to simply ignore the national voice and regard Wales as a western part of an indivisible Britain. The tensions was reflected by a division of views within its own ranks. Arthur Horner adopted the view of a centrist trade unionist, anything which threatened a unified national union of mineworkers was bad for Welsh miners interests. By contrast, Idris Cox and W. J. Rees became involved with writing in support of Welsh self-determination, as well as the Welsh Congress and, in turn, the Parliament for Wales campaign. The campaign was taken forward during the nineteen-forties by both the Communist Party in Wales, and by the party at the level of the whole of Britain. A number of booklets were produced displaying strong support for Welsh self-determination, suggesting representation to be developed at both the Welsh level and for the whole of Britain. In effect, the policy was for dual parliaments, an idea better understood perhaps when seen alongside the party's promotion of proportional representation.

The advance of arguments for Welsh self-determination coincided with the period in the 1930s when the party committed itself to what it called a popular front or alliance. In the case of Wales it is true that a then increasingly right-wing Nationalist Party was gaining some support. In this circumstance the Welsh CP congress could be understood as an alternative voice to either the then reactionary leadership of the nationalists or the dismissive views of the Labour Party. Clearly the Communists could have little in common with the nationalist's leadership which in the mid-thirties had come to sympathize with Salazar and Franco. Yet the party contained many with whom Communists could work, and who, in the spirit of the people's front, the party saw as potential allies. Yet on the other side the party had no wish to create any excuse for the Labour leadership to refuse co-operation. Certainly at a local level it was customary for Labour and Communist in South Wales to work together on a broad range of social issues. This desire not to upset Labour can be recognized in the hesitancy with which the Communists put forward their one parliamentary candidate in the 1945 election: Harry Pollitt in East Rhondda.

It is, though, the Communists' turn toward the nationalist cause that is the more interesting. In the decade from 1935 to 1945 the party published several pamphlets concerning Wales. Quite reasonably during the most difficult ten years of the twentieth century, the party policy did not remain entirely consistent. Neither was there unanimity within the party. In 1944 Idris Cox expressed a view more sympathetic to the nationalist view:

> Welsh language and culture will never reach its full status until the people of Wales take their full share in the fight to destroy fascism and then go forward for the abolition of capitalist ownership. This will not be achieved at one stroke. That is why we Communists support the demand for a secretary of state for Wales and a national advisory council (Cox 1944a 12–13).

Four years later the emphasis had subtly shifted such that the nationalist cause was viewed as deficient:

> The Welsh Nationalists are the modern counterpart of the nineteenth-century Welsh Liberals, but their programme and policy is far more confusing. They have advocated dominion status for Wales for over

twenty years, fumed against the mythical 'English' capitalists, and advocated economic separation for Wales (Cox 1948 18).

The Communist Party response was though not merely to dismiss the nationalists. Rather the latter's points were met with concrete alternatives:

> The remedy lies not in economic separation, but in the planning of Wales as an economic unit within the framework of the British economic system. The solution is not dominion status but a Welsh Parliament within a British federal system (ibid. 19).

Some indication of the structure of this federal system and Wales' place within it, is indicated by the party's reorganization of itself into a single all-Wales congress. Policy proposals of the new congress included the establishment of Welsh departments, which it argued could conduct affairs specific to Wales at a more strategic level than was possible with the existing arrangements of counties and boroughs.

That these initiatives came to nought is probably due to a simple explanation of their timing. The first initiatives were during the period of the people's front and would have been prevented from continuing first by the change of line to 'imperialist war', a change not initially opposed incidentally by Idris Cox, and after that of course the war itself. It should not be forgotten that national socialists in Germany established a Radio Free Wales early in the war, which would have compromised any Communist initiative about self-determination. The reawakening of the support for partial Welsh independence in 1945 would probably, like much else at this time, have been killed off by the onset of the cold war. In Gwyn Williams's estimation, the party's enthusiasm for self-determination waned after 1950 when it reverted to a position in line with that of the Labour Party. It was only after the CPGB had become a very different sort of party by the late-nineteen-seventies, that it again became possible to link up with Plaid Cymru and reaffirm a policy for Welsh autonomy.

3. Migrant London

Documented research of migrants in the Communist Party is virtually nonexistent, and as such it would be very difficult to provide a picture of the migrants in the Communist Party at any time during its history. Having said this we do know that for many years the London region included Jews from East London, and Cypriots from North London in its membership, and it is the second and lesser known of these that I am concerned with here. To get a better picture of migrants in the London branches of the party though, I shall first recall a little of the better known presence of East London Jewry.

Records for the settlement of Jews in East London extend back for many years. While antagonism would almost certainly have existed at various times during that history it was in the early-twentieth century that racialization of a Jewish presence in the area occurred. The result was the implementation of the 1905 Aliens Act, which with various amendments, continued to serve as the major immigration legislation until the Commonwealth Immigration Act of 1962. The Jews who entered Britain in the earlier part of the twentieth century brought with them a radical politics upon which they were to form their own labour societies and struggle for their own industrial conditions. Membership of the Communist Party seems to have become an increasing phenomenon from the early-twenties, following considerable activity in the East End by the party. Again Macintyre records that,

> One expanding base of support was the Jewish community of London's East End, most of whom had arrived from Europe during the second half of the nineteenth century. Prior to 1914 most Jews remained within their own community and created their own trade unions and socialist organizations; during the anti-fascist campaigns of the 1930s they became an important source of party recruitment. For the transitional period of the 1920s we lack the necessary research, but it is at least evident that several leading Communists came from this background (Macintyre 1980b 30).

It is difficult to know what reasons may have made for Jewish membership of the party distinct from that of English members. It has been suggested that it was the particular international situation of the thirties, the rise of fascism and victimization of Jews across much of Europe. While this would certainly have been a factor in the equation, it would have been but a variant of the reasons for many others becoming a Communist in this period. A second which would again require empirical research was the correlation between unemployment among East End Jewry and party membership. Macintyre writes of 'independent working-class consciousness emerging in distinct working-class communities united by a few large-scale industries' (ibid. 9). It may be possible to include East London Jewry within that formula, and add to it migration and resettlement as factors reinforcing the sense of distinction. This is not to diminish consciousness of a global community, but to suggest that this might itself be mediated by the experience of immediate community.

The case of Cypriot membership of the Communist Party has received even less attention than that of Jewish. Cypriot migration to Britain carries three distinctive features. It was the first numerically significant migration of colonial subjects to the UK; second, settlement was initially almost entirely in one area of central London only slowly moving northwards; and finally employment was heavily concentrated in the catering trades. As such, Cypriot migration too can be understood as creating conditions within which an identity centred around class could emerge, although it must be admitted that the catering trades made for a very different environment from coal or steel. In his 1969 *The sociology of British*

Communism, Kenneth Newton estimates that in the later-thirties the Cypriot branch of the Communist Party contained some sixty members. This figure is unlikely to include the many others who joined a series of sister organizations. Important among the latter was the Union of Cypriots in Great Britain which campaigned against Cypriot conscription to the army at the outbreak of the Second World War, a stance exactly in line with the Comintern's denunciation of the imperialist slaughter of the working classes of Europe. Later, when Communists had become active supporters of the war effort, the Cyprus autonomy committee argued for death payments for migrant Cypriot soldiers equal to those of the majority of British subjects from within Britain.

Links between anti-colonial and Communist activities in London were enhanced by the association of the Cyprus autonomy committee with the League Against Imperialism. The latter, according to Paul Rich, was a Communist-dominated association connected with a number of anti-colonial groupings in Europe, who had moved from Hamburg to London in 1933. In London, the League Against Imperialism brought together a number of individuals and groups and probably served as the most effective link between official Communists and anti-colonialists, and almost certainly enabled the party to become intimately involved in the activities of many different struggles beyond those of the, usually illegal, Communist Party in a colony.

The importance of the Cypriot branch was the manner in which it articulated the colonial circumstance of Cyprus with that of the Empire generally, and with the circumstance of Cypriot migrants in London. Connections were made possible through the imagery of imperialism and capitalism as the two elements enabling an English ruling-class to maintain its supremacy over the domestic working class and that in the colony. Where capitalism was the social relationship through which profit could be extracted from labour, imperialism was both the extension of that system and the ideology which divided the domestic working class from its colonial sisters and brothers. In this, the Cypriot Communist branch was at one with the general Communist line.

Cypriot migration to Britain had in large part been for economic reasons. Unemployment had long been a prevalent factor in Cyprus, and continued to be the experience of a large number of Cypriot migrants in the thirties. Unemployment could act as an immediate means through which the interrelation of capitalism and imperialism could be experienced. The Communist Party in those circumstances stood as a logical alternative, offering both explanation for the experience and a means by which to transcend it. The main alternative to the Communists for Cypriot migrants was the Greek Orthodox Church and its front, the Greek Cypriot Christian Brotherhood—salvation in this camp's repertoire amounting to gaining Enosis, or union with Greece. Enosis seemed a less immediate necessity in the context of London, and the brotherhood's appeal was further undermined by the liberal attitude of the Communist Cypriot branch toward attendance at Orthodox churches. In such a circumstance the Communist Party and the brotherhood competed for the allegiance of new migrants arriving in London, much to the distress of the imperial government. Though scant, evidence suggests that the Cypriot Communist branch was in contact with Indian and other communists and anti-imperialists in London. Certainly the two communist Cypriot newspapers *Kipriaka Nea* and *Vema* carried coverage of anti-colonial struggles in India and condemned English 'imperial aggression' there and elsewhere. Again, while this was fully in line with the CPGB, it carried a degree of immediacy that a purely domestic party could not carry.

The image of England produced by the Cypriot Communist branch and carried by *Kipriaka Nea* and *Vema* was one of a dictatorship exerting arbitrary rule over its colonial subjects. Continued economic exploitation was the norm, interrupted by episodes of violent repression. Against this, the Soviet Union was presented as the land of free workers determined to fight for not only their own salvation but that of all oppressed peoples. The call was always for the workers of Britain to recognize their common lot with the colonial subject, again a theme much in keeping with that of the main CPGB.

The Cypriot branches' articulation of communism and anti-colonialism attracted the patronage of a number of Communist and fellow travelling politicians including the Labour MP and lawyer at the Meerut conspiracy trial, D. N. Pritt. It also attracted the attention of the Colonial Office and other departments of government who sought to proscribe its activities. The colonial office and the Government of Cyprus maintained continual pressure to prevent either of the communist newspapers from being imported into the island.

The limited evidence makes assessment of the impact of Cypriot migrants on communist organization and strength in Britain, difficult to ascertain. During the later thirties the CPGB was attempting to create a people's front. Migrants coinciding with this period might therefore have received a warmer welcome as possible allies than would have been offered a few years earlier. The issue of anti-imperialism while a part of the party's propaganda from 1920, would in a period when the widest possible alliances were being sought, have been all the more attractive. Within Britain Cypriot members, because of their geographical migration, would have belonged to only a handful of CP branches in Central to North London. In this circumstance what influence they brought to bear would have been localized and therefore concentrated. However, the majority of the migrants were ill-educated and employed in irregular and unskilled employment. It is unlikely therefore that they would have engaged in the blooming cultural activities of Communists at this time. Their published record would be largely restricted to the two newspapers *Kipriaka Nea* and *Vema* plus a few pamphlets mainly regarding conditions in Cyprus and the activities of the colonial government, nearly all of which would have been in Greek. If, however, we place the Cypriot migrants together with the Jews in East London, and the many Celtic migrants from South Wales and elsewhere, then the presence of non-English members of the Communist Party in London would have been very much more than the histories have tended to show.

4. UNITY WHICH UNITY?

Previous sections of this chapter have dealt with particular elements in the cultural composition of Communists. I want in this last section, to review the broader circumstance of the Communist Party in Britain and its inability to transcend its own marginal existence. I am not suggesting this inability was due to a lack of effort. Rather the problem lay in a contradiction, inherent in the very formation of the party. On the one side it perceived itself to be heir to a radical lineage, yet on the other espoused an internationalism which aligned it with a hierarchical, bureaucratic and centralized world movement.

It is perhaps only too typical of the unfortunate history of the Communist Party that outside of a small group of ageing comrades the main theme of its 1956 congress is probably almost completely unknown or at least forgotten. The events which are remembered, the debacle over the CPSU twentieth congress, will be the theme of the next chapter. Here I want to approach the twenty-fourth congress from the perspective of its intended issue, that of unity in the Labour Movement and the extent to which this served as a vehicle for frustrations seemingly long held by at least some members. The official statements pertaining to the congress are contained in *The Report of the Executive Committee* (CPGB 1956), *Resolutions and Proceedings* (CPGB 1956) and a collection of speeches published subsequent to the congress under the title *The people will decide* (CPGB 1956). The theme of unity and its central place in the congress was clearly stated by the then vice-chair Rajani Palme Dutt:

> I want to say a few words on unity because I believe that it is the most important question before the congress. And I would like to make a special appeal from this platform to our comrades in the Labour Party, the trade unions and the co-operative movement.
>
> We believe that the present situation justifies and requires a fresh approach from all of us to the urgent question of co-operation and unity (Dutt 1956 249).

The call for unity at the 1956 congress was not a new departure. Its reiteration at this time had rather more to do with the recent triumph of the Conservatives at the polls, their second electoral victory since the war. The call for unity across the Labour Movement, and for affiliation with the Labour Party had been a long-term aim of Communists. Indeed at their founding congress in 1920 Communists approved, albeit by small margin, to apply for membership. Such applications continued to be made through the middle years of the twenties, meeting on every occasion with the same rejection. The turn toward what has been referred to as the 'third period' during 1928 meant that for several years relations between the two parties remained minimal and hostile. On the Labour side, concern with affairs of the Communist Party were likely to remain marginal less because of any cause of the Communists, as with the haemorrhaging of Labour following the 1931 defeat and formation of the national government. On the part of the Communists, however, the middle years of the thirties saw a change of attitude. While the suspicion of the Labour leadership may well have been understandable, the extent of its effort to prevent any collaboration occurring is at the very least surprising.

The forms of unity sought by radicals and socialists varied. Following the 1935 general election in which the national government was returned comfortably, the Communists again applied for affiliation. The Labour executive replied that as nothing had changed since 1922, when a similar application had been refused, there was to be no consideration given to any appeal now (Mahon 1976 199). During the nineteen-thirties, attempts were made to form wider collaboration on the left, the most memorable being that between the Communists, the Independent Labour Party and the small but influential Socialist League. The aims of those involved included getting rid of Chamberlain; forging an alliance between France, the Soviet Union and Britain; gaining state support for the Spanish Republic; and ultimately preventing a European-wide war. In each case the great rallies, the educational groups, and the publishing efforts came to no more than the cultural, artistic and intellectual influence, to which so many had given time and money.

Aid to Spain was one of the most popular of these activities. The reason may not be too difficult to guess at, since it required no special abilities to participate, and at the same time could be seen to be immediate and effective. Alongside this, the failure to convince the Labour leadership to give tangible support for the republic, alienated ever more people from the narrow parliamentary spectrum of politics. The rallies and marches, theatre and music of the peoples' front offered a means of doing something in a world when those wielding power and authority were either on the other side or apathetic about everything beyond their own immediate interests. Writing in his biography *Kingsley Martin*, C. H. Rolph cites the Labour Party's Southport convention in 1939, and states bluntly,

> At that time he [Martin] and Cole and Laski were deeply disturbed about what they saw as the total failure of democratic government (Rolph 1973 218).

Given what I said earlier about significant figures, Rolph's comment that three of the most influential people on the radical left were so distant from constitutional Labour politics, is at the very least startling.

The Communist withdrawal from a broad left alliance was the result of first the signing of the Soviet–German Non-Aggression Pact, and the subsequent decision by the Communist International to declare the eventual hostilities between Britain and Germany an imperialist war. The two were of course not unrelated, though the fact of the first in no way prepared the British CP for the denouncement that was to come. When it did, in mid-September of 1939, Communists were presented with a choice between their duty to maintain the unity of the party, and the close collaboration many had experienced with independent socialists and radicals.

Adoption and implementation of the Communist International position was problematic even among the leadership of the British party. In both the earlier John Mahon, and the more recent Kevin Morgan biographies of Harry Pollitt, the then general secretary of the party, there is no mistaking the tensions and conflicts. Briefly, the history was of an 'about turn' performed by the party. Where at the start of September a steadfast anti-fascism and anti-pacifism meant that the party was committed to fighting if necessary, by the end of the month, the line turned to denouncing an imperialist war which the working class of all countries should seek to end. Pollitt, it seems, had been much to the fore in the campaign for an international peace alliance involving France, Britain and the Soviet Union, and for replacing the national government led by Chamberlain with one more able to pursue the war toward democratic ends. It was from this aspiration that the term 'people's war' seems to have evolved.

The sudden and totally unexpected change to denouncing the war was at first not accepted by the majority of the party executive committee, but eventually Pollitt was left in a minority for whom the change of line over the war remained unacceptable. That only a short while later, Pollitt, having given up the post of general secretary, was able to campaign for a cause he apparently so detested has received two very different interpretations from his biographers.

For Mahon, Pollitt's actions are explicable because,

> There is a difference between agreement with a decision and acceptance of the obligation to carry it out. Political agreement is a matter of individual conviction, an intellectual attitude arising only from discussion, consideration and voluntary consent. The obligation to carry out a decision is a political necessity if the party is to act as a unified force. A decision is made after discussion by majority vote, the only democratic method. A member who thinks it is incorrect has the right to reserve his opinion and in proper course to argue for changing it, but he is nonetheless bound to carry out what the majority have decided (Mahon 1976 253).

At one level this might read as nothing more than normal regulations for any political party. Yet beyond this apparent reasonableness there is the strong sense of a martyrdom, the need for a small sect to maintain discipline. At this level, the Bolshevik creed reads little different from that of a sacred rite. Directed though it may be at the circumstance of 1939 and the figure of Harry Pollitt, Mahon's comments have a greater significance, as we shall see in the next chapter, since they mirror exactly those made about the Reasoners and other 'dissidents' in 1956. Then discipline was discussed through the more abstract terminology of democratic centralism. Individual members' rights were argued to be secondary to the greater good of the party, *The Reasoner* being on this calculation merely a mouthpiece by which individual consciences were being exercised.

Kevin Morgan by contrast pitches his explanation at a more empathetic level,

> It was because he knew that nothing was so certain to split his pals and comrades like [those] who made up the CP that Pollitt could not countenance the idea of defection (Morgan 1993 113).

There is no reason to think that Harry Pollitt believed anything other than that a Bolshevik party, was essential to the advance of socialism. At the same time, he carried with him a deep patriotism to the British working class. Though here placed within a single figure, it was a tension which ran right through the membership, and infused the conflicts and contradictions which were never far from the party throughout its history.

A decade after the war, the call for unity at the twenty-fourth congress in 1956 and the confusions regarding the aims of the party, can be traced back empirically against the electoral results since the end of the national government in 1945. The Communist Party had delayed its preparations for the election and even when finally committed, curbed their activities for fear of splitting the anti-Conservative vote. In the end the party put up only twenty-one candidates, a relatively small number given the party's apparent popularity during the war. Two candidates, Phil Piratin in East London and Willie Gallacher in Fife gained election. Harry Pollitt, standing in Rhondda, was only one thousand votes short of the Labour candidate. In local elections Communists did very well, achieving a total of 206 councillors by the Spring of 1946 (McKinnon 1980). There were also a number of labour MPs elected who were sympathetic to communists and in whose constituencies Labour and Communist were able to work together.

Yet the general election result was less good than the party had hoped for given its apparent popularity during the war. Three points need to be born in mind in understanding why greater popularity should not translate into votes. On the positive side was the fact that a considerable part of the Labour vote came from within the armed forces, many of whom were not yet demobbed. While Communists had continued to work in the services, this had to be covertly. It was then for Labour that party members encouraged soldiers to cast their vote when the time came.

On the negative side though, two points have been made by one-time party members. In 1945, with victory certain, attention increasingly turned to post-war considerations. The Beverage Report had been issued, and with their experience, particularly in domestic matters, the Labour leaders were keen to end the national government and force an election. The Communists by contrast, completely missed the popular sentiment behind the demand for an election and called for continuation of the wartime alliance. The party's mistake becomes even less explicable if the successful by-election results of Common Wealth and independents against the national government over the preceding years are taken into account. However, the deeper and far more important reason why the Communists may not have done as well in the parliamentary elections as they had hoped, was the legacy of their alterations of policy in 1939, their apparent unpatriotism, and the immediate change of view once it was the Soviet Union which came under German and allied attack.

Following the general election, the party's policy seems to have been to continue to give full support to the new Labour administration. Reciprocation by Labour was hardly to be expected given that many of the same people who ruled before the war continued to hold the centre of power in party and in the unions after. The left of the Labour Party, while not approving all the leadership's actions, continued to give their support both because it was unthinkable to undermine the first ever Labour government with a majority of substance, and because of the fable that this was only the first instalment of the socialism that was to come.

By 1950 in contrast, the Communist leadership had shifted its position to be a mirror opposite of that of the Labour leadership, and sought to fight a campaign for its own candidates nationwide. The change of line was indicated from 1947 onwards. In effect the change was parallel to the adoption of what came to be called the 'new line' in the nineteen-twenties. As with the earlier period, pressure for change came from inside the British party and from the world leadership, now under the name of the newly established Communist Information Bureau or Cominform. This outside pressure was stated in terms of a world division into two camps. The whole movement of policy is faithfully reproduced by Edward Upward in his 1972 novel *The Rotten Elements*. Upward had himself resigned in 1948 believing the party to be drifting away from its revolutionary principles. His two lead characters in *The Rotten Elements*, Elsie and Alan Sebrill, are in this respect autobiographical. Unfortunately, the latter seems also to suffer paranoia out of proportion to the reality of the couple's situation. What comes through though is that the leadership's support for the Labour government's policies in the post-war years, as exampled by its attempts to encourage work-place and other activities that would enhance the national economy over which Labour were attempting to exert some control.

By the time of the actual election in 1950, the Korean War had become a reality for the electorate. British soldiers were now involved in fighting an enemy referred to by the media as communist. In such circumstance it is hardly surprising that of the one hundred parliamentary candidates put forward, none were elected and only three saved their deposits. The failure meant that the two sitting MPs both lost their seats. Whether one looks at total votes cast for Communist candidates or at the percentage of the total vote going to Communists in constituencies where they stood, the whole turn of policy was a fiasco. A year later when an exhausted Labour leadership again went to the country, the period of the present 'new line' was ended. In the face of a real threat of a Tory victory, the party returned to the cause of electing a Labour government, putting up only ten candidates of its own. Substantially, the result was no better than a year earlier. For Labour the result was extraordinary. They both gained more votes than a year earlier, and more than the Conservatives, who yet managed to get more candidates elected and thus the right to form a government.

The twenty-fourth congress in the first quarter of 1956 followed only months after the second post-war victory for the Conservatives in the 1955 general election. Communist candidates had again failed completely. In such circumstances for the call for unity to regain the ascendancy at the congress is perhaps less surprising. Yet it could equally be said that the difficulty which members, including the executive, had in stating how unity was to be reconciled with building the party, is even less surprising given the history of Labour–Communist relations. We can gain an indication of this difficulty from the party's programme *The British Road to Socialism*. First published in 1951 the programme received some alterations during 1957, from which edition the following examples are drawn. Under the section 'Unity in Action' the document refers to 'the united action of all sections—Labour, Communist, trade union and co-operative', and 'The alliance of working class and progressive sections of the people' (CPGB 1957 15–16). In the shadow of a Conservative Party victory, neither of these statements are very surprising or apparently contentious. A little more difficulty might be thought to lie in a practical step by which this sought for unity was to be achieved, namely the 'removal of ... bans and prescription' (ibid. 15). These were a series of measures by which the Labour leadership sought to prevent Communists belonging not only to the Labour Party but to any associated body, although no such sanction applied for the co-operative movement to which many Communists belonged. Why the lifting of the bans might be problematic becomes clear under the last section of the programme, `The Communist Party and the Labour Movement'. Their removal is again cited, followed by:

This could lead toward further steps towards unity, including the possibility of affiliation, and eventually of a single working-class party based on Marxism when the majority of the movement has been won for a Marxist outlook (ibid. 30).

In short, the intention is for the establishing a single Marxist party. Or to put it another way, for the Labour Party to become the Communist Party. Given the dominant view of Labour, such an intention would hardly cause the leaders to place lifting the bans at the top of a conference agenda. In reality, the call for unity in 1956 was already far too late to be of any significance, even without the international events that were to overshadow the months and years ahead. The chequered history of Labour–Communist relations and their susceptibility to alien influences, had opened a chasm that had come to be filled with distrust and reproach. The potential that may have existed for a broader radical left in the later-thirties, and again though less coherently in 1942–44, had been buried beyond recall in the substitution of the anti-fascist struggle with the paranoid imaginings that severed relationships and stunted lives in the war of truth between competing ideologies after 1945.

The events after the end of the 'great patriotic war', during which was generated popular enthusiasm for the Red Army, came like a series of stones each building up that wall by which the years were so poignantly marked. The years between the Korean War and the invasion of Hungary can at best be described as contradictory. The death of Stalin in 1953 heralded in unspectacular yet perceptible changes. Where in 1953 the events in Berlin had only served to demonstrate the blind repressive character which had become so much the image of the Soviet Union, Khrushchev's renunciation of Cominform's charges against Tito in Belgrade two years later, were much more confusing. For non-members it is unlikely that following such outrages, any attempts at reconciliation would have any effect other than further confirm the hypocrisy of Soviet foreign policy and the superficiality which allowed leadership and party in Britain to so readily fall into line with any twist and turn that policy might take.

Domestically, the Communist Party of Great Britain saw itself as the heir to a noble radical tradition (*Arena* n.d.). Yet on its own it was in reality never in a position to influence history. The irony was that the only moments when that heirdom might have achieved some real existence were those when it in part subsumed its own identity within that broader left made possible by the existence of a common enemy. At no point was there ever the likelihood that such a left could embrace the leadership of the Labour Movement, and therefore the majority of the Labour members. It was one of the facts of history that the CP executive always found difficult to realize. It was, though, when those wider alignments were possible that many of the most able members were drawn within the party's fold. When yet one more call for unity was made in 1956 it was against a backdrop in which the very soul of communist life was being torn apart. Many of those same able members left, and found a new cause in the bomb. Or rather an enemy against which a new alignment bereft of discipline and central command could flower, however briefly, as an expression of genuine passion.

chapter six

RENEWING THE LIBERTARIAN TRADITION

1. MAKING REASONERS

We take our stand as Marxists. Nothing in the events of the past months has shaken our conviction that the methods and outlook of historical materialism, developed in the work of Marx and Engels, provide the key to our theoretical advance and therefore to the understanding of these events themselves; although it should be said that much that has gone under the names of Marxism or Marxism-Leninism is itself in need of re-examination.

History has provided a chance for this re-examination to take place; and for the scientific methods of Marxism to be integrated with the finest traditions of human reason and spirit which we may best describe as Humanism.

The opportunity may be of short duration. Once passed it may not soon return. It would be treason to our cause, and betrayal of our striving past and present, for a classless society, to let it pass in silence (*Reasoner* 1 1956 3).

Stated in the first issue, these paragraphs perhaps encapsulate in as fine a manner as any summary can the heart of the project that was *The Reasoner*. *The Reasoner* attempted not merely to express outrage, though it did that too, it sought first to change the Communist Party, and when that proved hopeless, to break open a new political space:

Communists all over the world are today being forced to consider the shattering implications of the Khrushchev speech (ibid. 4).

To date little has been written on *The Reasoner* and even less of its antecedents. However, there are a few accounts which require citing. Edward Thompson has offered some recollections, most particularly in his 1973 essay an 'Open Letter to Leszek Kolakowski'. Second is an important collection of essays contained in the 1976 *Socialist Register*, which collectively recall the events of 1956. Of these, the essay by John Saville deals directly with the politics of writing *The Reasoner*. Twenty years on from Saville's essay, his comment that, 'There will be a good deal more flesh on the bones when the complete story of 1956 is told' remains to be met (*Socialist Register 1976* 17). Malcolm MacEwen also contributed to the collection, and recently published his informative autobiography *The*

Greening of a Red (MacEwen 1991). A rather different sort of contribution was a conference, held by the party's history group in 1990, and published under the title of *The Communist Party and 1956* in 1993.

The trials of the left in the nineteen-thirties have received considerable discussion in chapter two. Whatever the long term consequences, the late-twenties and early-thirties were immensely wearing for those involved. According to the Communist Party historian James Klugmann, the shift away from the period of the 'Social Fascism' around 1935 was not at first fully conscious. Such qualitative shifts are always difficult to measure precisely and it is interesting that Miliband more than once suggests that when the young John Saville joined the party in 1934 the 'worst rigours' of the Third Period were over (Miliband 1979 19).

The ending of the sectarianism of the Social Fascist-period did not mean that being a Communist was easy during the remainder of the decade, but it was certainly very much harder from the middle of the forties (Fieldhouse 1985a). Between these times though was a crucial period when it was possible to be a Communist and be seen by some at least to be on the right side. The period of the popular front and the Second World War was certainly not unbroken—to have achieved that was too much for the leadership of the party to have managed. The months of the imperialist war following the Hitler–Stalin pact aside though, it was possible for Communists to find others in considerable numbers who were prepared to work with you even if you were in the party:

> From 1941 onwards the Second World War permitted a unique fusion of international and national causes on the left. Unconditional devotion to the international goals of communism could be combined with intransigent leadership of the fight for national liberation from German occupation (Anderson 1980 142–3).

Exactly how the circumstances of a period related to the action of an individual is difficult to explicate, as Miliband points out with regard to John Saville,

> Of course, what made this particular young man attend meetings of the left and join the Communist Party is an immensely complicated business, as is any large choice that anybody makes (Miliband 1979 16).

While Miliband's comment is certainly true, it is important to note that like other politically conscious young people of this period, Saville's own lower-middle-class background was not that of the dominant university culture between the wars, and, like Williams, his means to university was via a scholarship not wealth. For John Saville though, it was with the job of making Communists that he was most engaged, a university activity particularly apposite to a period when, in the perception of many, a Fascist attack might soon have to be fought:

> [People] were not placed in some pure climate of choice, but in the contexts of savage counter-revolution and military politics which none had chosen. If their choices had been wiser, world war might conceivably have been averted, or limited. If their actions had been more self-centred then the war could certainly have been lost. And it is difficult to see how the evidence of the thirties and forties (taken together) can be read as an irrevocable verdict on the human heart. The worst evil was defeated. And if every form of evil—power, lust, sadism and the corrosion of humanism, into abstraction of power—were displayed on the side of the victor, so also was self-sacrifice, heroism and every generous quality in superabundance (Thompson ed. 1960 169).

Three oft-cited elements in the history of this period were the general crisis of capitalism, the apparent forward strides of the Soviet Union, and the equally cited, though rarely connected, war in Spain. The first has been vividly set out by Branson and Heinemann in their heroic account of suffering and struggle. If the crisis of capitalism set up the negative pole then the many glowing reports of the rapidly industrializing Soviet Union could certainly serve as an alternative and positive pole. To this the events in Spain, the marching Blackshirts in London's east end and elsewhere, and the emergent popular front, provided the necessary romantic impetus to the formation of professional class Communists.

During the thirties many, both inside and outside the party, had come to view capitalism as inevitably doomed. Such a view could be derived from the sight of the unemployed and the hunger marchers alone. Founded on such direct experience such a view would be hard to condemn. The more contentious strand in the measuring of capitalism's economic failing though was the assurance of the inevitability of decline based on purely theoretical grounds. In this guise the last rites were being proclaimed on the basis of attaching present trends to abstract laws. After 1956 this positivist reasoning was to also come under attack from what was to become a sister publication, *Universities and Left Review*. There the criticism was that this concern with the tendencies of capitalist economies had marginalized the Utopian appeal of socialism. It is perhaps also ironical that a close concern with economics, enclosed as it was in a formula which declared capitalism's demise, may have meant that the real trends in, say, working-class living-standards were actually missed.

By contrast, the immediate political necessity to confront fascism both at home and abroad, and the unity created by such a threat, provided a very different emotional and intellectual response. What fascism threatened was not only an extreme form by which the capitalist state might manage itself but also a direct endangering of human liberties. The last was a critical feature in the formation of many of the dissidents of 1956 who came to support *The Reasoner*. Taking the scene forward to a comparison with the expectation at the end of the Second World War Thompson wrote:

> Stalinism confined this spirit, but it was never killed. Today it walks

abroad again in full daylight on the Polish streets. It was present in the Budapest barricades, and today wrests with anarchy for the future of Hungary. Never was there a time when comrades of ours were in such need of our solidarity in the face of the blind resistance of Stalinism, the black passions of reaction (*Reasoner* 3 1956 Supplement 7).

Thompson is invoking a spirit here which can be recognized from a decade earlier, first in the tribute to his brother, *There is a Spirit in Europe*, and then in the account of the building of the railway from Samac to Sarajevo. For the composers of *The Reasoner*, fascism and the people's front, the onset of Stalinism and the doctrine of two camps, were in the nineteen-fifties remoulded by the greatest threat to human liberties of all, the bomb. Overshadowing the years since the war this most lethal of all dictators was, under Thompson's pen invoking a new popular front against itself. The Campaign for Nuclear Disarmament meant that for first time since 1945 a real fraternity between Communists and Socialists could again be realized.

2. WHY WE PUBLISHED

I began to reason in my thirty-third year and despite my best efforts, I have never been able to shake the habit off (Thompson 1978).

With these words Thompson recalled the commencement of *The Reasoner* some twenty years later.

As I noted at the beginning of the chapter, compared with the volume of theoretical discussion of the arguments it inspired, there is a remarkable lack of empirical detail about *The Reasoner*. So much so in fact that in an interview with Eric Hobsbawm the publishers, *Marxism Today*, even managed to get the name wrong. With this in mind it may be as well to begin the present section with a few basic facts. There were in all three issues of *The Reasoner*; issue one in July 1956, issue two in September and issue three planned for October but not finally published till November. That there were only three issues could be attributed to a number of factors, not least the editors' pre-announced suspension on the issue of the third number. It would be only fair to recall the editors' own claim published in the last issue that 'We planned only three numbers in this form' (*Reasoner* 3 1956 44). While any such claim might be challenged it should be remembered in the following account.

Publication was carried out between Halifax and Hull, the Thompsons then living in the former and the Savilles in the latter. The published names of the editors were Edward Thompson and John Saville, though there were many others assisting with reports, writing, printing, and distributing. At the time Edward Thompson was an extra-mural tutor for Leeds University and the Workers' Education Association, a post which he had held since 1948. John Saville by contrast had gained a lectureship in the

History Department at Hull as early as 1947.

Printing was carried out from stencilled paper, mainly it seems at the Hull end of the operation. What is less clear is how the final product, priced at two shillings, was actually distributed. The last is not unimportant, since publication was as a dissident Communist voice, but internal to the party. As such it was directed first and foremost at other party members. The many pages of theoretical discussion about culturalism and socialist humanism have been directed toward projects other than the recovery of what was a remarkable historical episode, and therefore have left some of that history to one side. Yet unless the fact of *The Reasoner* being a dissenting publication internal to a Communist Party is remembered, there is little prospect for understanding the style or content of its pages.

The first, its style, is that of polemic. The first issue appeared some five months after the twentieth congress of the CPSU, and four months after the twenty-fourth congress of the British party. By this time Togliatti, the Italian party leader, had, in an interview with the non-party paper *Nuovi Argumenti*, given clear indication of there having been a 'secret speech' in which some significant facts had been disclosed. Recently Kate Hudson has claimed that:

> the French and Italian parties now acknowledge that their delegations at the twentieth congress (headed by Thorez and Togliatti) were given the text of Khrushchev's secret speech while still in Moscow (*Socialist History Society* 1993 4).

In addition, Eric Hobsbawm recalls that,

> ... it was clear to those of us who listened to the congress, or read the reports of the congress that even before the secret speech there were some rather notably critical remarks by Mikoyan. And one wondered what else was going on (*Marxism Today* November 1986 17).

By July, and the first issue of *The Reasoner* there was already considerable ferment in other parties, particularly in the United States, where *Jewish Life* had carried serious criticism of the suppression of Jewish culture in the later years of Stalin's rule. The international spread of discontent infused the urgency expressed through the pages by editors and contributors alike. However, *The Reasoner* is best understood for its role of carrying replies to debates and arguments published both inside the Communist Party and elsewhere. We can gain a flavour of *The Reasoner* from a quick review of the contents. In all, the three issues carried some seventeen letters and other correspondence. While many of these were in the form of replies to statements by other party members, they also include some items solicited by the paper's 'monitoring service'. In addition, John Saville contributed a longer piece replying to the various articles by Cole.

The Reasoner was in that sense a paper publishing alongside others, and only understandable if read in conjunction with official party organs. In 1956 these official party publications included the *Daily Worker, World News* and *The Modern Quarterly*. Alongside these was *Labour Monthly*, the exact status of which was apparently a little uncertain, a fact highlighted by the editors of *The Reasoner* in defence of their own act of publication. The purpose of each publication varied, and *The Modern Quarterly's* function as a scientific and cultural review meant that it played but a small part in the debates of that year. By contrast the *Daily Worker* was the foremost organ of the party since its inception in 1930. The most widely read publication within the party, it also commanded considerable sales beyond. In 1948, total daily sales had reached over one-hundred-thousand. While these had declined by 1955 to some eighty-thousand, this still compared favourably with a membership which in February 1956 stood at thirty-three-thousand and ninety-five (*Daily Worker* 2 April 1956 4, Harrison 1974 215, Thompson 1991 218).

For these reasons alone, what appeared in the *Daily Worker* must be taken as an important indication of the views within the party. Editorial control of the *Daily Worker* though was firmly in the hands of the leadership. At national level, King Street, the party was run by the executive committee. Subordinate to this, at least in theory, was the political committee, though there was suspicion that in practice the direction of command may have been in reverse. Either way, the overlap in membership between the two committees made agreement between them highly likely. Editorship of the *Daily Worker* was firmly slotted into this arrangement, as much by personality as by organization. During the trauma of 1956 its editor, Jonnie Campbell, maintained the executive's discipline with little short of an iron hand.

Reasons for its launch are variously identified through the pages of *The Reasoner*. In the final issue the editor set out in considerable detail their own reasons under the heading 'Why we Published' (*Reasoner* 3 1956 40), though the first paragraph can be taken as a fair summary of the arguments;

> We published *The Reasoner* because there was a political crisis both within the party and within international communist theory which was not being reflected in the statements and actions of our leadership: because the *rights* of comrades to take part in fundamental discussions were being violated by the E.C.: because the *facilities* for this discussion were inadequate and the editorial control not such as to safeguard the expression of minority views (*emphasis in original* ibid. 40).

While 'rights' may be the more fundamental factor in the decision to publish, the equal citing of facilities should alert us to the extreme pressure which party members felt under during this period. The eventual breaking of party discipline by publication of unauthorized literature critical of the political committee, was a direct response to the prolonged frustration at having items refused in effect by members of that same committee wearing the hat of editor of the *Daily Worker*. In a piece entitled 'What shall we do about The Reasoner', Ronald Meek wrote:

> ... all too often those of us who criticized these practices were threatened somewhat coldly (to say the least of it) by the leadership, and our criticisms remained largely unpublished (*Reasoner* 2 1956 8).

Focusing on the shorter period of March to October 1956 the editors state the same point more precisely:

> Can it be doubted that demands for an honest open forum, if raised through the 'recognized machinery' would have been subject to the same evasion and delay, so that today we would still be arguing at the same point on the official ladder, while events passed us by? (*Reasoner* 3 1956 42).

In discussing the case for publishing *The Reasoner*, the claim of a denial of a voice in the official publications cannot be separated from the difficult issue of members' rights. Situated somewhere between the party rule book and an abstract recall of a Painite tradition, arguments developed in direct response to executive statements, international events, and the content of official party publications. The first issue in July followed a letter in the *Daily Worker* by Cornforth and Dobb in March, an executive statement in May, and an exchange between George Matthews and Edward Thompson in *World News* in June. In similar manner the second issue in September needs to be read in conjunction with the establishing of two internal party commissions; the first on a redrafting of *The British Road*, and a second on inner-party democracy. Though the editors do not directly refer to the two commissions by name, their long editorial, 'The Case for Socialism', returns again and again to the questions of the rights of party members to effectively express their views and participate in the formation of party policy (*Reasoner* 2 1956). Similarly, the appropriateness of Soviet policy for conditions in Britain is again questioned, together with its effect in distancing the party from the majority of the Labour Movement:

> But in place of the clear analysis of imperialism, the agitational explanation of the Socialist alternative, which Engels and Lenin, Morris and Tom Mann, knew must be carried on alongside the heart of every struggle, we have increasingly substituted, for the first, an oversimplified myth of the 'two camps', and for the second, Utopian propaganda about the Soviet Union as the land of Socialism-realized (ibid. 3).

The issue of the rights of members to effectively express their views directly related to a central feature of a Communist party: Democratic Centralism. The concept may be taken as having been derived from Lenin, though it would be true to say that its inflection at any time was due more to the fears of the Executive Committee of the Communist International (ECCI). The main elements were set out in an article by G. D. H. Cole:

(i) that minorities shall accept the decision of majorities; and

(ii) that lower party organs shall accept the decision of higher party organs (*The Reasoner* 3 1956c 7).

The editors, perhaps not surprisingly given their professional persuasion, pursue the issue of how a minority might effectively express their views, by way of historical analogy. In an open letter to Robin Page-Arnot, John Saville refers back to the circumstance in the party in 1927–28 and the pressures brought to bear by a minority for a change in party ideology and practice. The change was toward what has since been referred to as the Third or Social-Fascist period. In summary, the party leadership had split. The majority, including William Gallacher and J. R. Campbell, had argued for continued co-operation with the wider Labour Movement. Against this, a new group, which included Robin Page-Arnot, William Rust, Ranjani Palme Dutt and Harry Pollitt, some of whom were at the time still members of the YCL, argued for the adoption of a new line. John Saville argues that the new line group defied the express forbidding of the leadership to pursue their aims through publication or any other means which involved active campaigning to gain a movement within the party for a change of policy. Saville notes also that this defiance of the orders of the leadership was carried out with the support of the Communist International. Given such a precedent, Saville concludes with the question of on what basis Page-Arnot can withhold his acceptance of the right of a new minority to also pursue the cause for a change in party policy?

3. DEMOCRATIC CENTRALISM AND THE SOVIET ROAD

In the case of Communist parties there is a further problem. Under the constitution of the Comintern (now defunct) each national party was required to regard itself as a branch or a section of the Comintern and to accept the orders, not only of an International Congress, but also of the Executive Committee of the Comintern (ECCI). Thus the international executive was treated as higher than even the congress of a national Communist party. It may be said that since the dissolution of the Comintern, this situation has ceased to exist; but how far was the place of the ECCI taken in practice by the central organ of the CPSU (*Reasoner* 3 1956 8).

The paragraph follows on from Cole's premise regarding the nature of Democratic Centralism. Here though the theme is extended so as to relate that content to the subordination of other Communist parties to that of the Soviet. The issue goes to the heart of *The Reasoner*, and indeed the unrest throughout the party. The July and September issues enjoined in the debate over the 'cult of the individual' explanation presented in the secret speech, and repeated by the British party executive, while the November issue included Thompson's 'Through the Smoke of Budapest' and the outrage expressed there at the leadership's endorsement of the Soviet intervention in Hungary.

The problem of members' rights, their frustration at being denied access to effective voice and the subordination of these to the practice of democratic centralism were themselves effects of the party's relationship to 'actually existing socialism'. In the pages of *The Reasoner* this relationship is doubly faulted. In the first instance it meant that the leadership of the British party had made the Soviet Union into an heroic shrine and more recently reduced the world into two camps, characterized into simple good and bad. The second followed from the first. A defence of all things Soviet had isolated the British party, and by association its members from not only the British Labour Movement, but also indigenous traditions of radicalism.

These two issues are addressed in a long review by John Saville, 'World Socialism Restated: A Comment', which appeared in the second issue. Again in the style of *The Reasoner*, the article is a response to another which appeared elsewhere. G. D. H. Cole had written calling for the International Labour Movement to re-examine itself and from this to seek greater unity (Cole 1956a and 1956b). Saville continues the discussion;

> I will confine myself to one important aspect of sectarianism … This is our attitude to our own history, … It is not simply a matter of estimating the degree of error in our own past policies, … but of analysing these mistakes in the whole contexts in which they occurred. … the whole period of Social-Fascism. Were we right in applying the New Line in this country. … Or consider what is a more vivid memory to us all— the change of line to the war in 1939. There is not a shred of doubt that this question is still exercising a considerable political effect. Many of our own members are now convinced that we were wrong to switch to the policy of imperialist war (*Reasoner* 2 1956 20).

Writing in 1993 Mike Squires has argued that in each instance, particularly the first, there had existed pressure from within the membership of the British party for a sharp separation to be made between itself and the rest of the Labour Movement. The argument in *The Reasoner* though had been framed in a different manner. It was not necessarily that a particular action followed an identifiable directive from Moscow, but that the conditions within which decisions were made by members in the British party were determined by a firm belief that the first priority was the defence of the Soviet Union. In consequence, even if the actual manner in which a policy was carried out reflected the views of Communists in Britain rather than just those of the Comintern, the thinking of those party members had already been conditioned to view any policy from the perspective of how it might affect the Soviet Union. Sectarianism need not be a decision to purposefully reject the Labour Movement, as in the case of the new line, but the thinking through of an issue in a completely different way to those outside the party. The disciplined Communist in the West, lived where they did not think, and thought where they did not live.

It was to break this stranglehold on thinking that *The Reasoner* turned to people outside the party for support. The significance of this move was perhaps only later understandable. As Thompson recollected,

> I was not then looking for that alternative space, though I can see now in retrospect that a few were trying to hold it open: ... Claude Boudet in France, in Britain G. D. H. Cole. The space did not open until after Stalin's death and the Khrushchev 'thaw'. In 1956 there was a world-wide effort both in the East (Poland, the Soviet Union itself, Hungary) and in Western parties. When this was checked within the old ideological and disciplinary norms, many thousands of Communists ... left their parties, and some of these sought to break open that alternative space. Many gave their support to CND and the new non-aligned peace movements of that generation. Some survivors from that moment put together the peace movement of today (Thompson 1985 17).

Contained in a much summarized manner here is a history of that independent left from the perspective of those who lost the openness of the earlier-nineteen-forties in the crushing deadness of cold-war discipline. Writing in 1961, Thompson addressed this history under a rather different guise of literature and culture. Taking the opportunity of a review article, Thompson discussed the conditions which had so effectively divided the Left in the years after 1945, and a figure who by 1961 he saw as having resisted the pressures of those years,

> the major intellectual socialist-tradition in this country was so contaminated that Williams could not hope to contest with reaction at all unless he dissociated himself from it: ... he did the only thing that was left to him: he took over the vocabulary of his opponents, followed them into the heart of their own arguments, and fought them to a standstill in their own terms. (Thompson 1961 27).

In addition to comparing the two quotes from Thompson given here, it is worth recalling his 1960 essay 'Outside the Whale'. In it he denounced the manner in which the pressure of the post-war years had been fuelled by the lurid images of Orwell's fantasy *1984*, and the rapidity with which Spender, Connolly and others had beaten a track to the doors of the BBC to tell the story of deceit and betrayal. The pressures of the period were also referred to in the review of *The Long Revolution*, only this time it was the manner in which they produced T. S. Eliot as their interpreter.

Interestingly, the ends of Thompson's review, is recalled by Williams by way of a reference closer to that of the first of the quotes here from Thompson,

> I met so many people on those Aldermaston marches I hadn't seen in

years, especially from a Communist background. It was like people who had been separated for a decade meeting up again in all sorts of ways (Williams 1979a 361).

The reference is valuable in that it returns us again to the actual context in which assessment of the post-war years was now being made. While though in these accounts and recollections the emphasis is on the ending of the time of separation and lost progress, there remains the justified complaint that the time had been so wasted when the opportunity for advancing a socialist movement had been available in the years after the cessation of war. At that time the call would have been made by those who were on the outside;

> If the intellectuals in the Communist Party had been moving toward our kind of project, as one could say many of them did in '56, they would have given it much more solidity on the political/economic/ historical side. ... But they of course had a completely different perspective—they still thought it was necessary to fight inside the Communist movement. The sort of formation that was necessary nearly occurred in '46–47. But it didn't happen (Williams 1979a 77).

With these examples we are brought full circle. Thompson and Williams present us with the agonies and failings of these years. When these different elements are pulled together in this manner, the real tragedy of the period between 1947 and 1956 can be seen. *The Reasoner* was a realization of that tragedy. The arguments to review the party's history, made by two members of the historians group, followed years of strain in defence of their loyalty and continued membership (ibid. 92). In an exchange between the 'Reasoners' during the crisis the historians group was spoken of thus;

> It is, I think significant that of all the intellectual groups in the Communist Party, the historians have come out best in the discussions of the past nine months—and this surely is due to the fact that over the past decade the historians are the only intellectual group who have not only tried to use their Marxist techniques creatively, but have to some measure succeeded. Letter from John Saville to Edward and Dorothy Thompson 29 November 1956 (*Socialist Register* 1976 7).

It is this uneven development, as represented between Raymond Williams and Edward Thompson, that makes the history of an independent left tradition since the war so problematic.

4. Responses to the Reasoner

The hostility of the official response to the publication of *The Reasoner*, with its threatened sanctions against the paper for breach of party rules, has already been noted. In view of the feeling of deep crisis searing through the party though it might be argued that the leadership's views counted for little more than that of the membership at large. Certainly if the letters forum of the *Daily Worker* and the specially opened forum in *Marxist Quarterly*, are taken as a symptom of that depth of feeling, then the response evoked from other members cannot be ignored.

The principal sources for much of the detail in the following paragraphs are the executive committee circulars for 1956. The executive committee's decision to raise questions soliciting responses from branches and individuals, was a sign of the turmoil within the party. To invite expression of members in this way was certainly extraordinary, possibly unprecedented, suggesting that the executive could not be said to be entirely deaf to the discontent. In the circumstances of 1956 it may even have been that *The Reasoner* symbolized a potential for fracture of the membership, eliciting apprehensive respect from the executive. Just such a splitting of the membership was what was called for by Sheffield students in their reply to the executive's questions;

> Attack on the Soviet army in action in Hungary for deceitful and barbarous action. Call on the E.C. to demand withdraw: if not, recommend all branches to dissolve themselves as branches subject to existing leadership, but to form honest and independent Marxist party (Executive Committee Circulars 1956 Box.)

The replies are listed as coming both from branches and individual members. The great majority of the branch responses are dated between the 20th September and the 8th November. Those concerning the Hungarian situation came from both branches and individuals and are nearly all dated November. Otherwise individual letters tend to start from the 12th September and finish at the end of October.

The headings under which branch responses were listed were several. The first, 'The Reasoner' was divided into three categories. The first totalling thirty-nine replies included those 'in favour of E.C. attitude'. The second group, those 'against the E.C. attitude' totalled seventeen. An additional twenty-four were 'noncommittal'. The number of the replies in the last category make it hard to claim the responses offer decisive support one way or the other. To further complicate matters, branches expressing a 'noncommittal' attitude to the rights and wrongs of *The Reasoner* do not form a uniform stance. Rather they range from that of the South-east Midlands District Committee's 'Report of discussion on "The Reasoner"; most comrades support the E.C. but no vote', to Golders Green's 'Against disciplinary action; call for special party journal.' Perhaps the most intriguing was that of the historians' group, which read 'Against disciplinary action; have asked T. & S. not to publish 3rd number'. This last clause is supported by entries in the group's minutes book.

Of those taking a firm stand one way or the other there was a strong tendency for London branches to be 'in favour', but for several to also oppose disciplinary action. As such nearly all the opposition to the E.C. would appear to come from outside London. The picture for London though might not be so clearly one way. The majority of the 'individual letters' come from London and the great majority of these oppose the executive committee. One final significant finding with regard to *The Reasoner* were replies from cultural groups and universities. These totalled twelve, of which only two supported the E.C. The remainder were evenly split between 'against' and 'noncommittal'. In total there were some thirty letters from individuals, of which only two could be said to support the E.C. One other, from Peter Sedgwick was 'Against continued publication of *The Reasoner* but critical of the E.C.'. More significant was the inclusion among the letter writers of three members of the historians' group and two members of the staff of the *Daily Worker*. In every case the response was against the E.C.

Finally, under the closely-related heading of a party 'Discussion Journal' there were twenty-six replies, nearly all of which were from branches. The view of these contributions is not in doubt, only one identifying itself as 'against'. Cultural groups and universities were again well represented among those favouring a new journal, Cambridge graduates declaring themselves 'For a journal of free discussion in agreement with T. & S'. This radical stance of Cambridge is maintained in responses listed under 'Hungary' where students and city branches condemn the *Daily Worker's* presentation of events. A submission also dated 6-11-56 from Cambridge U. Senior Branch, but listed under 'Miscellaneous' read—

> E.C. members should express individual views so as to show membership where they stand: accounts of differing views in E.C. discussions should be published (Executive Committee Circulars 1956 Box).

It would be wrong then to declare that in the crucial period of September to early November at least, a coherent voice one way or the other was being expressed by party members. Rather views shifted between issues, many responses seeking a compromise that might keep the party together. Once again we are presented with a picture of a party membership and indeed executive deeply distressed and fearful of events which many felt to be personally threatening. As in other situations, the mood has been best caught in fictional portrayal, on this occasion Doris Lessing's *The Golden Notebook*.

Unevenness of response during these months allowed for, there are identifiable periods during which the crisis in the party took on different forms. The first was from March 1956 through to late September. The primary focus during these months was the Khrushchev speech and the response, or lack of it, from the British leadership. Fuelling the feelings of members at this time were the statements from within other Communist parties, of which the United States was particularly critical. The build up of tensions first in Poland and then in Hungary dominate the thinking during October, creating a heightened sense of anxiety. The entry of Soviet tanks into Budapest then serves as a break at which point a large number of members leave the party. The last phase is that from the beginning of November through to the special congress held in April 1957, at which point a number of those who had continued to view the fight for change in the party as worth pursuing, also resigned. This last phase, of course, post-dates *The Reasoner*, but was perhaps the moment when a real potential existed between those retaining party cards and those already outside. It was in this period of flux that serious discussion of an alternative to the Communist Party was floated, and when the *ad hoc* socialist forums seemed to present an opportunity to speculate on the future.

We can trace these responses of party members through the pages of *The Reasoner* and *Daily Worker*. Earlier in the chapter I noted that in the last issue of *The Reasoner* the editors claimed that it had been their original intention to only publish three issues. In the end, the exactness or otherwise of that claim was made academic. To get a better understanding of the closing of *The Reasoner* we need though to move back several months to the 14–15th July when report of *The Reasoner* was first formally recorded by the executive committee. The response at that time was to refer the matter back to the Yorkshire district committee. Following a meeting of the latter on the 18th August, to which both Thompson and Saville were invited, the following resolution was passed:

> The district committee asked Comrades Thompson and Saville to cease the publication of *The Reasoner* (*World News* 22 September 1956 600).

The two editors refused to comply. In consequence a further meeting held on the 26th August passed a longer resolution the effect of which was to pass the affair back to the party centre. Recalling the previous request this second resolution continued;

> The district committee takes a grave view of the declaration made by these two comrades that they will not carry out the decision of the district committee. The continued publication of *The Reasoner* constitutes a breach of party rule, practice and discipline, harmful to the party. As the principle involved is of national importance and there are comrades involved with the journal outside Yorkshire, we bring these facts to the notice of the executive committee and ask them to deal with the matter (ibid. 600).

In actual fact the next act was played out by the political committee who invited Saville and Thompson to a meeting on the 31st August. The aim was apparently to clarify the situation before the September executive committee meeting. It might though be suspected that the formal relationship at least between the two bodies might better place the political committee to intervene, while still leaving a way out by way of referral yet further up the party ladder of authority. Certainly the leadership was already going to extraordinary lengths to prevent any final show-down with the editors of what was a clandestine journal. The political committee, as might be expected, repeated the call made by the district.

We can understand this sequence of events very differently depending on the position from which the scene is viewed. From the point of view of party discipline the increased strain could be said to result from the defiance of the previous resolutions by the editors, and their publication of the second issue in September. Such a view would be perfectly reasonable on the basis of a summary view of the paper work. In a letter dated 5 September, and published in *World News* for 22 September, Saville and Thompson had replied to the political committee that, '... the second number is in active preparation'. Not unsurprisingly the September executive committee reiterated the call for no further publication of *The Reasoner*. The reply from the two editors, though in part conciliatory, remains a clear defiance:

> While we appreciate your general assurance about the intention of the leadership to promote and extend discussion, we are not at all satisfied that this can in fact take place adequately in the present forms: ... We therefore propose to bring 'The Reasoner' to a close at the third number (Thompson and Saville to Gollan, Letter dated 7 October).

Apparently attempting further clarification the executive duly replied that it 'specifically instructs you not to bring out a third number of "The Reasoner".' (Letter from John Gollan, undated).

Yet the most remarkable turn of this long and tense exchange did not come until the end. When the third issue did eventually come out the political situation had of course entirely changed. What is difficult to understand is the manner in which the executive so speedily and radically shifted its own position. Certainly the change bore little relation to the events of Hungary, although if the events surrounding *The Reasoner's* closure are viewed singularly in terms of party procedures, this should not be surprising.

For the moment we need only note that it was the apparent call to work actively against the party leadership that lay at the centre of the executive's concern. To the executive it was not clear whether the editors were urging the formation of a faction inside the party or a new socialist grouping. The former was as completely forbidden by Communist, as it is by most other party's rules. The latter would seem to speak for itself. Yet to assume that this flouting of party rules was simply wilfulness on the part of editors of a dissident paper would be to edit out the political context within which these meetings and exchanges took place. The resentment of the British party's executive was being reinforced by the publication elsewhere of repression of Soviet Jewry, the seeming coolness with which Tito and the Yugoslav party had been readmitted to the Soviet fold, or the attempt to explain Soviet history of the past two decades by way of a 'cult of the individual'. Looked at from this perspective, consideration of party rules was not simply irrelevant, but deeply mischievous.

Whichever view is adopted, publication of these exchanges in the 22 September and 17 November issues of *World News* can only be viewed as exceptional. Following the circulation of the second issue, a deferred suspension was set in place should any further publication take place. The editors decision to go ahead with such publication in the form of the third and final issue automatically caused the suspended penalty to be invoked. The circumstance of the suspension arose from a meeting between the editors and the executive committee on the 31st August. Writing retrospectively in the 1976 *Socialist Register* John Saville recalls that he and Edward Thompson 'drafted our letters on the train going home'.

Defiance of an executive committee instruction while not unique in the history of the CPGB was at best rare. Defiance in the midst of the most traumatic period of the party's history could understandably be regarded by many as treachery. Yet ironically, it was precisely the nature of that crisis that made it possible for two long-serving intellectual activists to take such a step. John Saville's recollects:

It was a complete failure of minds to meet; on our side we wanted to discuss politics, what the crisis was about and why we needed a much more serious analysis of the twentieth congress; while the P.C. talked only with the narrow framework of party organization and the way in which we had violated its rules. After three hours we adjourned for lunch and after we re-assembled we re-affirmed our decision to continue publication (ibid. 11).

We are in one sense back again with the issues of Democratic Centralism. Yet we are also in the presence of a much greater question of whether a party can ever avoid the decline into what I shall describe as bureaucratic scholasticism which seems to epitomize the CPGB in the mid-nineteen-fifties. To the editors, the executive's response seems to have been one of 'while Rome burned'. But it would be false to suggest that the resignation of the editors and with them the ending of *The Reasoner* was the result of an intensification of existing tensions in the party only. There had after all been plans made for the editorship to pass on to a series of pairs of individuals should Saville and Thompson be expelled, and after them, each of the subsequent editors. Rather it was the eruption of one of those tensions, the developments in the Hungarian Communist Party and its relations with the Soviet party, that effected the closure of *The Reasoner*. Once again writing in the 1976 *Socialist Register* recollection, Saville comments '… we both resigned.'

Given the centrality of events in Hungary to the story, it would be as well to review *The Reasoner's* response to those events. Briefly, the sequence of events was that Imre Nagi, leader of reforms two years earlier, had been returned to the position of prime minister around the 23rd October. By this time Soviet tanks had already entered Hungary for the first time. The exact position of Nagi is hard to pinpoint given the fighting, though what was clear was that pressure was being exerted for Moscow to effectively recognize the possibility for Hungary to choose its own path to socialism. Pressed on by apparently popular sentiment, Nagi served as a focus at the head of the uprising. Soviet tanks had first entered Hungary in late-October but held back from the vicinity of Budapest. The stalemate between the uprising in support of the Nagi government and the Soviet troops was short-lived. Within hours of the French and British troops' invasion of Egypt, Soviet tanks entered Budapest. The uprising was put down and Nagi taken. The days and nights of the 3rd and 4th November were moments when a response was demanded. In the pages of *The Reasoner* that response was to call for a new Communist start. Of course, more generally in Britain, it was the Suez situation which was of the greater import both at the time and subsequently. This said, the wisping smoke that blew away from the barrels of Soviet tanks also effected as it did elsewhere, a change in the British political landscape.

5. Last Minute Changes

The third issue of *The Reasoner* had been planned and written during October. During this time the conflict in Poland had been eased by the strength of the reformed Polish party to resist Soviet threats of intervention. This said, the political unrest in Poland was greatly intensifying the tensions felt by parties across the world. The attack by French and British troops on Egypt on the 30th October had tremendously contradictory effects. Loyal and dissenting Communists were pulled together while each was at the same time brought together with others outside the party. In Raymond Williams's *Loyalties*, the tensions are played out in a Trafalgar Square anti-war demonstration, talk of comparison with Hungary, raising the question of the authenticity of the appearance of a single-minded crowd. It should not pass our notice that it was precisely in the name of such common cause that the accusation of divisiveness was levelled at *The Reasoner*.

Any careful compilation the third issue may have enjoyed to that moment was thrown into disarray by the Soviet entry into Hungary. The existing editorial criticizing the party executive for its continued failure to ensure adequate means for open party discussion was moved to the rear of the issue where it was renamed a 'Statement by the Editors'. In its place was inserted Edward Thompson's 'Through the Smoke of Budapest'. Even then a further change was required. 'Through the Smoke of Budapest' responded to the *first* Soviet entry into Hungary. At that moment the possibility that 'Reasoners' may have stayed to fight in the party was slim. The night of the 4th November, and the re-entry of Soviet troops, this time into Budapest itself, turned that doubt into a call for all Communists to leave. In the final published version of this last *Reasoner*, Thompson's article was pushed back two pages and another editorial inserted.

At one level differences between the pieces are obvious. Previously, while views had varied as to its possibility, the argument had been conducted within the terms of reform. The final editorial sought no such compromise:

> ... we urge all those who will like ourselves dissociate themselves completely from the leadership of the British party, not to lose faith in Socialism, and to find ways of keeping together (Editorial *The Reasoner* 3 1956).

There is also something of a shifting idiom in the manner in which the last items are written. The first, the 'Statement by the Editors', was a planned article, written during October. It was, as I say, originally to be the editorial for the last issue. The principal themes are—a resumé of the main events from March to October, the conflict in the party over rights of members to discuss political and historical issues, the shifts in the executive committee's response to mounting pressure for publication of dissenting views, the 'revelations' stemming from other Communist parties and a defence of the rightness in principle for the publication of *The Reasoner*. The arguments, however critical in tone, continued to be conducted within the framework of the party. To put it another way the article remains as one written by Communists to Communists: a contribution to internal debate. The statement was dated the 31st October.

'Through the Smoke of Budapest' takes a step beyond this position:

> I had intended in this article to attempt some definitions of Stalinism, to enter into some questions of theory which our British leadership refuses to discuss, and to consult with readers upon the best way to rid our party of Stalinist theory and practice.
>
> But these points of theory have now found dramatic expression in the great square of Warsaw and amid the smoke of Budapest. It is difficult to speak at all in the teeth of a whirlwind. And if we have helped, in some small degree, to sow that wind, do we have the right to speak? (*The Reasoner* 3 1956 Supplement).

The shift cited in these paragraphs sets the theme of the whole article. Before, the situation had been a 'crisis'; world communism was deeply divided. The necessity was for the truth to be told, for questions to be answered. But if this could be achieved, then the possibility remained for the International Communist Movement to regain its respect. The issue had been the rectifying of a circumstance past and present. The assault by Soviet tanks on Budapest had, I would argue, changed the circumstance. It was not simply that a present situation had got quantitatively worse, but that a new situation, qualitatively different, was now present.

In the preceding months one of the threads of argument pursued in *The Reasoner* had been that the Khrushchev speech and to some at least, the actions of Soviet party, had made for a situation where a new beginning could be made: In 'An open letter from a "premature anti-Stalinist",' the

141

writer argued:

> ... history, or Khrushchev, has presented you with your great opportunity to break with the past ... The Soviet party, by the method it has chosen to renounce its Stalinist past, has given the initiative to the British and other parties to do this in an independent way, suited to the particular needs of each national party. (*The Reasoner* 1 1956 18–19).

For the editors too, the Khrushchev speech stood for a potential frank exchange of views on Communist theory and practice, past, present and future. Indeed, it was precisely the perceived failure of the British leadership to respond adequately to the opportunity presented by the speech that had evoked the publication of *The Reasoner* in the first place. As such, the final act in the closure of *The Reasoner* is appropriately confusing.

In September the executive committee had issued a suspended suspension should the editors publish a third issue. In a circular dated 10/11 November was carried the message that:

> The executive committee of the Communist Party has considered the position of E. P. Thompson and John Saville in the light of the publication of the third number of 'The Reasoner' (Executive Committee *The Reasoner* Circulars 1956 Box).

The circular concluded that,

> The executive committee cannot therefore ignore the undemocratic, indisciplined and disruptive activity of E. P. Thompson and John Saville. It decides to expel them from the Communist Party for refusal to carry out party decisions and for conduct detrimental to the party (ibid.).

No more than one week later, this time in *World News*, the conclusion reached was that,

> The executive committee cannot, therefore, ignore the undemocratic, undisciplined and disruptive activity of Comrades Thompson and Saville.
>
> It decides to suspend them from the Communist Party for a period of three months for refusal to carry out party decisions, and for conduct detrimental to the party; and to review their position at the end of that period of suspension (*World News* 17 November 1956 726).

The similarity yet fundamental difference between the two executive statements is at the very least extraordinary. Events in Hungary were far from 'returning to normality'. Inside the British party divisions were hardening into divorce. The decision to commute a sentence of expulsion to a not over long suspension and to review the position thereafter can only be a reflection of a people in anguish.

These still bureaucratic procedures had for many, by this stage, become meaningless. Whatever hope for reform that had still flickered had been extinguished in the smoke rising above Budapest. No longer was it a case where the advance made in one part of the Communist Movement might be met by mutual exchange from another. The tanks had destroyed the ground upon which the struggle for openness might be mounted. Saville and Thompson were but two of many thousands of resignations from a Communist Movement inside which there was no longer anywhere to turn.

chapter seven

RADICALISM REAFFIRMED

1. STIRRING THE EMBERS OF REVOLT

For the first post-war generation the Campaign for Nuclear Disarmament (CND) was the most significant movement for creating radical protest. At the same time, the campaign offered a new start for those of our inter-war generation who had recently left the Communist Party. Finally, the campaign presented those many other socialists and progressives, whether in the Labour Party or independent, a cause with which to identify and inspire their arguments for a radically different society. Politically, the antecedents of the campaign was the response to the invasion of the Suez Canal by Israeli, French and British troops in October–November of 1956. Recreating elements of the people's front style of politics, the Suez protests were the first popular expression of radical dissent in the post-war period. This is an important link in respect of the inter-war generation. Albeit different in nature, the Bomb, like fascism, symbolized a threat to humanity. The events of 1956 only reinforced this sense of a shared danger. While the initial invasions of Suez and Hungary were coincidence, once under way they became calculated. The Soviet forces had withdrawn, and advanced again only when the actions of the British and French governments made Western protest untenable. While Suez was undoubtedly the primary focus in 1956, the combination of outrages influenced the development of the protest. Ban the Bomb was inspired by the idea of humanity itself being in peril, in which circumstance sides were seen to be irrelevant. The fact that both of these sides had in 1956 shown a disregard for human rights, could only have enhanced that sense of common risk. In the last chapter I referred to a libertarian tradition. The protests against the invasions of 1956 and Ban the Bomb, also link back into a longer tradition of dissent. Whether figures such as Edward Thompson would have eventually shifted their allegiance from the Communist Party to the anti-nuclear movement without the events in Hungary is not possible to know. What though can be asserted is that in the thirties, fascism was perceived to threaten the values of freedom and liberty, in response to which many of this inter-war generation entered the Communist Party because communism appeared to offer the one real alternative to the degeneracy to which capitalism seemed inevitably destined. The Campaign for Nuclear Disarmament was a similar cause in a world where values of liberty were being suppressed for nuclear military expedience. These links and similarities mean that this chapter traces a subject of special significance in the lives of the inter-war generation as they have been traced here.

The invasion of the Suez Canal by first Israeli and then French and British troops have been the subject of various books, including Paul Johnson's 1957 account *The Suez War*, Terence Robertson's *Crisis: the inside story of the Suez Conspiracy* in 1964 and Hugh Thomas' *The Suez Affair* in 1970. The Suez attack could be related back to the withdrawal of British troops from Egypt in 1953 and the transfer of power from King Farouk to President Nasser. From the perspective of a French government waging war in Algeria, President Nasser's rapid rise to unofficial leader of Arab nationalism, placed him as nothing less than an undeclared enemy. During the summer of fifty-six the mounting crisis surrounding Suez came increasingly to dominate the minds of a cross-section of the politically-conscious population. In this context the re-entry of Soviet troops into Hungary created an indignation of a different quality to that of Suez. Writing in the *Socialist Register* in 1976 Mervyn Jones recollected;

> I well remember the Sunday afternoon of 4th November, when we demonstrated for a Suez ceasefire. While we were pressing toward Downing Street ... someone said to me 'Do you know the Russians have sent the tanks into Budapest?' I was filled with rage against Eden, not so much for what he had done as for forcing me to waste my time on him (ibid. 70–71).

Similar recollections might be repeated by many thousands of people. Estimates of the extent of opposition to the invasion are imprecise, but it was certainly considerable. The opposition cause fitted exactly with the tradition of radical, pacifist and socialist dissent from state aggression and imperial acts for a hundred years and more. President Nasser while not guiltless in areas of human rights, did nonetheless hold a leading role in the development of a non-aligned movement. In the context of advancing Arab independence, the unilateral nationalization of the canal was understandable. By contrast, the invasion was carried on by two European powers determined to maintain an imperial dominance even if that required the use of force. It was this violent ruthlessness that united a Left which events in Hungary was otherwise sharply dividing.

Opposition to the invasion by some sixty-thousand British troops and thirty-thousand French, was swift. Its first manifestation was a demonstration in Trafalgar Square on Sunday, 4th November at which both Gaitskell and Bevan spoke. The fact that the two wings of the Labour Party could be seen standing together on the platform has been taken as signifying the sudden unity which the Suez invasion had evoked on the left. Further demonstration of the new-found agreement was expressed the following Tuesday in a public meeting at the Royal Albert Hall, reminiscent of the people's front. The extent of popular support was made evident by the number of people, requiring adjacent halls to be quickly hired, between which the lead speakers had to rotate. The spontaneity of the occasion, especially on the Sunday, seemed to mark the cultural change from the quiescence of the post-war decade that was now ending. The flavour of the occasion is well caught by one women in a letter of appreciation published in the *New Statesman:*

> As one of those who last Sunday walked about ten significant miles through London, may I offer a pat on the tired back to the man with the guitar? ... at several points when there was a definite difference of opinion about which way the column should go, a general rallying round 'the music' saved the situation (*New Statesman* 10 November 1956 588).

The reference to music foretells the style of protest that was to occur two years later under the banner of Ban the Bomb. It would be wrong to imagine that the presence of popular music meant a lack of seriousness in the new arena of protest. The stand against the Conservatives' action in Suez brought together people from across the political spectrum, from the generous progressive liberal to the committed communist. The nature of the issue was fortuitous in that respect. Imperialist aggression was straightforward, it was an evil to be opposed as a matter of principle. A range of reasons for both the atrocity committed and the necessity for opposition could be generated, ranging from the moral principle to the logic of capitalist competition. Examples of each, and many points in between could be gleaned from the pages of the *World News* and the *New Statesman*, each of them weeklies on the left of the political spectrum, though separated by the chasm dividing attitudes toward the Soviet Union. In the days before the involvement of French and British troops in the Canal Zone, the *New Statesman* carried an article by G. D. H. Cole which sat very firmly between the liberal and Communist. Cole ran through the arguments presented by French and British governments for threatening action, dismissed them, and proceeded to offer what he considered to be the real reason for the threats:

> I feel sure that the real object of the French and British governments is to overthrow Nasser as a dangerous potential ally of the Soviet Union against the western block (Cole 1956d 509).

It is ironic that the article, appearing in the issue for 27 October should carry the title 'Midway Thoughts on Suez'. A few days later and midway was looking potentially a long way off. There is an interesting history in Cole's thoughts. Israel, he pointed out, had enjoyed special favour in the left's view since 1945. Looking back from the end of the century the reasons are difficult to empathize with. Crudely, they had rested on a belief that the Arab world had proved to be reactionary anti-socialists. Certainly there had been Arab volunteer troops serving with the Germans in the Second

World War. By contrast, the Jewish refugees from Europe were known to include many socialists and communists. Quite reasonably they might be expected to bring a progressive influence to bear in a potentially reactionary area. For Cole in October 1956, i.e., before Israeli troops had entered Egyptian territory, there was certainly the hope that Nasser would not be armed to the extent that he might be a threat to Israel. Politically, Cole sums up his views on the matter thus:

> My conclusion is that socialists must acquiesce in no settlement with Egypt that does not assure the opening of the canal to the vessels of all nations; and that in order to make possible a settlement that does, they must insist on effective steps being taken to settle the refugees and must guarantee to Israel whatever arms are necessary to its defence (Cole 1956d 509).

Turning to the other weekly, *World News*, and an article in its issue of 28 July 1956, accent is placed on Israel achieving a neutralist position with regards to the Soviet Union and the United States, and blame attached to reactionary views within Israel for inflaming hostilities with Arab countries. In the same vein, the article concludes that no solution can be lasting that does not take care of the refugee problem. However, there is no mistaking the stress placed in the article on the need for Israel to be guaranteed a right to exist, and for public recognition of that right to be made by Arab states. There was thus a degree of uniformity, albeit with some difference of emphasis, between these publications as to the causes of tension in the Middle East prior to the Suez invasion.

When it came the denunciation was based on varied grounds. Legally, the point was made, Egypt had acted within its rights and taken possession of an asset to which it had lawful entitlement. In similar manner, argument was made that the actions taken by British and French governments were without any legal justification. However, the technical detail of such argument was unlikely to create a sense of outrage. More able to cause protest was the mastering of these points within the more general denunciation of aggression by more powerful imperialist nations against a Third-World state attempting to express its rights. The call was to moral outrage, and the opposition in the thirties to invasions of Abyssinia and Spain bear obvious parallel.

In this cause the *New Statesman* followed a difficult path. The events of Suez and Hungary sat side by side in the pages of the magazine. The stance was to condemn what might quite reasonably be presented as two instances of imperialism. But from here distinct differences entered. The events in Poland and Hungary were contradictory. For much of the year they could be celebrated as advances of liberty, and even in late October a headline could be run proclaiming 'The Cracking of Stalin's Empire' (*New Statesman* 27 October 1956). Within days this line had given way to denunciations of aggression:

> The flame of liberty, once the inspiration of communism and the terror

147

of reactionary regimes, today threatens the empire the Communists have built. The rulers of the Soviet Union have discovered that the conditions of revolution, which Lenin once diagnosed so accurately in capitalist society, may also exist under communism which has deteriorated into bureaucratic tyranny (*New Statesman* 3 November 1956).

By contrast the build-up toward the Suez invasion could be condemned from the start. Or rather, the posturing of the French and British governments could be condemned; Israel's preparation could be excused as a response to extreme provocation. When eventually the actual invasion came, the *New Statesman* headline for the 3rd November ran 'Britain's Act of Aggression'. In the ensuing days the chief part in the planning of war was found to have been taken by the French. In this context the Conservatives could be lambasted as pathetic obedient poodles, or as colluding plotters taking the chance to act now that a strong ally was present.

The effect on the Commonwealth of the British Government's action was viewed with alarm. Reckless imperialist action, it was feared, undermined Britain's moral leadership of a free and equal Commonwealth of Nations. The international standing of both Britain and France was brought under severe strain. Both, members of the United Nations Security Council, yet each disregarded the opposition expressed within this small circle and the much stronger protest of the General Council. In the context the *New Statesman* appealed to,

> All those liberal-minded people who have laboured for two generations to establish the authority of international organizations ... (*New Statesman* 3 November 1956).

The course of events made the actual power relations of the post-war world savagely clear. The activities of declining colonial powers was tolerable providing it did not disturb relations between the United States and the Soviet Union or their respective interests. Though still some ten years off, the end of Empire was becoming an ever more obvious inevitability. The Suez campaign was an attempt to, if not turn back the clock, then at least to stop the rot. Viewed alternatively, a political party that revealed itself to be capable of so losing touch as to attempt such hopelessly outdated imperial action, could prove a threat to the new and determining experience of the cold war. Actually, existing reality was reaffirmed by the demonstration of economic power by the United States and political power by the Soviet Union. The run on the pound that rapidly followed the troops' entry into the Canal Zone proved much more potent than any possible military and political humiliation. The event revealed the economic reality that since 1942 Britain had become ever more reliant on the United States' economy in the most stark manner.

148

Domestically, the humiliation of Suez had in the view of the *New Statesman* made the future of the Conservative Party uncertain. Its ability to remain in government was in question and the magazine advised the Labour Party to be ready to take office. The reasoning behind the magazine's thinking rested on the damage the Conservatives had done to Britain's international standing, and the ignominy of the manner of the army's retreat. Yet Suez was not the only signal of change. The sense of the Tory's possible decline and their replacement by a new government was also brought on by the deeper social and cultural changes that paralleled the Suez war. A number of ventures signalled the sense of change: Jimmy Porter was railing against the establishment, empire and mummy; under the guidance of Joan Littlewood, Sheila Delanie was contesting assumptions of love, sex and perhaps even childhood; Kenneth Tynan was assembling the disparate group that were to make a 'Declaration'; and a statement about 'Conviction' was in press. In this context, Suez was a register for fears and even perhaps some hopes that the existing order was not in control and potentially therefore not permanent. Cracks in the edifice of what by this time was being referred to as the Establishment were becoming clearer. Caught between the idiocy of Suez and the outrage of Hungary, a part of the population sought a new political consciousness. One possibility was for Britain to assert a moral leadership, yet the action in the Suez Canal made that possibility deeply uncertain.

2. CONNECTING UP AGAIN

A year later, though, developments had created a cause where moral strength was precisely the issue. The obviously political events are, perhaps as always, easier to recite; the Khrushchev secret speech, the invasion of Hungary, the attack on Suez, and the mass resignation from the CPGB. The 1957 demise of Bevan as the political leader of the Labour left was a new dimension. Of course, these were critical to the deeper changes that were to alter for good the social and cultural patterns of the population at large. About these we are correct to use Williams's term of 'a way of life'. What is more difficult is to understand the relationship between the more obviously political events and those deeper trends. In the present context that relationship may usefully be understood in the effect a political event has. The underlying trends can either insulate the political, nullifying its potential influence, or they may amplify the effect, even taking it in directions that the political agent could not have foreseen. Certainly, there is evidence that this was what happened to what became Khrushchev's very unsecret speech.

Yet it is in examining the consequences of the political events, and the relationship of these to deeper social and cultural trends that the most interesting patterns and questions may arise. In viewing CND in this manner, we might employ another of Williams's terms: that of a structure of feeling. I use the term here to refer to that which is new and yet to mature; a movement that has not yet evolved its institutional presence nor its routinized means of communication. The form of the campaign, its spontaneity, its mixture of fun and deadly seriousness, its refusal to defer not only to the authority of the state, which after all was its prime enemy, but its own leadership, were each microcosms of the deeper social and cultural trends. They were what I call part of the secularization of post-war British society. Though Williams was using the term to refer to a different grouping, we might adapt the point to say that CND represented 'the comprehensive irreverence for established ideas and institutions, in the earliest phase' (Williams 1980a 155). At the moment we are talking about, it was not clear what fate might have overtaken the campaign. Certainly, had it remained in the form envisaged by some of its leaders, it may well have suffered incorporation; an understanding reached as to how pressure was to be applied and reacted to. Alternatively, it could suffer subjugation, reducing it to a cell of militant activists, easily represented as outsiders from civil society and duly criminalized.

A year after the Suez invasion the Labour Party conference dealt a further blow to the cause of liberal peace campaigners and the left. The real defeat was the overwhelming vote in favour of Britain retaining a nuclear capability. Historically though, the significant event was the parting of the ways between Aneurin Bevan and the left of the party. The comments about 'emotional spasm' have been recorded often enough. Here it is the effect of the speech on top of the Suez campaign in creating the first popular movement in post-war Britain which I want to emphasize. The conditions making for the Campaign for Nuclear Disarmament were wide and complex, though the changes then happening in post-war culture signified in music, theatre and film were noted at the time in such publications as *Universities and Left Review*. The link between Suez and Bevan's speech, and the inspiration which set the formation of CND in motion, was a piece in the *New Statesman* for 2 November by J. B. Priestley. In fact, Priestley's article was shortly followed by an 'Open Letter to Eisenhower and Khrushchev' submitted by Bertrand Russell in the *New Statesman* for the 23rd November. Indeed the latter may well be argued to have had the more substantive impact, drawing as it did replies from Khrushchev and the United States Secretary of State, John Foster Dulles. Certainly in the strategy of the Left's most influential weekly, Russell's contribution was fundamental, but it is the Priestley article which is remembered as galvanizing people into action.

Before discussing the content of the article in detail, it might be worth mentioning that it has not always received fair treatment. James Hinton, for instance, has misrepresented the content to suit the ends of his own work. Far from Priestley being 'redolent with Britain's war-time glory' and speaking 'highly of the Queen' (which Priestley does not), these are only the finishing sentiments of an otherwise well-reasoned thesis (Hinton 1989 158–159). The central core of Priestley's argument would seem to be summarized in the following paragraph:

> The only move left that can mean anything is to go into reverse, decisively rejecting nuclear warfare. This gives the world something quite different from polarized powers: there is now a country that can make H-bombs but decides against them. Had Britain taken this decision some years ago the world would be a safer and saner place than it is today. But it is still not too late. And such a move would have to be 'unilateral'; doomsday may arrive before the nuclear powers reach any agreement; and it is only a decisive 'unilateral' move that can achieve the moral force it needs to be effective (Priestley 1957 555).

The reference to polarized powers is in response to the speech by Bevan who claimed that it was by Britain's retention of nuclear weapons that the world was prevented from becoming divided. In Bevan's view the British bomb offered an alternative to the two superpowers. Priestley's response was contemptuous, and quite contrary to the image presented by Hinton:

> If there are little nations who do not run for shelter to the walls of the White House or the Kremlin because they are happy to accept Britain as their nuclear umbrella, we hear very little about them (ibid. 555).

Priestley based his argument on the quite different and clearer reasoning, that a country which had the ability to make H-bombs but decided not to do so, was clearly making a statement to others seeking the technology. Were that country to go further and reverse its policy and disband its weapons unilaterally, then, the statement became all the stronger. That it is Britain which Priestley cites, need at one level be no more than a reflection of his residence. Yet there is beyond that a case for such citing which again is based on sound reasoning. In 1957 there were only three states which possessed the bomb, the United States, the Soviet Union and Britain. The other two significant nuclear powers in subsequent decades, France and China, had yet to develop their capacity. Priestley points out that the major nuclear powers, the U.S.A. and the U.S.S.R., could not of course make a unilateral decision to disarm. Very simply, that left Britain. Priestley it must be admitted, does not develop an analysis of the more complex international history necessary for a coherent disarmament proposition, tending instead to fall back on a history of Britain. He still arrives though at the logical conclusion that of the three countries, Britain was the only one that could make the decision to disarm, and yet still make that decision influential. It was at the point at which the ability to act unilaterally and make that action count, that Britain became the only possibility.

Bertrand Russell's Open Letter, appeared three weeks later. Its point was simple. At the heart of the circumstance of the Soviet Union and the United States there was very much more that united them than divided them. Russell listed the points of common interest in numbered paragraphs, after stating that,

Although you are, of course, both well aware of the points in which the interests of Russia and America are identical, I will for the sake of explicitness, enumerate some of them (Russell 1957 683).

In turn, the propositions were that each side wished to see the 'continued existence of the human race'; and that the continued existence of nuclear weapons would lead to a diffusion as a result of which more and more countries would become nuclear powers. In this second point, Russell was all too correct in his predictions. France and China, both of which he cited, were to gain nuclear technology. His third point was that resources were being constantly diverted towards the development of nuclear weapons, leaving other scientific and social needs less than fully met, a fact that was probably more damaging for the Soviet Union than the United States. Finally, Russell points out that each side would benefit from an easing of the fear that currently dominated action and thought. To this, and indeed each of the points, Russell argued the necessity for dialogue of the 'conditions of coexistence', foreshadowing in these words discussions that were to take place in years to come. The most remarkable fact of Russell's Open Letter was that it drew a reply from one of the two addressees, Khrushchev submitting a long detailed reply which appeared in the *New Statesman* for 21 December 1957. Some months later a letter was eventually received not from the president, but from the United States Embassy.

It is perhaps remarkable, certainly questionable, why the Communist Party's weekly paper *World News* ignored both Priestley's and Russell's contributions to a nuclear debate that was otherwise prominent in the pages of the Communist publication. The approaches to peace in the *New Statesman*, and *World News* were, not surprisingly, somewhat at variance. Views expressed in the former ranged between those who identified with a 'western' perspective but saw atomic weapons as unacceptable, and those who saw atomic weapons as wrong in principle and not an issue that could be debated according to military blocks. By contrast, discussion of the bomb in *World News* was part of the party's assessment of national and international politics.

The Labour Party Conference for 1957 was reported with little partiality or comment in *World News* for the 12th October, the coverage including the resolution for unilateral action on nuclear weapons. The reservation to comment is made up for the following week, in an article entitled 'Communists and a United Labour Left', which argued that the left of the Labour Party needed the Communists. As such the article continued the unity theme of the party's 1956 congress. The question of nuclear disarmament was now relegated to little more than a passing mention, despite the comment in the previous week's report that

Thursday morning's debate on Foreign Affairs and Disarmament was the most tense and emotional of the whole week (*World News* 12 October 1957 645).

Given this subordination of disarmament to the party's unity theme, it is less surprising that the moves to start an independent movement following the conference defeat received little mention. Indeed, perhaps the only citing in the months after Suez was a photograph on the front cover of *World News* for 30 November 1957, in which appears a banner with the name of the then small National Campaign for the Abolition of Nuclear Weapon Tests. Inside the same issue, a report by Nora Jeffery to the executive committee on the general issue of military activity and disarmament instead concentrated on the British Peace Committee. Cited perhaps not altogether fairly as a Communist front, the Peace Committee had in 1950 taken forward the initiative of the Stockholm Appeal and succeeded in collecting not far short of a million signatures calling for the 'unconditional prohibition of the atomic weapon' (Cox 1981 192–193).

The effect of Priestley's article was to draw a number of responses in the correspondence pages of the *New Statesman* and in that manner ignite debate. In the last weeks of 1957 the letters were filled with points directly relating to the content of Priestley's article, though a discussion between varied contributors developed almost immediately. A principal aim in Priestley's article had been to continue the weapons argument with the leadership of the Labour Party, and in particular Aneurin Bevan. From within the parliamentary party, Konni Zilliacus, claimed,

> The 'official' line taken at Brighton was merely a question begging and unrealistic compromise between Labour leaders who still clung to national unity with the Tories on foreign policy and defence, and those who agree with the rank and file that we should carry out the foreign policy to which the party is committed on paper. That policy ... rejects the incalculable risks of H-bomb power politics that follow from assuming a will to war by the Communist countries, and accepts the calculated risks of inviting the Soviet Union and China into partnership in organizing peace by means of regional agreements based in the Charter (Correspondence *New Statesman* 16 November 1957 650).

If the policy of the Labour Party was one theme in the correspondence, then another was what people could themselves do. For some this took the form of preaching personal example,

> We must not put the blame on others. It is we as individuals, who are responsible for stopping the drift to nuclear war (Correspondence *New Statesman* 30 November 1957 730).

By contrast, another letter appearing in the same week sought to express the newer feeling of people who had no political experience but desperately wanted to 'do something'. The first suggestion of a broad-based popular movement against the bomb is suggested in a group letter published in the first week of December. Several of the people who did eventually form the initial leadership of CND were called upon in the letter to take on this role, and a proposal made for each new member to pay a subscription. The letter concludes by stating that 'We the undersigned should like to be the first members of the organization.'

Existing organizations, whether small and little known anti-nuclear groups, or larger and more general peace bodies or pacifist organizations, began to participate in the sort of discussions suggested by correspondents to the *New Statesman*. CND was not in that sense a wholly new start, rather the passage from Suez via the 1957 Labour Party conference to Aldermaston was made by existing activists. What was new was the popular appeal which for the first time since 1945 a movement was able exert in Britain. The result was for the new generation to make the movement in its own image, a state the older campaigners had little choice but to accept. The views which had dominated both *World News* and *New Statesman* were taken up and represented in the form of songs, poems and even drama which arguably came from a commitment less to change the structures of society than to expressing a freedom of spirit and challenge to historical witness.

The Campaign for Nuclear Disarmament was the most significant radical movement from the mid-nineteen-fifties to the early-nineteen-sixties; indeed it has remained the gravest cause for the remainder of the twentieth century. While CND appears in diverse books and articles; there are also several works devoted entirely or primarily to the campaign, and I draw on these in the following discussion. The first of these is Frank Parkin's *Middle Class Radicalism*. A work of political sociology, Parkin's is a study of the social basis of the movement and its ideas. Similar themes are returned to by Richard Taylor and Colin Pritchard in *The Protest Makers*, which compiles the results of a study of the campaign, primarily through the lives of several of those involved, and some who opposed the unilateralist cause. Of the personal histories, Peggy Duff's *Left Left Left* offers an insider's account from one of the campaign's most able figures.

The name 'CND' was not adopted until 1958, by which time several small campaigns had been organized. These had tended to consist of either one-off events, or attempts to bring pressure on authorities through letters, etc. The latter had tended to be confined to scientists and clerics, as indeed was much of the early concern about the bomb. The general lack of awareness among a wider public was nowhere more obvious than in the almost complete silence which greeted the Labour Cabinet's original decision to begin manufacture of a British atom bomb in 1948. Reasons for the absence of any notable response to the 1948 decision are not clear, though certainly the secrecy surrounding the issue was a significant factor. For certain members of the Labour Cabinet the bomb was an essential component in the struggle to maintain global status. As Ernest Bevin, the post-war Labour Foreign Secretary put it;

> … we've got to have this thing over here whatever it costs … We've got to have the bloody Union Jack flying on top of it (Hinton 1989 147).

The beginnings of CND are informative for examining the composition and views of the leadership. CND itself was produced in 1958 out of an amalgam of existing movements, the most important of which was the Direct Action Committee (DAC). The DAC consisted of dedicated activists operating primarily on the basis of public witness. The tactic of direct action was in part based on a Gandhian philosophy of nonviolence and the political device of civil disobedience. Much of the propaganda was directed at workers in the armaments industries, a practice based on the belief in building a campaign out of people in their own localities. The members of DAC were concerned not immediately with influencing established authority, which they tended to see as irredeemably lost, but at 'ordinary people' who, following Gandhian lines, were thought to be the only constituency capable of forcing change. A mark of such an approach was in the first Aldermaston march which, marching from London to the weapons' site, tried to carry the message to the people. By 1959 and the takeover of the event by the main body of CND, the route was reversed to take the message to the capital.

The contradictions of attempting to provoke a mass movement against the bomb while at the same time demanding a high degree of commitment in action, were inherent in the DAC. The almost complete failure to gain support from workers in the nuclear or military industries reflects the difficulty of a movement which ultimately was concerned with affirming a moral and individual commitment against what was seen as a denial of humanity. In summing up the main ethos of the DAC, Taylor and Pritchard set it directly in the line of radical dissent:

> The central focus was thus the traditional pacifist concern with conflict and war. And the ideology underpinning this was the radical individualism of the ILP—a secularized Christianity: a politics based on the moral appeal and teaching of the sermon on the Mount—partially impregnated with Gandhian ideas. The upshot was that the DAC never took its own propaganda for creating a mass movement seriously: it remained a small, dedicated, radical pacifist grouping—bubbling over with fresh ideas for protest, passionately committed to the cause, but lacking any clear ideological or strategic grasp, and destined to remain a small and exclusive group dedicated to the principles of nonviolence (1980 79).

It was this same practice of direct action and civil disobedience that set the DAC in direct opposition to the leadership of CND. The original intention of the latter was to form a pressure group comprising of people from the church, politics and intellectuals. Not intending a mass organization, the group thought it was possible to operate at a level in society sufficient to ensure influence on decision making, an attitude which may appear either extraordinarily naïve or appallingly arrogant. The assumption becomes perhaps more explicable if it is put into the context of the group's feeling about the role of Britain in the world.

On the one hand this was still believed to exist in some vacuum where autonomy of action was still possible on matters of defence; on the other that what Britain did regarding its nuclear defence counted in global terms. The former was clearly becoming out of date. The latter though was more complex. In terms of global nuclear capability Britain's action counted for little. In terms of the principle that a country with a nuclear capacity decided not to exercise it, the effect was of considerable potential. The leaders were almost certainly aware of these limitations, but in a sense this only spurred on their belief that it mattered what Britain did, since part of their concern was to establish a new post-imperial role for the nation. In this, their attitude was not entirely naïve. What they recognized was that in the late-fifties the history of the Empire was still sufficiently recent to provide the government with more subtle forms of influence, precisely in the manner relied on by the Foreign Office. In this sense the leadership of CND were in accord with the establishment to suspect a possible leading role for the rapidly approaching ex-imperial power; a role demonstrated in the manner successive governments have attempted to maintain Britain's place at the top table.

We can better appreciate the views of the wider campaigners from their composition. According to Parkin the Campaign for Nuclear Disarmament acted as a catalyst for a varied range of disaffections with contemporary British society:

> In fact one of the main arguments to be developed here is that CND is not to be understood wholly as an expression against the bomb, but as a somewhat more complex affair. It will be claimed that much of the movement's attraction derived from the fact that it also served as a rallying point for groups and individuals opposed to certain features of British society which were independent of the issue of the bomb, but which the latter served dramatically to symbolize (Parkin 1968 5).

This argument slightly contrasts to Taylor and Pritchard who are keen to emphasize that, except for the minority of politically-committed activists, usually of a Trotskyite or other Marxist persuasion, the majority placed the cause as their foremost concern. One reason for the contrast of views here is Parkin's approach, which seeks to use the movement as a means for examining a series of concepts around class identity or consciousness in political sociology. A consequence of Parkin's approach is the division of attitudes to the bomb by the designations moral and political. Parkin ascribes the former to the majority, limiting the latter to two minorities. The first of these was the familiar small committed sect, sustained by a very specific version and vision of revolution to which converts were to be won. The second was that looser political milieu which may be termed New Left . However, for those engaged in building a New Left , the idea that the moral and political could be divided was false. This was apparent in the founding of *The Reasoner* and the call for a new association of socialism with humanism. Similar expression occurs in the *New Reasoner*. Although surprisingly little space is given to the campaign, D. G. Arnott's pieces link the unilateralist demands to a detailed examination of governmental talks and the science of nuclear weaponry (*New Reasoner* 5 Summer 1958, *New Reasoner* 9 Summer 1959). Further evidence against Parkin's view of the New Left profiting from the campaign is offered by Stuart Hall, who points out that, having no party card or prescribed set of rules, the New Left, far from using the campaign to enlarge its own ranks, was more likely to be expedient to CND. Peggy Duff has gone so far as to suggest that the New Left was itself exhausted by the campaign.

However, Parkin's discussion of the social basis of the campaign does point to possible links between it and a longer tradition of dissent and radicalism. Parkin divides up campaigners into Christians, Communists, Trotskyists, intellectuals and the Labour Party. The Christians may arguably be fairly directly associated with those traditions of dissent cited in chapter one, though by the mid-twentieth century this could no longer be assumed to follow any strict divide of Nonconformist versus Anglican. Having said this, Parkin particularly highlights the considerable involvement of Quakers, quoting frequently from *The Friend*.

The main point from Parkin's study though is that as with others, Christians may have entered the campaign as a continuance of existing grievances toward, in this instance, organized religion. Such protest is in line with a long line of dissent cited earlier. Whether we return to the English Revolution, critical philanthropists, or the early church, an example itself often cited in the letters of clergy writing in support of the campaign, we find a belligerent voice condemning the existing order in the name of Christ. The campaign worked, according to Parkin, to afford a means for expressing deeply felt, but socially inhibited, emotional and intellectual needs:

> One noticeable feature of the campaign against the bomb which gave additional stimulus to religious participation was the form in which the protest was organized. By largely avoiding orthodox political channels and overt party allegiances in favour of public demonstrations, marches, fasts and vigils, with the physical discomforts or deliberate acts of self denial they often entailed, responsive chords were touched in those whose religious beliefs had strong puritan roots. The Aldermaston march, in particular with its Easter setting, and its overtones of moral dedication and pilgrimage made a deep impression on socially-committed Christians. It provided, too, a yardstick against which to measure the shortcomings of the church's own radical witness (Parkin 1968 68).

The argument here is couched in more obviously religious terms, though the more general point of public witness and personal sacrifice is firmly in the tradition of moral revolt, from which not only CND emerged but, it may be argued, socialist and radical liberal traditions alike. The bomb symbolized a world of technological advance but ethical regression. Opposition to the bomb could draw on a rich wealth of protest against injustice and inhumanity. The difference in the late-fifties was that protest was now all that stood in the path not of an individual's fate, but that of the whole of humanity.

Whatever the effect of CND for socially-minded Christians, the influence of the churches on CND was critical. If the 'political' side of the divide was represented by Marxists or members of the Labour Party, the churches'

> influence on the Movement, not least at leadership level, was profound, … Middle class, respectable, committed, constant, centrist, the Christian believers at the head of the Movement were a counterweight to those of a strongly structural and political persuasion, and were an extremely important influence on the policies, attitudes and 'image' of CND … (Taylor and Pritchard 1980 40).

As against a structural interpretation which might situate the bomb in terms of military and industrial complexes, or economic and political institutions, the stress from the leadership of CND was on the moral responsibility of people to oppose the bomb. The composition of the original group makes clear why this emphasis should have dominated; Kingsley Martin, J. B. Priestley, Bertrand Russell, Jacquetta Hawkes, Peggy Duff, Canon Collins and A. J. P. Taylor. The first meeting was held in Canon Collins' home in the shadow of St Paul's Cathedral. Most of the leadership might best be described as a radical contingent of the Establishment, a position more usually presented in terms of eccentricity than political conflict. Several of the executive and others closely connected had been in radical causes before CND. Bertrand Russell had been in pacifist politics since the First World War, and was an early member of perhaps the most influential of the bodies against nuclear weapons, the grouping of physicists and other scientists known as Pugwash. Although Russell became one of the most committed anti-nuclear campaigners he never connected this with an overt politics, socialist or otherwise. By contrast, Donald Soper, more than any other of the leadership, represented the quintessential combination of pacifist, socialist, and non-conformist. Organizationally, Soper was crucial in being a columnist for *Tribune* thereby linking the campaign with one of the organizational pillars of the left in Britain. Though not involved in the hierarchy of the CND, Soper provided the campaign with a passion and an integrity which few could realize. Both Priestly and Hawkes had been involved in UNESCO and while the latter was influential in establishing women's CND, both were archetypal representatives of the moralist wing of the movement. A. J. P. Taylor had displeased the state some years earlier to the extent that he was removed from broadcasting on the BBC in 1941 for raising questions about the management of the war. Marganhita Laski while herself less easily disposed to the radical turn that CND as a popular movement was to take, did provide one of the earliest feminist arguments in her assertion that the bomb confronted women with a specific set of concerns. Trevor Huddleston provided not only a link to the radicalized international wing of the Anglican Church, but from this a cross-over from the campaign to one of the longest-running human-rights causes in the post-war decades, the Anti-Apartheid Movement. Finally, and least fitting the description of establishment, was Peggy Duff. Already a skilled political activist, she had been involved in campaigning for the abolition of capital punishment, previous to which she had worked for the radical war-time party, Common Wealth. Less concerned with making any personal statement, Duff was, of all the figures mentioned here, the most obvious activist in actually leading an organization from the front.

The executive of CND represented that crucial combination of radicalism and authority. If not all practising Christians, the leadership were unlikely to differ strongly from the churches, thus enhancing the latter's ability to sustain a continued influence on the philosophy and practice of the movement as a whole. It was on the basis of their place in the establishment that the faith in bringing about a persuasive influence for change was based.

The leadership provided an image for the movement. While it raised criticism of the bomb, there was no suggestion of opposing Britain's general international position. That Britain should discontinue her membership of NATO was a decision not reached until 1959. Even then, the judgement was not inspired by the leadership, though some might have agreed on pacifist grounds, but under pressure from the mass of active campaigners. Even then there were still those who opposed nuclear weapons because of what they saw as the potential detrimental effect they might have on conventional weapons and with this, on jobs.

The decision to press for withdrawal from NATO should not be read as an entirely new departure by the movement. There had ten years previously been those who had viewed alignment with the United States as the wrong move, preferring instead a stronger unity of independent European countries (Schneer 1984). Unilateralism and a proposal to withdraw from NATO at the end of the fifties had considerable political repercussions on an already divided Labour Party. The division has sometimes been popularized as between Hugh Gaitskell and Aneurin Bevan, who we noted earlier were to be seen standing together at the time of the Suez invasion. Whatever interpretation may be put on the period between the Autumn of 1956 and the Brighton conference of 1957, or judgement made of the people involved, there can be no denying the influence on either the Labour left or the campaigners against the bomb. The reference to 'an emotional spasm' followed by Bevan's claim that the unilateralist's resolution—

> will send a Foreign Secretary, whoever he may be, naked into the conference chamber (quoted in Jones 1987 145).

have taken on the status of myth. The myth includes the judgement that Bevan forsook his erstwhile comrades and turned back on his own convictions. Yet this may not be the best interpretation. Peggy Duff has shrewdly suggested that Bevan may not have reneged on his former beliefs. He had emerged as the lead figure of the Labour left in the nineteen-forties, so presenting many others of similar persuasion with the title of Bevanites. The closely associated *Tribune* newspapers had served as the Labour left's principal mouthpiece since the end of the thirties. The view both of *Tribune* and the Bevanites had been that Britain should remain closer to the United States than to any non-aligned movement. Peggy Duff suggests that the Bevanites were never part of a non-aligned movement. There was little if any suggestion that Britain should withdraw from NATO either in the 1947 manifesto *Keep Left* or in the later *Tribune* document *One Way Only* published in 1950. Instead, the image was of a Britain which would act as a responsible elder statesman to the new superpowers and an example to the emergent Third World. When there had been criticism of the United States this had frequently been expressed in terms of the possible detrimental effects this could have on relations within the emergent Commonwealth. The objection to the South East Asian Treaty Organization (SEATO) had been very much on these grounds. Alternatively, the criticism was couched in terms of leading the British Labour Movement into a situation where it would have to support US policies for which it had not voted. Indeed it was on the strength of the British Labour Movement that Britain's ability to mediate was at times claimed by Bevan.

Since the first sirens about the atomic bomb were sounded, *Tribune* had been sympathetic to opposing the weapon. Bevan's stance had been not that Britain should not possess the bomb, but that she should not test it, nor deliberately escalate a war by its use. At no point did the Bevanites reject the possession by Britain of atomic weapons. The argument had always been that they should not be used first. That they should argue for a ban on testing, was, Duff points out, a little contradictory if the possession of them in the first place is accepted. The break in 1958 by CND was beyond Bevan. It is perhaps no coincidence that the campaign was from that moment beyond the Labour Party. In effect Duff argues it was a renewed libertarian and non-aligned left that for perhaps the first time moved beyond Bevan, first in rejecting the holding of nuclear weapons and then a year later, of continued membership of NATO. The ensuing confrontation between the Labour left and peace activists shaped discussion on the bomb, the immediate issue of tactics, and the more erudite subject of Britain's post-war and rapidly post-imperial status, through to the defeat of the unilateralist position at the 1962 Labour conference and even beyond.

Peggy Duff's view of a non-aligned and libertarian left going beyond Bevan after 1957 is a useful description of the history presented here. The preceding chapter was concerned with how that renewal of the Left was effected by the lessening authority of the Communist Party. The present chapter has concentrated on the inspiration arising from the Suez invasion which was so important in creating the Campaign for Nuclear Disarmament. In the next chapter the campaign reappears in the activities of those around *Universities and Left Review*. For a number of my inter-war characters the campaign was a genuine cause. Edward Thompson is the most obvious figure, his opposition to nuclear weapons being the most widely remembered part of his life. Against this memory, the minimal coverage of the campaign in the *New Reasoner* in the late-1950s might seem surprising. However, there is no doubting the inspiration behind Thompson's article 'The New Left' (*New Reasoner* 9 Summer 1959):

> The young marchers of Aldermaston, despite all immaturities and individualistic attitudes, are at root more mature than their elder critics on the Old Left (ibid. 3).

Elsewhere, Thompson contributed pieces which took the potential of the campaign and the New Left clubs to considerable heights. In an article entitled 'Revolution', Thompson mused,

> Should the protest in Britain gain sufficient strength to force our country out of NATO, consequences will follow in rapid succession (Thompson 1960b 307).

'Revolution' appeared in the collection *Out of Apathy* which appeared two years after the 1958 collection, *Conviction*, each being very much part of the political ferment in the years after Suez. In an article which uses the subject of the bomb to reflect on his generation, Mervyn Jones raises a series of questions about attitudes and changing circumstance. Linking fascism and the bomb, Jones questions whether some of responses to the former, may have contributed toward a justification of the latter:

> I am persuaded that the only hope for the Labour Party and for our country is a revival in modern terms of Socialist pacifism (Jones 1958 198).

It is interesting that Doris Lessing, writing at a moment when, 'Now, in March 1957, the British Government decides to continue the hydrogen bomb tests', felt a 'real gap between people of my age and to choose a point at random, people under thirty' (1957 19–20). At the moment when Lessing is writing this for the collection entitled *Declaration*, published one year before *Conviction* in 1957, CND was still evolving. Within a few months her inter-war generation would join with the under-thirties on the road between Aldermaston and Trafalgar Square, so that just as the campaign was a turning point for her generation, part of that change was the linking up of people separated by a series of experiences and varying responses.

We could extend the examples of the many who responded to the threat of nuclear annihilation and the campaign. However, the foregoing offers something of the sentiment of many who either participated personally or were affected by the campaign's appeal. CND was the most significant marker of a turning point in the biography of these inter-war characters. A. J. Davies has presented the point succinctly in his very readable *To Build A New Jerusalem*:

> Until the 1950s the Roundhead tradition largely dominated the British labour movement, reflecting the Nonconformist strand which had contributed much to the early days and provided a bedrock of support for the new Labour Party (1966 271).

We can draw a direct parallel between Davies identification of an end of puritanism, in the Labour Movement, and the suggestion of Victor Kiernan, cited in chapter two, that religion's capacity to be one of the taproots of politics, had dried up. Where the parallel ends is in the consequences the two writers draw. For Kiernan the effect was potentially negative, a loss of commitment and engagement.

> is it possible to recapture the kind of socialist enthusiasm of an organized and disciplined form that we had in those days?

Davies is perhaps less sympathetic to this tradition. Turning to that 'organized and disciplined' party with which Kiernan and so many of my inter-war generation were associated, Davies continues:

> The Communist Party too had frowned upon culture as a diversion. It was something to be dealt with after the Revolution. Instead, comrade, why aren't you out selling the *Daily Worker?* Following Lenin's example, the party called for asceticism and orthodoxy in members' private lives. Morality was subservient to the dictates of the party ... (ibid. 271).

CND was not the cause; more powerful features of post-war capitalism must take that responsibility. However, it was a marker both of the end of this asceticism and the beginning of a new manner of political behaviour in which neither the party nor anybody would take precedence over personal life.

chapter eight

A NEW CHAPTER OPENS

1. RAISING THE POLITICAL TEMPERATURE

This penultimate chapter turns to focus on a number of younger socialists who were directly influenced by the generation of characters with which this work has been concerned and on the figure of G. D. H. Cole, a member of a still earlier generation. It will be with the direct influence of Cole together with Raymond Williams on the Socialist Society at Oxford, for which the institutional connection was the Extra-Mural Delegacy, that the first section of the chapter is concerned. The second and larger section examines the contents of the magazine *Universities and Left Review*. In the process, links with earlier partially non-aligned socialists' initiatives are drawn, and most particularly that with the Coles' early experiments with guild socialism. In *Universities and Left Review* this last is translated into the language of Workers' Control. Paralleling the first part of the chapter, a link is also made with the work of Raymond Williams, and in particular the attempt to envision culture as material relations patterning everyday lives. Perhaps the most notable element of *Universities and Left Review* was its freshness and vitality, seeking to use visual and written text to examine a wide range of topics and issues; youth, the post-war generation, Wolfenden, disputes within the Labour Party, the Campaign for Nuclear Disarmament, the Royal Court Theatre and Free Cinema.

If the rejection of the Communist Party by some of the inter-war generation was provoked by affairs on the far side of Europe, the younger New Left were more directly concerned with matters closer to hand, the long years of Conservative rule, and the struggles within the Labour Party. This said, the composition of those in the Socialist Society from which the ULR group came, meant that their interests were unlikely to end at the English borders. Made up of figures from ex-colonial states and the Celtic fringe of Britain, the society was linked through G. D. H. Cole to the International Society for Socialist Studies (ISSS), a body which could draw in not only figures from across Europe, including Claude Boudet, but beyond. However, the emphasis here is more specific, addressing in particular change and continuity of class cultural experience, and consequently the need to develop a deeper understanding of these processes.

The guiding thread in the following sections will be the *Universities and Left Review* group's attempt to engage the new, and assert its place in the continuity of a libertarian and democratic tradition. We shall try to follow this guide by first examining the organizational relations that made up *Universities and Left Review*, both club and magazine. From this we can begin to explore some of the themes that made up the discussions and articles. Expressed as a series of key terms these would include class, culture and commitment. Serving in turn to contextualize these was a concern with the nature of post-war capitalism. Chapter seven discussed the major cause linking the inter-war and post-war generations. The present chapter returns to the kind of detailed study, more characteristic of the book, and seeks to demonstrate the full influence of the inter-war generation in shaping post-war Left politics.

The origins of the *Universities and Left Review* group was the Socialist Society at Oxford, itself partly a continuation of a Cole seminar. The boundaries were, on the one side, Left politics at Oxford, and on the other the attempt by Cole to reopen an international socialist dialogue that was not determined by Communist or any other party. The socialist club comprised of people potentially marginalized by their relationship to England, to the elite culture of Oxford, and the dominant political ethos of the English Establishment.

This sense of marginality was not new. It was certainly important for those in the nineteen-thirties who either entered from the outside or, though nurtured within, felt estranged from much of the ethos in which they found themselves. From an earlier time, D. H. Lawrence and Orwell had come to represent these experiences, as in a different way did F. R. and Q. D. Leavis, and many women since. The tensions of belonging created by the experience of confronting this dominant culture were given expression in Hoggart's discussion of the scholarship boy, and which Williams went on thinking through, through the idea of the border.

Though arriving from different routes and at different moments, Raymond Williams and Stuart Hall's experience had much in common:

> I joined the union as a life member, but only after some embarrassment, since I knew no one who could propose me. In this and in other ways, over the first week I found out what is now obvious: that I was arriving, more or less isolated, within what was generally the arrival of a whole formation, an age group, which already had behind it years of shared acquaintance, and a shared training and expectations, from its boarding school (Williams 1989a 5).

Stuart Hall's recollections have the added usefulness of being made in relation to Williams:

> I still experience that indefinable sense of being placed and put down even today, whenever I cross the threshold between Oxford railway station and Broad Street, gateway to the 'dreaming spires'. In the light of these pages, I know just what is meant by thinking of this as a 'colonial' experience (Hall 1989 57).

That Stuart Hall was referring to Raymond Williams when making this comment was not entirely innocent, the two having first met at Oxford in the mid-fifties. For Williams's part we sense there was a felt contradiction with regard to the New Left, drawn by age and experience to those around the *New Reasoner* yet by concerns to the younger group around *ULR*. It was after all the younger New Left who pursued the theme of culture and contemporary British society more closely, while the *New Reasoner* was more concerned with continuing questions of Marxist theory and politics.

Because of the dominance of the universities in the production of knowledge, the place of adult education in the New Left has been largely ignored. In reality the Workers' Education Association, university extra-mural delegacies and similar bodies provided ready-made constituencies from which both CND and the New Left could and did draw. The Oxford Delegacy provided the link between Williams and those at Oxford, where Williams was appointed, albeit briefly, in 1960 as a resident tutor. Before then though his position as a staff tutor provided contact with the younger socialists, some of whom were themselves to take up posts in adult education. We have already cited this linking role of adult education in chapter four, Raymond Williams maintaining working relations with both Labour people and Communists.

It is something of the same circumstance that Hall refers to when speaking of the relations between those in the Labour club and others on the left at Oxford in the mid-fifties:

> We are talking about the depths of the cold war. We are talking about a period when it was not possible to be both a member of the Communist Party and go to an Oxford Labour group meeting. It was forbidden to do so. ... To move a little bit left of Centre was to be in danger, instantly, of falling into the grip, yes, of the Comintern, becoming a subversive agent. You had dangerous thoughts. You were clearly paid by Moscow. That was the form of talk (Hall 1985 6).

The sense of marginality and the questioning of how to understand the dominant cultural reading of history, are not unrelated, and discussion of Williams's earlier post-war enquiries into the idea of culture from chapter four, will be continued in examination of the contents pages of *Universities and Left Review*.

The Leavises and *Scrutiny* were naturally important to the project of the New Left. Their importance, Hall recalls, was less their interpretation of the received culture, than the seriousness with which they approached their work:

> It is difficult now to convey to those who only know the conservative afterglow of Leavis and the *Scrutiny* tradition, the paradoxical nature of the influence of what Williams quite rightly calls Leavis' 'cultural radicalism' ... Certainly in the 1950s, *Scrutiny's* seriousness about serious issues contrasted favourably with the dilettantism of the Oxford

approach to literary and cultural questions (Hall 1989 57).

In its organization, a small number of people producing a periodical aimed at drawing into a debate a larger population, the *Scrutiny* project offered a model for *Universities and Left Review*. The analogy can be taken further if it is remembered that where *Scrutiny* was especially directed at English teachers, *ULR* was, at its inception at least, aimed at students at other universities, an intention which seems to follow from a forerunner distributed within Oxford. Culture became the prism through which much debate was be carried on, because of the configuration of influences informing *Universities and Left Review*, *Scrutiny*, the pedagogic practices brought from adult education and the relation of the younger New Left to the established order.

It would, however, be a mistake to assume from this that the New Left can be defined in terms of culturalism. That is to abstract a term from the conditions in which, what were political arguments took place, a key site for which was the ISSS around Cole. G. D. H. Cole had been a relatively marginal political figure for several years, generally identified as somewhere left of the Labour Party, not unsympathetic to the Soviet Union, as so many others were. As Tony Wright says,

> His starting-point was a belief in the central unity of different forms of socialism … from which he concluded that it behoved Western socialists to regard with sympathy and tolerance the developing situation in the Soviet Union. While never disguising his own personal antipathy to Stalinism … he refused to pretend that his own preferences counted for anything when compared with the force of the national imperative … Thus his firm belief was that Soviet communism represented a necessary and appropriate form of government not merely for the Soviet Union itself, but also for countries at similar stages of economic development and with similar types of social structure (Wright 1979 251).

A much briefer summation of Cole's politics would be Williams's recollection of a comment Cole made at an Oxford Delegacy meeting, to the effect that he was not interested in Adult Education but in Workers' Education. Cole's attitude about education might be understood as a continuation of the earlier examination of the possibilities for direct worker participation in guild socialist schemes, and stood in contrast with Raymond Williams who, as I noted in chapter four, was already developing his ideas in another direction.

Cole's disillusion with the direction of the Labour government contributed to his apparent isolation in the forties and his turn toward a new International Socialism in the fifties;

> it was Cole's acute sense of the post-war malaise of democratic socialism and of his own theoretical isolation which, above all else, prompted his embrace, both practical and scholarly, of a vigorous internationalism

during the 1950s (Wright 1979 257).

The formation of the International Society for Socialist Studies was one result of this embrace. An informal grouping the ISSS was able to draw people from both across Europe and from ex-colonies. Its key function was perhaps that of a forum for making contacts and forming new alliances and exchanging ideas. The principle of the organization for Cole was that it should be able to cut across the divides of the cold war, making possible discussion beyond the constraints of power blocks, East and West. Whatever its success or failure, and Margaret Cole in her 1971 biography of her husband suggests the latter was the greater, the ISSS did provide a means through which the Socialist Club at Oxford could begin to engage in debates on colonial politics outside its own circle.

It was through the ISSS that Hall and others from Oxford first met Claude Boudet, who at the time was leading a grouping in France called the Socialist Unity Party, and from whom the term New Left was taken. The importance of this connection was that it not only provided a link with another grouping dedicated to finding a 'third way' in politics, but a link with the very present colonial war in Algeria. Following on the complete defeat of French forces in South East Asia, the Algerian war was creating acrimony with strong feelings both for and against its continuation. The Socialist Unity Party was a consequence of the Socialist Party's prosecution of the war, which the former continued to oppose.

To the Socialist Club at Oxford the Socialist Unity Party represented a rejection of colonialism in a manner not demonstrated by either the Labour Party or the Communists. In government the former had offered little alternative foreign or colonial policy from that of the war-time coalition. In the fifties, its left wing though subscribing to anti-colonial principles, in practice spoke of the need for Britain to consider her responsibilities to the colonies and of providing them with a moral lead. As such, the Bevanite position was more in line with the pre-war emphasis on a socialist commonwealth than any genuine third way involving Britain aligning herself with the non-aligned states. Even in 1956 the Labour Party, while opposing the British and French invasion of Egypt, continued fully to support membership of NATO, and the division of the world into power blocks, with Britain clearly to the fore on one side. The New Left, by contrast, had been deeply involved from the beginning with CND and had provided space for the argument against the bomb to continue through the magazine as well as in the clubs. In such manner the Socialist Unity Party represented a significant departure closer to their own aspirations than did any major political party in Britain. With this in mind it would be useful at this point to briefly consider the question of internationalism for the New Left as a whole before returning to the question of the younger New Left and available radical traditions on which to draw.

It has been customary to see *ULR* and the *New Reasoner* as somehow collaborative ventures slowly working toward each other. Perhaps though this perception is apt too quickly to cover over what might otherwise be considerable differences. In his 1973 'Open Letter to Kolakowski', E. P. Thompson refers to the notion of 'communist revisionism'. Here and elsewhere the inference is that there existed contacts between both party and non-party Communists across Europe possibly prior to the *New Reasoner*. Elsewhere in the essay a series of names are cited but the concern seems to be to demonstrate the existence of an internationalism, and little is said about what form any communication or contact between these people might have taken or what it meant. However, in 'A Handful of Scoundrels', published in 1985, Thompson is more precise, citing Claud Boudet and G. D. H. Cole amongst others as 'trying to hold open an alternative space'. The tribute echoes that Thompson paid to Raymond Williams, which I cited in chapter four. In similar manner to Thompson's sense of separateness from Williams, he writes he was not at first looking for any such opening. Yet Thompson's suggestion that other international links already existed, remains, together with the proffered but not pursued claim that;

> '1956' was an international confrontation within the communist movement, and the first New Left developed, for a brief moment, an international presence (Thompson 1978 iii).

'for a brief moment'. But between whom and to what end?

Thompson went on of course to be at the centre of END, explicitly emphasizing the need for European solidarity in the face of the common threat of nuclear weapons. That Thompson should work on an international, not national level, was of course part of his whole life experience, from the influence of his brother in Bulgaria and the Yugoslav railway line, onwards. Given, therefore, the context of CND, its is not unreasonable to suggest that the reference to a brief moment, in the above passage, was the instance when the project of END could first be imagined.

This would certainly be in line with Duff's comment that the peace movement exhausted the New Left. Its energies created not a new socialist grouping independent of the main parties, but an international peace movement; in other words a peace movement that differed from CND precisely in not being locked into the limitations of the nation, but which expressly saw itself as being about forming unions beyond the national community.

Within the larger campaign against the bomb, figures from my inter-war generation played varied parts in the New Left. The names ranged around the publications; *The Reasoner, New Reasoner, Universities and Left Review, New Left Review* and slightly later *The Socialist Register*, were many and varied. In his 1991 autobiography, Malcolm MacEwen recalls that after their work on one style of publication, the *New Reasoner*, Edward Thompson served as chair of the editorial board of a vibrant *New Left*

Review while he served as vice chair.

The adaptation of some to newer forms of politics, notably Raymond Williams, looked very much to the future politics of communication and media. By contrast was the continuation of more traditional format from 1964 in *Socialist Register*, edited by Ralph Miliband and John Saville, and published by Martin Eve. Together the examples merely demonstrate the variety of influences which people were to provide. The remainder of this chapter turns to the contents of *Universities and Left Review* as perhaps the most original of the developments.

Universities and Left Review was a wildly adventurous continuation of a student newspaper commenced at Oxford. The original aims were simple enough: to provide a channel through which the discussions that were taking place at Oxford and Cambridge could reach a wider audience at other universities. The distance travelled in the early months of 1957 can be gauged from reviewing the first editorial published in the Spring. The purpose by this time had expanded to meet the need 'to take socialism at full stretch' (*Universities and Left Review* 1 1957 ii). Within the terms of the editorial the phrase was made to stand for considerable and very varied events and pressures: the regeneration of the Labour Party; the apathy of welfare capitalism, the consequences of Hungary and Suez; the Campaign for Nuclear Disarmament; and the new cultural impetus in drama, music and film. In one of a number of dramatic summaries, these many and varied elements were part of a moment in which 'the age of orthodoxies has, once again, been outstripped by historical events.' (ibid. ii).

It is often as difficult to pinpoint precisely why a particular group should come to fulfil a particular political function, as it is to say why an individual should come to a chosen political viewpoint. In the case of *ULR* though that function was as expansive as the perceived need in response to which it had been created:

> This journal has no political 'line' to offer: it cannot have, for it seeks to provide a forum where the different fruitful traditions of socialist discussions are free to meet in open controversy (ibid. ii).

The magazine *ULR* was born alongside the commencing of a series of fortnightly meetings at the Royal Hotel in central London beginning in April 1957. The first saw Issac Deutscher speaking on the transformations in the Soviet Union leading to a red sixties. Given the political differences between himself and most of the organizers, Deutscher's appearance at a New Left meeting was a good example of different traditions freely meeting. The fortnightly talks in part served as a central focus around which a New Left constituency could be formed. The intention was for each meeting to be addressed by a keynote speaker who would have further opportunity to present their arguments through the pages of the magazine. Forty years on, the list of those early speakers reads like an all-star-cast of the Left: Hyman Levy, Raymond Williams, Doris Lessing, Issac Deutscher,

Barbara Castle, Edward Thompson, Clive Jenkins, Ralph Miliband, Richard Hoggart, John Berger, Thomas Hodgkin, Michael Foot, and Wal Hannington.

While we may joke about rainbow coalitions, the fact that such a coming together has been unimaginable at any time since the Universities and Left Review Club, has coincided with a virtual demise of any serious left. Perhaps the second point to examine is the list of topics covered in these talks; the Mass Persuaders, Crisis in France, the Managerial Revolution, second thoughts on the Jewish Question, European democracy, NATO neutrality and survival, crisis in Africa, workers' control, the Thirties, the Welfare State, theatre and social class, and sex and socialism.

At first glance it is perhaps the extensiveness and lack of theme, that is so noticeable. The only guide seems to be to try to cover all that was contemporary, contentious or potentially mobilizing at a given time. Yet this randomness and the wild assortment of people is completely in line with the self-image of *ULR* as a forum through which different socialist traditions could meet. The inclusion of Richard Hoggart and Raymond Williams talking about the mass media, and the Mass Persuaders is not perhaps unexpected. The Mass Persuaders had been the title of the New Left exhibition at the 1958 Labour Party Conference at Scarborough. Yet it was perhaps those other less likely entries which were the more significant; Wal Hannington on the Thirties, or Hyman Levy on the Jewish Question. A few years following in 1962, a suggestive fictional reference to Hyman Levy appeared in Doris Lessing's *Golden Notebook*. Underlying the engagement with post-war consumer capitalism is a recognition of the need to examine change as part of a longer process, though the emphasis, as we shall see, varied between different contributors. At its best, as in the articles by Edward Thompson and Raphael Samuel in issue six, *ULR* could offer people a position from which the new could be assessed in an historical manner.

The club and magazine reinforced each other. Advertisements for the former would appear in the latter, while printed articles could emanate from talks. An indication of the breadth of subjects which this arrangement produced, can be gleamed from the promotion in *ULR* 5, Autumn 1958. Within one paragraph we are told that;

> *ULR* is a young movement of ideas and people, seeking to renew and rediscover the sources of their socialist conviction. The club has become the centre of the 'New Left', asking some of the big questions about contemporary capitalism and capitalist society. We try to have challenging speakers, and to ask them awkward questions. The purpose of the club is to push and probe 'beyond welfare capitalism' (*Universities and Left Review* 5 Autumn 1958 6).

That the New Left could envisage itself in the role of a forum was in large part due to the influences from which it sprung, the background of the people involved and the range of parties on which it built itself. The first two, the influences and background, have been addressed already. We can summarize the key elements as the Socialist Club at Oxford, its international composition and leading figure in the form of G. D. H. Cole. On the question of who made up the activists and constituency of *ULR*, very little has been written. One recent exception is an article by Ioan Davies who had been a secretary of the, from 1960, renamed New Left Club. In it Davies comments that:

> By 1961 there were thirty-nine New Left clubs across Britain, with the London Club holding weekly public meetings as well as having a series of discussion groups based on education, literature, new theatre, race relations. The clubs also acted in many cases as the organizing centres for the Campaign for Nuclear Disarmament, and in many other cases were created out of the local groups of the Workers' Educational Association and the National Council of Labour Colleges. The New Left was therefore borne along by the animated presence of existing bodies of labouring intellectuals (Davies 1993 118–119).

Davies' suggestive comments of voluntary education groups forming the basis for similarly voluntary political groups, was previously encountered in connection with the Left Book Clubs, and in reference to Roger Fieldhouse's discussion of adult education during the cold war. In practice this association between adult education and radical politics, stretches back to the start of the twentieth century and beyond. Its formative link across the generations has been traced here through the Oxford Delegacy, in particular G. D. H. Cole, Thomas Hodgkin and Raymond Williams. Edward Thompson provides the most noted link here, between politics and the Yorkshire adult education tradition, which threw up such notable figures as Sydney Raybould and George Thompson, the latter long expounding the view that the purpose of adult education was to create leaders in the Labour Movement in all its facets. However, alongside these should be placed the Leavises and *Scrutiny* the influence of which permeated not only adult literature classes for many years, but, as we noted in Williams's early experiments in teaching film, much beyond. Yet when we come to *ULR* it is not only these obvious influences, but in the figure of Michael Barrett Brown, the editor of the collection of New Left essays, *Out of Apathy*, a direct family link to A. Barrett Brown, one-time principal of Ruskin College, where of course another member of the group, Raphael Samuel, was later to teach. It is an interconnection if this kind that Raymond Williams referred to in the *New Left Review* interviews for *Politics and Letters:*

> After *Culture and Society* was finished but before it was published, I was invited through mutual friends in Oxford to speak to the Universities and Left Review Club in London. These were well attended,

lively meetings which opened up quite new areas of discussion. The *ULR* people tended to treat the conflicts of the cold war as a past phase. They were much more orientated to what was happening now in the rapidly changing society of contemporary Britain … The 'New Left' cultural intervention, incomplete as it then was, outlined a necessary new kind of analysis (Williams 1979a 361–362).

The last sentence again points to the project nature of *ULR*. The attempt to pick up from past efforts, adapt them, and then take them forward to meet the changing conditions which faced the New Left. One of the principal means by which *ULR* defined that new circumstance was in terms of class and culture.

2. A DIFFERENT STYLE OF MAGAZINE

We can begin to get a better understanding of why *Universities and Left Review* made culture a spectrum through which to analyse class by briefly recalling one key contemporary work. Though not published till 1958, Raymond Williams's *Culture and Society* had been first completed in 1956. Its influence on the thinking of the Universities and Left Review Club was, therefore, present from the very beginning. Here I want only to seize on one or two key points. Towards the end of the book there is the section 'Marxism and Culture' from which two points are worth recalling. On the one hand there is a discussion of what the content of a Marxist cultural theory might be like. Of course, what Marxist cultural theory was to be like was in large part to be the result of Williams's own work over many years. Yet there is also a discussion of what writers in Britain, writing from within a self-claimed Marxist tradition, had themselves made Marxist cultural theory.

Pulling these contributions together, a Marxist cultural theory offers, Williams suggests, a number of contradictory arguments:

> Either the arts are passively dependent on social reality, a proposition which I take to be that of mechanical materialism, or a vulgar interpretation of Marx. Or the arts, as creators of consciousness, determine social reality, the proposition which the Romantic poets sometimes advanced. Or finally, the arts, while dependent, with everything else, on the real economic structure, operate in part to influence this structure and its consequent reality, and in part, by affecting attitudes towards reality, to help or to hinder the constant business of changing it. I find Marxist theories of culture confused because they seem to me, on different occasions and in different writers, to make use of all of these propositions as the need serves (Williams 1958a 274).

Viewed from the outside Williams's observation of contradictions in Marxist (which prior to the mid-fifties meant communist) writings is accurate. However, what may be lost is the extent to which apparent contradictions were actually arguments between communists. The tension may have been periodic, but it separated a minority for whom cultural issues were of real importance and a majority who focused on narrower bread-and-butter matters of industrial and communal life. At times the division could erupt into heated argument over the nature of culture and its part in the class struggle, as when a debate appeared in the *Daily Worker* at just the time Williams was beginning the *Idea of Culture* in 1950. The argument took place in the letters' section of the paper, beginning with a piece entitled 'Culture or Snobology' (*Daily Worker* 4 September 1950 2). Debate centred on whether there were bourgeois and proletarian cultures or a common culture. The contributions amounted to several hundred letters over a few days, and included arguments concerning the nature of culture, whether there were different levels, e.g., material and super-structural, as well as whether culture would distract workers from the class war or equip them the better to fight it. The verdict, laid down by Emile Burns, chair of the national cultural committee, was that there were indeed two cultures and that the bourgeois version was rotten thus offering nothing for the advancement of the workers. Yet the more remarkable was that culture was able to raise such heated debate in a daily newspaper, the contradictions, which certainly there were, being produced through a lively exchange of views.

At one level the whole attempt to work through the problem of post-war cultural change was a continuum from the thirties, though as ever, changes of language and perspective interrupted the dialogue. The post-war generation of socialists were faced not only with a loss of role models from which to build but a positively hostile environment in which to even attempt to build. In Stuart Hall's words, it was like trying 'to raise the political temperature right off the floor.' The dilemma that had confronted the thirties' literary Marxists needed still to be addressed, but from a different direction. Thirties cultural Marxism had, it was felt, remained class-bound. It had argued that culture was important, but ironically failed to offer an understanding of culture which could encompass the patterns of life of the majority of people. The crucial feature about *Culture and Society* was the space it opened up through its challenge to that selective culture. *Universities and Left Review* and *The Long Revolution*, particularly the third section, were two projects, moving beyond that challenge to elite culture to examine the totality of post-war change in Britain; a totality that included the working class, and therefore needing a redefinition of culture which could include that very different way of life.

One way of presenting the New Left's focus on class cultures is as an argument which attempted to forge a path between two contending interpretations. On one side was the argument that capitalism was the same as ever and that therefore class was the same as ever. Against this was posited the theme of change premised on a notion that poverty was finished and that with the prop of the Welfare State everyone would become steadily better off. In some versions of this imagery, youth were a vanguard. Overstepping the old class barriers, youth were to be a new classless generation whose expectation was for ever increasing material prosperity. Between those views the New Left tried to find a midway point.

The development of a New Left way of thinking about class and culture was the result of a particular circumstance which reflected more general contradictions. The development can be traced in Raymond Williams's account of his experience in adult education after the war which I have already referred to in chapter four. At a number of points Williams suggests that a common problem with Fabian and Marxist thinking was a tendency to forego any attempt to think through what might be understood by the word culture. Marxism retained an adherence to the class struggle in a very particular way, while Fabianism talked about the gradual improvement of the workers' lot but without thinking fully about what that might entail.

The Fabian argument had been presented during the decade through a number of publications. In retrospect the most influential of these were *The New Fabian Essays* published in 1952 and Anthony Crosland's *The Future of Socialism* which appeared in 1956. To these we might add a 1961 Fabian tract in which Richard Wollheim responds critically to Raymond Williams with very standard assumptions about the cultural level of people. In summary, Wollheim's argument is that change cannot go ahead of the population's cultural standards, which in turn are limited by natural capacity. While recognizing itself to be at odds with the Labour left's perception of society, the New Left also defined itself against the perceived revisionists in the Labour Party:

> We were directly engaged, locked into the revisionist debates going on the Labour Party. We wouldn't let go hold of it for a minute, we would track Crosland at every meeting, we insisted on arguing with him, we knew his book, the pages, we knew the Crosland dream, where it came from, the amalgam of the United States and Sweden descending into the new towns and we were determined to track that argument because that was where the debate was breaking (Hall 1986 20).

Intervention in the debate about post-war social change necessitated addressing the nature of what that change was. Few people would doubt that in 1945 there was a real desire to avoid the conditions of the thirties as they had been experienced by so many. The aim was to alter the real material conditions of people's lives, and in large part this was achieved. The mistake was to view this as a simple matter of affluence, rather then the outcome of prolonged efforts to develop institutions to address poverty head-on and seek at least a minimal redistribution of wealth. In Stuart Hall's view, what made the matter complex was that if you only looked to the 'relations of production' then nothing appeared to have changed. If on the other hand you only looked to culture, in the rather limited sense of fashions, etc., then, with a bit of careful editing of focus you could say; 'everything's changed!'

Reworking the idea of culture, reflected felt changes in the experience and expectations of post-war society and a sense of inadequacy in the responses of both Labour Left and Marxists' accounts. What seemed to be missing equally, though differently, from each, was recognition that there were real changes happening and that these needed to be examined. The reason they were missing them was because they were happening elsewhere from where they were looking. To put it another way, their theories tended to focus on the economic, but this was defined either in terms of class relations or with reference to welfare and the distribution of wealth. They did not have a space where what they might perceive as the non-economic could be seen. The development of New Left thinking around culture resulted from a necessity to recognize change to be occurring in society while still seeking to maintain an understanding of that society in terms of class. The need was to demonstrate that changes in culture were not only the superficial (superstructural) elements beloved of an emerging consumer advertising, but were part of the pattern of life in which class was experienced.

This meant a simultaneous political intervention which argued the importance of the changes in post-war society, substantiated by a theoretical reworking in which culture as a part of class was shown to involve real material forces and relations. Changes in culture were therefore changes in experience of class, though not necessarily the relations between classes. The point is absolutely crucial, indeed in a very real sense it is the point. The relationships between classes were locked into the nature of capitalism itself and therefore did not show up on charts plotting the changes in tastes because the axis by which the charts were framed was located inside the relations. On the other hand, the experience of class included not only improved material standards of living, but, and crucially, the representation of those living standards in the glossy magazines, the advertisements of a new commercial television channel and now indeed in the very language by which much of the Labour leadership was describing society to its own followers.

Pertinent here was Raymond Williams's suggestion that those wider changes, changes of cultural formations perhaps, were reflected in the particular project of adult education. There was arguably already at work here an understanding of culture as material. Now there are different ways of understanding that idea. The problem is if we think of it only to mean, that it involved the production of material 'objects'. Of course, it does mean that, but if we limit ourselves to that, we are arguably not going to be able to understand this prism of class and culture very well. We are not going to understand why the recognition of cultural change in post-war Britain was important. Even more, we are in danger of only seeing that change in terms of the artefact. Or, if you prefer, the alienated product of the capitalist mode of production. What we will completely miss is the depth of cultural change because we will not be able to see the active productive process. And in that case we certainly will not see the relations of class and culture.

The New Left tried to develop a means by which to avoid these pitfalls by altering their understanding of production. Production needed to be seen as real human labour, activity, energy. These in turn are part of what Raymond Williams called a way of life. What is then being emphasized is that the material of culture is us; real human beings. The changes that were being expressed and struggled over in adult education were part of that very deep sense of change in the production and reproduction of ourselves. Williams's point could perhaps be said to be that culture is material in the sense that it is the pattern in which our lives are led; and that pattern has to be lived in consciousness as well as behaviour and therefore changes in culture are also about changes in ourselves and our self-perceptions.

One of the standard contributions to the post-war change debate involved an argument about false consciousness. Now that was certainly better than anything from the Fabian side which did not seem to have anything to say other than that we were either rapidly on the way beyond class or that people remained working class but that it was different. The point about the development of the New Left was that it was in effect a development of seeing class not as something separate from culture, but as lived in patterns of life. The attempt was to keep penetrating the depth at which culture is lived and therefore, the way in which to talk about changes in culture is also talk about changes in class.

What is called the New Left then was in part an attempt to think through culture in a different way and that the necessity to do this was experiential. It was a need to develop an understanding of class and culture which was more substantial because otherwise you would end up in a situation where either class remained the same as ever in which case it has very little bearing on how people experienced life; or the advertising agencies took over then class was cultural alright, but the cultural was only the artefacts. But since these were changing, and since society was only what you saw, then society was changing, and so too was class. It was the felt political necessity to explore these social changes, for which neither Fabian categories nor existing Marxist cultural theory were adequate, which led to the projects between 1945 and 1960 which I have traced out in this and preceding chapters.

Another way by which changes in society were approached by the New Left was through the idea of commitment. During the life of *Universities and Left Review*, commitment came to be discussed through several different avenues. An early statement was that made by Lyndsay Anderson in the first issue of *ULR*. The original article appeared in 1956 in *Sight and Sound*. That it should be reproduced in *ULR* two years later suggests the latter's preparedness to explore a range of materials perhaps beyond the expertise of the editors and certainly beyond that found in any strictly political periodical of the time. Anderson's objective theme was that of cinematic criticism, both its right to exist alongside other art criticism and the need for explicit and definite standards. Appearing alongside Anderson's article in *ULR* 1 was a sister piece on art criticism by Peter De Francia.

Though including a great deal on particular features of art, under the title of 'Commitment in art criticism' De Francia finds space also for more general argument. Identifying what he refers to as a, 'cultural crisis [which] can only deepen during the next few years: and with it the crisis in criticism', De Francia suggests that a prime cause is, `the growing shrinkage of the range of European bourgeois culture.' A familiar theme is perhaps echoed when De Francia suggests, that, `This range can only decrease in exact ratio to the frantic affirmation of individuality'. Against such failure De Francia develops a polemical critique:

> Within the past five years a great deal of discussion has gone on concerning painting and sculpture. All other arts are involved, but the visual arts have been the focal point of debates concerning commitment, realism, social questions and a whole set of associations which these ideas immediately touch off.
>
> Nothing has been of greater service to the retreat into ambiguity, non-commitment and fear than … the perversion of Marxist cultural ideology, the basic premise of which seems to me more valid than ever. True realism, which is the expression of that which is essential, has almost completely eluded [Soviet art].
>
> The imaginary and the real are not irreconcilable enemies. They can be united for the purposes of hope and action. The nature of committed criticism is to effect such unity, here everywhere, and with ruthless honesty.

Appearing in *ULR* the De Francia's piece connects the journal with other radical expressions of the fifties, while at the same time aspiring to ends redolent of progressive polemics of the thirties.

Socialism at full stretch, it was felt, needed to engage the present with uncompromising honesty. It was therefore necessary to recognize that which was essential in the present, in order that that engagement might be effective. Commitment was a recognition and alignment of that essential reality. Realism was an expressing of that which was essential and thus a necessary preparation for commitment. But socialism at full stretch required also the bringing to bear of the possible on the actual. Committed criticism, the unifying of imaginary and real, was a means of effecting such a unity. In this way realism, commitment or committed criticism can be seen as component parts of taking socialism at full stretch. But the thesis can be seen to extend further in the whole project of the New Left. The concern with change and working-class culture has already been introduced. Realism and committed criticism linked into this as devices for separating out the ephemeral, the glossy magazines and the pop music from the true and sustained pattern of working-class culture; separating the surface changes from the underlying continuities.

There were several contributions to the debate, most notably Stuart Hall in issue five, and Edward Thompson and Raphael Samuel in issue six. The latter were responses to the previous issue of the magazine generally and to Hall's article in particular. The theme around which the argument lined up, centred on Stuart Hall's sense that the working class were being contaminated by a crass materialism. That 'the club' and the media were in some way effecting a new and overwhelming negative influence on the class, and that the resilience necessary for it to resist was being eaten away. We can quickly get the flavour of Edward Thompson's response if we remember that it was at about this time that he was commencing research for what was to become the *Making of the English Working Class*. A flavour of that later masterpiece is present in the following response to Gordon Redfern's article 'The Real Outrage' which had appeared in the same issue as Hall's.

> Here the working class is seen as the passive object of social transformations which take place with geological inevitability. 'The industrial conurbation grew quickly. Masses of the population drawn from the countryside became meaningless as human beings, but important cogs in the means of production.' Meaningless to whom? Surely not to themselves? Are working people to be allowed no consciousness of themselves, no power of moral reflection, no agency in shaping industrial society? The period to which (I take it) Gordon Redfern refers was meaningful enough in working-class history; it is the period of Luddism and Peterloo, trade union experiments and Owenism, the ten-hour movement and Chartism, and the proliferation of popular religious, educational and co-operative societies.

Perhaps though the underlying theme of both Thompson's and Samuel's critiques is that the sociological image present in some *ULR* articles fails to place their subject matter historically. Were this done, Samuel points out, then the message of the media, for instance, may be recognized as but a modern version of what was preached from the Methodist pulpit in the nineteenth century.

> The means of persuasion were in some ways more powerful than today, for they were anchored in a shared social and religious ethic. Nonconformity was both religious doctrine and shared morality; it was a common bond between the entrepreneur and many of his workers; a shared religion imposing, as the imperatives of religion, the social norms of the risen industrialist. ... The media of persuasion were the chapel and the characteristic institutions of self help and thrift: the savings bank and the mechanics institutes.

As for the apparent materialism of today's working class, Samuel points out,

> The piano in the front parlour was a far more powerful index of status

than any of the more diversified range of household goods that are almost universally consumed today.

Committed criticism was the picking out of that which was essential from that which is ephemeral. Or as Edward Thompson put it,

> I do not know what moral and cultural values are attached to the kitchen sink, a washboard, and the weeks wash for a family of five. But if we are getting more washing machines, we should recognize in that fact at least the potential of greater emancipation for working women.

In Thompson's view there had perhaps been a little too much of the uses of literacy and not enough of the uses of history. Prefiguring an argument that was later to be used in a more famous episode in *New Left Review* in 1961 when the target was Raymond Williams's *The Long Revolution*, Thompson suggests that Hoggart's stress is too much on the working-class 'way of life', and insufficiently on a 'way of struggle'. The point allows for the development of an argument for the importance of the conscious minority, the 'poor bloody infantry' in history, and for the need for intellectuals (the dashing cavalry), to make connection if an adequate socialist struggle was to be mounted. Commitment, alignment, allegiance and even affirmation were in effect all part of an effort to confirm in the present the attempt to take socialism at full stretch.

Raymond Williams posed the question of where the historians and social scientists were, when he and two other English trained graduates were editing *Politics and Letters*. In fact, as we noted the earlier journal was not without contributions from people like G. D. H. Cole, but they were only sufficient, as we shall see below, to take *Politics and Letters* into discussion of social and economic issues on the rare occasion. *ULR*, despite the majority of its editors coming also from English academic backgrounds, was less constrained. Worker's control still appears though as a surprising subject for the *ULR* to tackle. However, that an interest in industrial issues was by no means a passing whim, is evidenced by what turned out to be one of the most in-depth studies of contemporary capitalist society collectively undertaken by the New Left. 'The Insiders', appeared inside issue five in 1957, and it is from this that the following quotes are drawn. The thrust of the work was an analysis of the Labour Party's 1957 conference publication *Industry and Society*. In reply, the editors and others associated with *ULR* and the *New Reasoner* carried out a study of the nature of ownership and production in post-war Britain, concluding that there existed a high degree of centralization and minimal democratic control.

Under the heading 'The Democratization of Power' we read,

> One of the fundamental aims of socialism has been to do away with ... the acquisitive society, and establishing in its place an industrial democracy, a society where workers would have some control over their own life as producers. But since the crash of 1929 socialist thought

has moved away from the problem of industrial democracy to focus on the inefficiency and predicted collapse of the capitalist system. For many years our major criticism of capitalism is that it does not work. Consequently we have found ourselves theoretically disarmed in the face of a capitalism which manifestly, within its own terms of reference, is 'working'. Yet the fundamental socialist critique: that capitalism treats [people] as things, that it atomizes social life is not dependent on whether the system happens to be booming, slumping, or equilibrating. It has not lost its relevance in the age of the giant oligopolies.

The accuracy of the dating, 1929, or even the extent to which such a move had actually taken place, is perhaps less important than that such a loss was felt to have occurred. The attempt was to regain a perceived earlier position. The New Left's relation with the thirties is ambiguous, but a desire to renew traditions other than that of the Labour or Communist parties, may in part be responsible for the central place that a moral critique had within the pages of a magazine written by a group of editors apparently unconnected to any such tradition.

Further on though, that apparent unconnectedness becomes a little suspect. The critique of a lack of industrial democracy is aimed not only at the private sector. The nationalized industries too are seen to have improved the degree of industrial democracy only marginally at best. The attack is directed at what had come to be seen as the form of nationalization associated with the name of Herbert Morrison:

> The substitution of the state for 'the Boss' accomplishes little: ... It is pointless to try to re-establish the dignity of labour without allowing for some form of workers' control, for a real participation by workers in the management of industry; and it is impossible to achieve a democratic control over the large-scale institutions of our society without breaking into the circle of oligarchy—be it that of a capitalist power elite or a state bureaucracy—from the base.

Turning to a presentation written well before 1929, we find:

> The proper sphere of the industrial organization is the control of production and of the producers' side of exchange: its function is industrial in the widest sense, and includes such matters as directly concern the producer as a producer ... its right rests upon the fact that it stands for the producer, and that the producers ought to exercise direct control over production.
>
> The proper sphere of the state in relation to industry ... has no claim to decide producers' questions or to exercise direct control over production. G. D. H. Cole 1917 (quoted in Coates and Topham (eds) 1970 46).

G. D. H. Cole had been associated with the guild socialism movement before the First World War, and his association with the socialist society at Oxford University provided editors of the review with a direct connection with the issue of workers' control.

As such, the link to the moral critique and the demand for a socialist morality was in part constructed through a critique of a version of socialism that was seen as guilty of robbing the worker of precisely that full humanness that socialism should have made into a weapon with which both to condemn capitalism and construct its own alternative image of society. Cole's guild socialism or workers' control provided just such a link.

It may also be possible to see in this condemnation of Morrisonian nationalization that other New Left enemy, Stalinism. The common fault in the perception of some at least was that each prioritized the planning of social and even personal life. A not untypical form of scorn for such endeavours was the claim that human creativity was too diverse, its potential too great to be fulfilled by any Soviet-style five-year plan. Indeed the latter, far from providing a means of using human intellect and energy, was a limitation, a strangulation, of that capacity.

In the pages of *ULR* the theme of intellect and human creativity linked into a series of issues which we might put under the general heading of the individual and society. The tension that ran through so much of the magazine and associated writings was how the two concepts could be reconciled such that each enhanced the other rather than serve as a detraction. The twin projects of *Universities and Left Review* and *The Long Revolution*, can again be seen to be moving in tandem, the latter devoting a large part of its first section to a theoretical working through of the problem.

We can see an example of this twin project in issue four, which carried an article, 'Realism and the Contemporary Novel' which later became a chapter of *The Long Revolution*. In this 1958 article, Williams, working through a series of forms of the modern novel, asserts the legitimacy of each within its own terms. Each though also represents a breakdown of a certain tradition in the novel which Williams suggests, 'are the symptoms of a very deep crisis in experience'. Having made this connection, Williams is able to go on to suggest that the manner in which individual or social is prioritized or marginalized resembles a breach in sensitivity; a present fracture which renders it difficult to think the social and the individual as a totality, in which the latter is both expression of a specific inflection and yet continuous of that which composes the whole.

However, it was not in Williams's theoretical or even historical writing where problems of writing are most acutely met, but in his own fiction:

He put down the paper. He was aware, suddenly, of the distance he had travelled, and of how urgency, unnoticed, had been slipping away. The crisis of yesterday, the tension of the journey and the arrival, seemed suddenly far back. Now, in so short a time, on this ordinary morning, even the purpose of the coming had slipped away. It had been easy and normal to talk to a neighbour, to look out at the day from the door of the kitchen, to eat breakfast, to read. The paper had been the decisive stage, removing him, as so often, from all the immediate situation. He knew, of course, just why he was here. But it was not what he had expected: to sit at his father's bedside. He was here to be in the house, to settle into it as if he had really come home. But it was reluctantly now that he got up from the table: a reluctance that Ellen noticed, and quickly interpreted in her own terms; she had dragged him from print so often. Now that he was on his feet again the situation changed. If he could not talk to his father, at least he could do what was necessary; not only the extras, but the things Harry himself had intended to get done. He was here not only to be in the house, but as a kind of replacement, to carry life on. Standing now, holding the list, he thought again about the reluctance of which he had just been ashamed (Williams 1960a 73).

Border Country was part of an unfinished struggle to develop an adequate narrative form, which always came back to tensions cited in the *ULR* article. In this extract two worlds are caught in the tensions between forms of experience. The immediate human presence and that contained in the form of the written word. There is no necessary priority in value between them. Each has its part to play. The difficulty seems to be in negotiating the relation between the two worlds, finding a means by which each can be accommodated in regard to the other. In the passage there exists a sense of shame that one world should have encroached somewhere it did not belong. On being discovered there, it is quickly dismissed.

Stuart Hall has referred to Williams as engaged not in a mere 'cerebral activity of thinking' but in a necessary 'lived activity of thinking' which makes 'socialism at full stretch' possible (*Raymond Williams—A Tribute* 1988). The central place of *Border Country*, and indeed all of Williams's fiction in working through that idea of socialism at full stretch, is rarely recognized. What we have here is not a concept, a thought, a terminology, but rather an active process of living. There is, as it were, a stitching together, a connecting up, so that the words are a pushing forward of experience. In cerebral activity there is the experience which is later recalled in thought for some purpose; the examination question or conference paper. Thinking as a lived activity is when the words themselves are a part of the experience of which they are at the same time a description. Socialism in cerebral activity is the plan, the policy document or the journal article. When Stuart Hall spoke of socialism at full stretch he seems to referring to thinking and speaking socialism as a lived experience in the present—a thinking through of what socialism is as an experience here and now, because of being part of an active living.

If this is accepted as a basis for the existence of the club and magazine then it may be a little easier to see why planning could never be more than a necessary but not sufficient condition of socialism. It is also necessary to understand this attempt at thinking 'beyond actually existing forms of socialism', to recognize that such critique was entirely different from that outcry defined by the fashionable phrase 'angry young men'. *Universities and Left Review* was not seeking a rejection of the existing social order because it was a social order. Rather it was seeking to replace what existed with an alternative, but an alternative that existed neither in blueprints or a body of theory, but which needed to be produced as part of the process of arguing for it. The call in the first editorial was not for support for an idea, a schema, already set down, but for participants in a project of construction. For the New Left socialism was a 'huge act of common imagination' (*Raymond Williams—A Tribute*). If Herbert Morrison represented what needed to be ended, William Morris represented what needed to be continued.

Arguably the distance between that fashionable, angry young men label and the New Left should not need stating. That it does is in part because of the manner in which 1956 has been mythologized. In the theatre and in prose the theme had been that of the 'outsider' against society. The politics were certainly not uniform; Colin Wilson's 'superman' for whom other people were but 'ants', could not have been more opposite to the deep human pain that was Osborne's Jimmy Porter. Both are marked off though, by a certain blockage. Jimmy Porter is only able to voice a negative aspiration. The present order is rotten through, but he has no alternative with which to replace it. It is interesting in this respect that in *Drama from Ibsen to Brecht* Raymond Williams identifies that apparently new theatre of which *Look Back in Anger* was a part, not as the beginning of something but rather as the end. In this there is a connection with Williams's analysis of the realist novel. Where at one level the theatre seemed to be breaking away from a certain limitation of horizon which had confined it to the middle-class drawing-room, at another it simply transferred what happened there to the working-class kitchen. The continuity carried over was that of blockage. The despair remained that of the individual enclosed by a society. The individual remained separate, alienated, unable to recognize their surroundings as a part of themselves. The theatrical device of the room for which the audience composed the fourth wall, had been but a means of making visual that separation and ultimately isolation.

What Williams seemed to be saying was that this solitude was carried over on to the working-class character, but that this was in one sense almost necessary because 'true'. Just as there was a barrier impeding the ability of the novel to present a new social relationship, so to the necessary dramatic forms for such presentation were also bared. Ultimately, it was a blockage of experience. There existed a certain structure of feeling but, as yet, the social including the literary and dramatic conventions, did not make possible any more substantial realization. The point perhaps begins to not only differentiate between the New Left and the so called angry young men, but demonstrate why the New Left devoted so much time and space to cultural expression. The recognition was of the place of cultural forms in the changing composition and experience of post-war society. The frustration with what Osborne and others were doing was precisely because it seemed to be wasting a precious chance to literally invent new possible relationships. The manner of the waste was in the offering of a critique of what was, without the presentation of what could be.

There is always a danger here of falling over into polemic. However, there existed a genuine urgency in the project of the New Left inspired by the feeling that the Campaign for Nuclear Disarmament and the developments in drama, music and literature, were signs of a political renewal which might circumvent what was felt to be a moribund Labour Party. The wide coverage of issues and the emphasis on the present running through the pages of *ULR* were witness to this urgency. More than this the diversity of matter in the magazine, reflected a feeling that the nature of politics was too restrictive to address those issues which the New Left felt to be important. That there was felt to be a tension between the social and the individual was in part because existing political dialogue was perceived to ignore much of personal life leaving tensions and pressures unspoken. While at times over sociological, *Universities and Left Review* did seek to explore these tensions and create a language in which they might find expression.

By way of a final example of the breadth of *ULR* I need to return to a discussion in chapter four. There I placed together the themes of post-war town planning and community, and reviewed examinations of these in *Politics and Letters* and *ULR*. In fact, the *ULR* concerns were informed by a still further influence; the recent recovery of early writings of Marx on the idea of alienation. However, here it is sociological arguments of the relationship of the new towns with perceived senses of working-class experiences of community that take first priority.

Once again, that discussion of town planning should even appear in a magazine edited by humanities' trained graduates might be a little surprising. One reason for its inclusion seems to rest on the attempt by the editors to provide a forum for the widest discussion of radical traditions. However, a second, and more substantive reason was the obvious importance of new town development in the fifties. The approach to the discussion seems to start from a question of the nature of social relationships that were or could develop in these new environments. The theme was paralleled by the more recognizably sociological discussions of the period and in particular those carried on by the Bethnal Green Institute for Community Studies. The comparison was in part, with the extent to which the new towns might transform a supposed close-knit set of community relations that were thought to exist in urban working-class areas. The latter proposition was itself the result of a recent reaction against a romantic and conservative model which counterpoised an idyllic rural closeness with an alienating urban fragmentation. The paradox of such a critique was a possible replacement of a one-sided rural romanticism with an equally romantic urban imagery.

The concept of alienation can be seen as part of an argument for the continued relevance of socialist critique of capitalist society noted earlier. Rather than a focus on the inability of capitalism to maintain living standards, the emphasis was placed on the inhumanity and immorality of social relations under capitalism. Alienation offered a theoretical means by which the perceived inequity of capitalism could be further explored. The examination of community was a yardstick by which to index the extent of alienation in a given society, the latter being the subject of Charles Taylor's 'Alienation and Community' in issue five.

Debate on the character of new towns encompassed therefore the sociological as well as the architectural. However, the latter had the advantage of initiating the more positive and programmatic points. Rejected was the manner in which new towns tended to merely provide more space for 'living'. New town houses provided greater opportunity for acquisition of new 'consumer durables', leading in turn to increased individualism, which those items could enhance. Charles Taylor's parallel in 'Alienation and Community' is a critique of a utilitarian view in which he claimed experience was equated with consumption. In a sociological view, the parallel can be seen in a concern with the privatization of life. Implicit in several *ULR* articles on new towns is a fear that an authentic working-class sense of community, characterized by sharing and togetherness, was to be fragmented by a greater interest in the home and private forms of entertainment.

The fear of individualization marked part of the complex of themes that made up discussion of the changing character of class cultures among the New Left. If culture were understood to include the institutions and material means for the reproduction of a way of life, then changes in the expression and experience of everyday relations were clearly a significant change in the pattern of culture and class. The issue was, then, whether the new towns were actually changing the composition of the working class to such an extent that its consciousness of itself as a class might be eroded.

In placing the question in that manner we return to an arguably romantic presentation of working-class experience. The picture of the close-knit community based on togetherness fails to appreciate the extent to which those relationships were created within conditions set by a free market and ruthless capitalism, against which they were erected as a defensive barrier behind which to survive. Between the two views exists a tension running right through the New Left.

chapter nine

CONTINUITY AND CHANGE

1. THEMES AND CONNECTIONS

The greater part of this concluding chapter is given to reviewing some of the underlying themes of the book and, particularly in the last pages, a weighing up of the events and reactions recorded across the different chapters, together with an initial assessment of the people who have formed its core. In keeping with the contextual approach of the work, one conclusion which may be offered now is that the conditions which gave rise to this cultural formation, their beliefs and manner of living those beliefs, do not presently exist, thus negating the possibility of reproducing such a generation in the foreseeable future.

The story composed here has been that of a generation of radical intellectuals moving forward from the mid-nineteen-thirties to the end of the fifties. Behind the story have been a series of themes by which I have sought to define their lives. Having defined the term 'generation' in terms of common experience, I have suggested that the historical context through which they negotiated their response created a remarkable political formation. Powerfully informed by a sense of seriousness which carried within itself a combination of puritanism and voluntarism, inherited from a late-Victorian lower-middle-class, this generation yet formed a bridge toward a secularized society where conviction and commitment would attach themselves to disparate causes and to different effect. The reasons for this shift of emphasis are varied, and later in the chapter I shall return to them in greater detail. They must include though the effect the Second World War had in convincing many people that the degree of regimentation that they had had to endure for five years was one they no more wished to repeat than the experience of poverty which had been the lot of so many before 1939. Instead the post-war years brought the security of a welfare state, full employment and consumer goods of a quality and price which made them available to virtually all. Since my argument is that it was the context of the inter-war years, and the influences of discipline and commitment, religious or otherwise, that induced the structure of feeling that informed the inter-war generation, so I conclude that the different context and influences of the years after 1945, called for a different manner of response from that prompted in the dark days of the 1930s.

The start of the book coincides with the war in Spain and the unwillingness of the national government in Britain either to admit that a legitimate government was being attacked or that non-intervention agreements were being blatantly breached in support of the insurgents. The uniqueness of the Spanish Civil War was that it provided the one opportunity for direct engagement when in so many other respects the thirties was a decade of defeat. The Labour Party was unable to mount a serious threat to the mastery of the national government for much of the decade, the security of which was wonderfully caught by G. D. H. Cole in 1937:

> They voted 'National' because the government was not asking them to think, or to plunge into unknown adventures, or to do anything they had not been used to doing—or in fact to do anything at all except just vote. Whereas these Labour men, if you could believe the newspapers and the leaflets and the kind ladies who dropped in to call, were up to all sorts of dangerous tricks. If you voted Labour, before you could say Jack Robinson you would find yourself out of work of because of these socialists upsetting things. In a jiffy you would ... find that the government had confiscated your money, in order to give it to the slackers who hadn't worked as you had. ... If you voted Labour, your house—the house you had been buying by instalments through the building society—would be taken away, and you wouldn't be able to save anything for your old age, or leave it to the children if you did (ibid. 59).

In such a context, the national government's outlawing of volunteering to fight for the republican government, only made the cause seem all the more righteous. The romanticism which rapidly grew up was important in inspiring action among younger people.

Continuance of a dissenting moral outrage was, however, not the only spur to action; alongside sat another prism through which the world was understood. Class offered a defining measure and category in both Labourist and Marxist understanding. Class enabled populations to be divided and numbered into named groups, which represented power and exploitation, and existed either in some hierarchical manner or as opposing armies. Essentially these conceptions of class were based on socio-economic criteria, and the workplace was the pivotal site where they were articulated. Yet while not for one moment losing hold of that socio-economic foundation, class was also used as a political category; the measure of a person's being and their allegiance to one side or another. The working class uniquely stood for the side to be allied with either because of the inequality inherent in society, or in the more intellectual Marxist argument, because in this class lay the resolution to antagonism inherent in the present social order. Siding with the working class was siding with the future; interpreted and predicted according to scientific reasoning.

By the thirties moral outrage had already been yoked to a class politics for three generations past. However, class was not an uncomplicated explanation which could be employed at will. The struggle for Spain, the war-time and post-war participation in Yugoslavia, the Suez affair or the emergence of the Campaign for Nuclear Disarmament were each situations where support across class boundaries was essential. At the time of Spain what was called the 'class against class' period had been superseded by a front uniting all progressive people against a larger common enemy. At this moment, moral outrage had taken the lead role. In Yugoslavia, the situation could be more easily explained in terms of working peoples, though class in that then largely rural region, might have been a little more difficult. By the middle-fifties, the Marxist-Leninist use of class as a political weapon was finally felt by many Communists, as it has for long been felt by many socialists, to be a travesty. The new anti-nuclear movement which exemplified protest at this time was far from founded on a working class in any socio-economic sense. The younger New Left, meanwhile, was bemoaning the decline of what some of its members imagined to be the working class, while some of the older generation were trying to reach for an understanding of class which was less reliant on a quantitative economic measure. I have sought to illuminate these cases through chapters four, seven and eight.

We should pursue this issue of class a little further, placing the question in the context of an altering society as this grew out of the war and the policies of the post-war government. The growth of a welfare state meant that the sharpest economic indicators of class were largely eliminated. Note, the sharpest indicators are here taken to be those of poverty, not wealth, which the welfare state only enhanced for those already among the 'haves'. The advance toward some degree of equality was real, and the welfare state coupled with general economic growth, ensured that for the vast majority of the population, visible material poverty became a thing of the past. However, and this was the point which in large part inspired the New Left, the advance was quantitative and not qualitative.

In a manner that only the war could bring on, the conditions to which socialists were responding underwent a considerable alteration to that of a few years earlier. There was the visible increase in government planning and direct intervention. The circumstances were such that unless the majority of the population were drawn into the work of total war there was serious risk of failure. In such circumstance morale was as important as military hardware, and to sustain this, a widely diverse cultural effort was needed. The forms of this were discussed in chapter three. Here we need only note that nothing of the like has been even attempted since. There were, it is true, some continuities and new initiatives; the transformation of the ABCA into the Bureau of Current Affair and, in 1946, that of the Council for Encouragement of Music and Drama (CEMA) into the Arts Council, the founding of the Third Service also in 1946, and the Festival of Britain in 1951. However, these were either short-lived or took on a different cultural form from that of the war, so that, as I discuss in chapter four, the potential for a popular cultural advance was not met.

There was no Beveridge Report for culture.

Instead the Labour government rightly placed the first necessity on the meeting of material need. The National Health Service was the most durable validation, while the extension of statutory education for all children in the form of the new tripartite system was, for all its weaknesses, a great advance on inter-war provision. The new welfare state did indeed go a long way to abolishing the great evils of want, idleness and ignorance, however, not in equal measure or to the same effect. To a degree unimaginable in the years before the war, physical poverty in the forms of food, housing, health, etc., was very nearly eliminated. The post-war economic boom effectively provided for all the extra material desires once the basics were supplied by the state. Meanwhile, idleness in the form of prolonged unemployment became a thing of the past (and future). Unemployment, family, child and sickness benefits and pensions, together with the NHS, social services and housing provided a cushion whereby people were no longer reliant on only earned wages. Income became to a degree separated from employment, and a space created within which more people could begin to enjoy 'leisure' activities unimaginable before 1940. Yet having met material needs and thereby creating this opportunity Labour viewed its job completed.

Arguably it was this failure of which Williams spoke in the interviews for *Politics and Letters*,

> I still believe that the failure to fund the working-class movement culturally when the channels of popular education and popular culture were there in the forties became a key factor in the very quick disintegration of Labour's position in the fifties (Williams 1979a 73–4).

There was a gap between what the Labour government was doing and those arguing for popular culture and education. The former saw meeting the material needs of the time as the end of its responsibilities. An alternative argument was for continued support for a genuinely popular education that war-time experience had made possible. That this was not pursued with vigour was partly because even those in adult education who were political radical, did not, at the time, see the need to campaign for such support.

The gap between the government's ends and this much deeper need was the ground upon which *Horizon* stood. As a literary journal with sympathies for the Labour government but a conservative idea of cultural decline, *Horizon* marked a political space, which it articulated not in the terms of daily newspapers, but through a language which resented the fact that the masses did not pay enough attention, or give enough money, to the cultivated. The standard retort that the mass of the population did not want cultural education, was one familiar to adult education tutors, and fails on even the simple commercial test that for a product to sell, demand must first be created.

These post-war arguments about culture and education informed the new radicalism as this emerged after 1956. Thus chapter four on Raymond Williams in the ten years after 1945, connects directly to chapter eight and the emergence of the New Left. That Williams felt nearer to this younger generation was precisely because of the failure of others of his own generation to recognize the importance of the cultural. Even Cole, when he commented that he was not interested in adult education but in workers' education, revealed the same failure of imagination. The economism which informed thinking across the left for a number of years, though only subsequently given that title, prevented recognition that an advance in material standards and the greater degree of equality which this afforded, could only be sustained if popular support were won for reforms. That this did not happen has been an important factor in the direction of my argument. The political 'line' has always been difficult in this matter, and the present work has suggested that cultural politics, indeed cultural poverty, remained always outside of the Labour Party's vision. That the blame should so squarely be placed upon this one body is justified not merely because of the Labour Party's betrayal of the visions of the earnest working class, but because it alone could have brought the resources of state to bear in support of such an aim. This refusal has contributed to the decline of that seriousness, and the continued limitations to the advance of cultural aspirations since.

What developed instead was a new departure in adult education. Many of those socialized into a broad progressive movement through the Left Book Club and similar bodies were drawn after the war toward adult education. Inside the latter they developed a new departure wherein the idea of culture was extended to include the patterns of life of many of the students. The work is caught up in the cold war divisions with which it had far from simple relation. The attempt to include the patterns of working people's lives in the understanding of culture was inspired by socialist sympathies. The cold war in adult education from 1948 made the pre-war unity which the Left Book Club, etc., induced all the more difficult to preserve. After 1956 the situation changed very considerably; however, the years before then required a sustained working out of a new argument amenable to neither established views of cultural heritage or the Communist Party and completely beyond anything understood by more than a very small number in the Labour Party.

Working out a new understanding of the link between culture and politics was not an academic exercise. Rather the work should be read as a response to a renewed assault from conservative or radical conservative positions, now most readily associated with the names of the Leavises and Eliot, and for which *Scrutiny* and *Notes Toward the Definition of Culture* marked rallying calls. On the other side was a reviving consumer capitalism which brought a very different set of cultural values. Added to these pressures was a reaction against supposed Communist influence in adult education and elsewhere, making any intervention which deviated from accepted parameters suspect to the charge of defending Moscow. I addressed some of these issues in chapters three and four, and here stress only that the arguments for supporting progressive cultural education constantly had to find their way through this hostile terrain. *Politics and Letters* was a product of those limits and pressures, as too should be read some of Williams's essays written between 1948 and the eventual birth of what came to be called the New Left.

Here, however, I want to pursue a rather different trajectory by way of a comparison of the analysis of the Communist Party with that of the Campaign for Nuclear Disarmament. There is no doubting the commitment which activists brought to each. The monstrous horror of fascism in the thirties and of the bomb in the later-fifties, invoked a sense of earnestness expressed through witness of the potential threat posed to humanity. The influence of religious behaviour in the actions of people whether holding street corner meetings as Communists did, or the Easter marches of CND, was noted in chapters five and seven. The continuity stressed by reference to the call to witness does not mean no differences existed though. In part the alterations were in social patterns and behaviour. The movement from one period to another which informs the difference between the CP and CND, is caught in Phil Cohen's reflection of growing up the child of Communist parents:

> It was the 1950s then, when some political and ideological certainties remained intact, together with the hope that the old order might be swept away. But already, unbeknown to me, the cold war had cast its spell over the Communist Movement and many individual CP-ers who had made their clear political choices in the halcyon days of the 1930s were beginning to have doubts. Even then I was reflecting a certain cynicism about the ritual aspects of CP culture: the marches, the speeches and the time spent away from more hedonistic pursuits (Cohen ed. 1997 13).

The quote comes from *Children of the Revolution*, a collection of interviews edited by Phil Cohen, from which I draw several examples over the next few pages. Too often this trait of commitment, coupled with a sense of discipline, has been ascribed to the Communist Party's adoption of 'democratic centralism'. However, such an explanation leaves out any context within which such a process might exist. Instead I would suggest that this practice only reinforced a culture of respectability as this was worn by both lower-middle class and skilled-working class. Similar to the present work, some of the accounts collected by Phil Cohen attribute this sense of discipline to chapel and a religious manner of behaviour. Running through the extracts below are recurrent emphases, linking people who grew up in various places, were born of different social backgrounds yet shared similarities in their experience. Ann Kane comes from a mining background in South Yorkshire. Her family include migrants from Ireland and Scotland. Kane makes the point simply; 'Being Irish they were a Catholic family'. What is clear though from her account, is that Catholicism and communism formed an inseparable thread that ran through family life, informing manners of behaviour and relationships with those outside.

Martin Kettle's description of his family background was very different from Ann Kane in that it was solidly middle-class and intellectual. Yet even that atmosphere was not closed to emotional interruption. Speaking of his parents he writes, 'My judgement is that they wanted a church, they wanted a religion'. Further on he comments on the effect of that desire, and its expression. Margot Kettle, his mother, stood for local elections:

> I think my parents saw themselves, certainly in my mother's case, as bringing the good news to the masses. She had a missionary zeal (ibid. 180).

Pat Devine, whose parents were involved in the early days of the party, spoke of going,

> with my father to the local pitch where he used to hold open-air meetings, and as I got older I would sometimes get up and take a turn at making a speech (ibid. 82).

In another vein, Jude Bloomfield talked of a moral responsibility:

> I felt injustice was wrong and that you had to do something about it. ... Being Jewish you had this sense of moral responsibility (ibid. 69–70).

The last short clip is from Nina Temple who led the reforming of the Communist Party into a very different sort of organization. Her background was of the strictest Communist kind where a zeal existed to maintain the light of the party and the Soviet Union against all comers. Referring to her father, though speaking of the party generally she contends, 'There was a kind of Calvinism in the Communist tradition, a prudity, which affected him deeply' (ibid. 94). However, by far the most in-depth discussion is that by Hywel Francis who grew up in South Wales, the son of a mining family. For him, 'The culture of the CP in the valleys of south Wales was still very much shaped by that chapel background' (ibid. 125). The themes of chapel, piety and puritanism run through much of his contribution to the collection and it would be worth quoting a section at length since it conveys so well the sentiment which this book has identified with this perhaps last generation of socialists—

> My mother encouraged me to go to a Nonconformist Chapel as a child and to Sunday school; my father never objected to that. The interesting thing about him was that he himself had quite a religious upbringing: he had been a Sunday schoolteacher, but had left the Chapel around the time he got married and joined the Communist Party. So with one step he went from being a Sunday schoolteacher to a member of the

Communist Party—people say of him that he took a lot of those kinds of values with him into the CP. ... he carried with him a profound knowledge of the Bible and of Welsh hymns. He had an incredible memory and was able to quote in speeches parts of the Bible or hymns, much better than ministers of religion themselves (ibid. 1997 125).

The foregoing accounts sustain my contention regarding the nature of generation. Though the reference was sometimes directed back towards the writer and at other times toward their parents, in each case was the influence of a cultural ethos stemming from the past wherein chapel or other context instilled a sense of discipline and commitment. Welding together otherwise disparate people, in each age group, was a common experience which elicited a particular manner of response. Socialism, in the manner presented in these extracts, was a structure of feeling located in a particular historical contexts.

Turning to the Campaign for Nuclear Disarmament we effectively relocate ourselves in a different historical identity. The material hardship of the past has been replaced by a welfare state, complete with universal education. Increased possibility for people to progress beyond school meant a new generation with high expectations, little fear of poverty and a misalignment with many who might be a teacher in one manner or another. When, then, a minority took up the first popular political cause of the post-war the cushion provided by this welfare state contributed to a restlessness with what was in effect a self-appointed leadership of the campaign, and a reluctance to follow where they did not wish to be lead. I have suggested that the war too contributed to a decline of the imposed discipline characteristic in the Communist Party. In these respects the generation gap between several of the leadership and some of the membership arose from a divergence of experience across which there was inevitably a difficulty of communication. The direction of CND was largely influenced by its grass roots. This is not to say there was no co-ordinated action; clearly there was; but rather that the manner in which people took part gave very much more to spontaneity than to instruction. Neither did CND expect or attempt to form a close-knit membership with systems for the carrying of information or relaying of decisions. Membership was very much more the expression of individual desires and beliefs and thus not susceptible to central direction. Arguably, this individuality might be seen to parallel the drive toward personal expression in wider social patterns ranging from consumer capitalism to modes of school learning. Self-expression was more closely met by Existentialism than Marxist-Leninism and it was not perhaps an accident that CND part followed, part coincided with a first take up of this new manner of philosophical expression.

Where the Communist Party continued to exhibit the hierarchy and discipline apparent in relationships before 1940, these were superseded in the practice of CND. Far from the leadership setting the agenda, they were taken in directions never intended, by a rank and file who displayed anything but deference. People would not give up their life to the extent of allowing others to dictate what they should do. Moral outrage would be an expression of a personal belief and personal witness, not something which could be orchestrated by a party or self-perpetuating leadership. It was perhaps something of this sort which Thompson caught in the polemical articles of the time. Commenting that 'It is a difficult generation for the old left to understand'. Thompson summarizes some of the formative experiences of these new political beings; Belsen, Hiroshima, the repressions in Cyprus, Algeria and Hungary and the absurdity of Suez. He continues,

> A generation nourished on *1984* and *Animal Farm*, which enters politics at the extreme point of disillusion where the middle-aged begin to get out. The young people who marched from Aldermaston, and who are beginning in many ways to associate themselves with the Socialist Movement, are enthusiastic enough. But their enthusiasm is not for the party, or the movement, or for established political leaders. They do not mean to give their enthusiasm cheaply away to any routine machine. They expect politicians to do their best to trick or betray them. At meetings they listen attentively, watching for insincerities, more ready with ironic applause than with cheers of acclaim. They prefer the amateurish platforms of the Nuclear Disarmament Campaign to the method and manner of the left-wing professional (Thompson 1959 1–2).

If, as I claim, religious affiliation can be set alongside that of political, and that each exhibited similar behaviour, then I think it is not inaccurate to suggest that a process of secularization set in after 1945. The historical context had altered and therefore the nature of the political formation. If, as in the case of religion, secularization may be taken to be a substitution of doctrinal certainty with greater circumspection, then political developments may follow a similar path. If we move on to chapter eight we can perhaps recognize this process in action. Centred initially in Oxford, the younger New Left, while respecting the Marxist tradition, were not in the main members of the Communist Party. Instead the greater influence was G. D. H. Cole. It was his seminar and international connections which provided the ground out of which a New Left could grow. The Coles afforded several links, through guild socialism to the alternative tradition of Morris, to adult education and more lately to independent socialists abroad.

With this personal and organizational widening went that of ideas. *Universities and Left Review*, the journal of the younger New Left, developed a number of discussions which draw on ideas outside of those characteristic of Labour or trade union traditions. Some of these, such as the idea of alienation, derived from parts of Marx's writings not significant in Communist Party readings. However, those concerning the nature and structure of the state, clearly owed more to guild socialism and decentralist traditions. People around *ULR* presented their ideas as an attempt to find a way between Stalinism and contemporary welfare capitalism, their shorthand for the Labour and Conservative leaderships of the time. This deliberate breaking away from either Labour or Communist by some of the London-based New Left might be interpreted as an example of a declining political certainty. The positive pole, post-colonial independence, to which some, including Stuart Hall, might have aspired, was not available to others, such as Raphael Samuel, for whom the loss of faith was real—a fact not forgotten in the celebrations for Raphael following his death.

To conclude I want to review certain of the connections between the different chapters, some having already been made in the closer analysis above. The aim is less to provide a final authoritative statement, such is never possible in any history, however desirous, than offer a weighing up of some events and responses which have filled the proceeding pages.

2. HISTORY IN THE BALANCE

Chapter two recorded the threat of fascism and war, opposition to which in the immediate context of the popular front of the thirties, was a complete failure. Even the heroic struggle for Spain, which, whatever the wider political manoeuvrings, was still for the ordinary combatants an act of extraordinary self-sacrifice, proved little more than a gesture in the face of an overwhelming enemy. Worse still at the end of the decade, the unity created in the cause of educating people about fascism was broken asunder by the sudden turnabout of the Communists. If just the major events are weighed, there is little to counter the conclusion that the causes which the generation of inter-war radicals took up, were unequivocally defeated. Yet beneath these headlines existed a considerable volume of activities in which people developed skills of learning and teaching, propagandizing, organizing and agitating. The Left Book Club was the most successful, though Unity Theatre, Kino Films and much else besides could be added. The skills were taken on into army education classes and later adult education which became a site for progressive politics after the war. The extent of influence of the Left Book Club and similar ventures is, by their nature, impossible to measure though we can be sure that the spreading of education and propaganda through a myriad of communications between people, would have taken the effects far wider than any count of members and readers would provide. In these less spectacular ways a claim of success for these new young radicals might have some substance.

Chapter three begins with the Communist Party reversal over the nature of the war to which I have just referred. Part of the chapter though was concerned with the varied war-time experiences, ranging from Christopher

Hill's high-level intelligence work to George Rude's service in the London Fire Brigade. Front-line military service on the other hand was the lot of Raymond Williams and Edward Thompson, who between them saw action in France, Germany and Italy. Space was also given to the very different war experience of Basil Davidson and the Partisan Movement in Yugoslavia, a movement and a country that was influential in the lives of several figures. There is toward the end of the chapter a return to Yugoslavia by way of the international youth project to build a railway from Samac to Sarajevo. On balance, the partisan cause and the unity of Britain with the USSR were high points for many. It was arguably a circumstance when a party political line could not hold. Too many disparate activities were occurring over too wide a canvas for one expression to be uniform.

Yet there was another side to the after-war experiences which I try to capture in returning to Cambridge. Raymond Williams had already moved away from the Communist Party before the outbreak of war. On returning, he undergoes a partial but progressive withdrawal which reaches its peak in 1948. Much later in the interviews which, in 1979, became *Politics and Letters*, Williams recasts this personal experience in terms of historical circumstance, relating it with what he feels to have been the political decline of the Labour government. The decline from the hopes of the thirties is acutely felt by Williams in what he perceives to be a change in the cultural politics of Cambridge, which he feels to have become conservative with a detectable increase in religious sentiment. More perceptibly perhaps than people within the Communist Party, Williams is influenced by the new conservative authority in cultural expression, and a sense that the post-war aspirations were running in a different direction from that which Orwell celebrated at the beginning of the forties. True, adult education did make for one means of pursuing a progressive programme yet it is not clear that initially Williams's own teaching took that form, nor, when he does begin the redefining of culture, does this form of employment offer any simple way forward. It was, of course, some years before Williams left immediate contact with the Workers' Education Association, yet it is clear that he was always circumspect as to the possibility of social change coming through what was essentially a liberal body.

We are left thus with a delicate balance from the post-war accounts contained in chapters three and four. Certainly there existed a potential for social progress, real enough in the reforms carried through by the Labour government. Meanwhile, Communists could feel their party had gained a greater level of respect because of the sufferings of the Soviet people during the war. Internationally, the establishing of new forms of government in several European countries seemed to vindicate the charge that socialist planning was the way forward. Yet Williams perceived the counter pressures both of a renewed conservatism in cultural expression and a new commercialism created by the peculiar turn of the post-war settlement as this took hold in Europe.

Parallel with the account offered in chapter four are parts of chapter five. In total though the chapter encompasses a longer time-span, turning back to the end of the First World War in order to gauge the culture of the Communist Party. It is in this chapter, more than anywhere else, that I address a culture of discipline and commitment leading to a perceived need for hierarchy and stable authority. The culture of the party was always complex, and no doubt variable as between one place and another. However, as the cold war came on there seem to be freezing over so that forward movement ceased. Martin Kettle recalls,

> I can remember my father saying, years ago, that the trouble with the Communist parties of western Europe was that they all got stuck at the start of the Cold War ... (Cohen ed. 1997 184).

There is, I believe, in the accounts offered in chapters four and five a difference of perception which can only partly be explained in terms of whether a person belonged to the Communist Party or not. A deeper division existed which stemmed from perceptions of change and the order of primacy ascribed to features of a society. For many of those in chapter five there was a concentration on a limited set of primarily economic activities and relationships. Economic relations remained central to Williams too; however, his understanding of economic activities was inextricably linked with an evolving theory of culture. This meant that no simple division could be made whereby one part of human reproduction could be assigned a primary and therefore causal role in relation to some other part. For Williams, an intricate web existed weaving together housing, cars, consumer purchasing, television, to increased individuality and with it privacy. Such pressures rendered the old appeals to workers' solidarity incompatible with the experience of contemporary life, necessitating a wider set of identities to be addressed if a positive response was to be gained. It was this deeper division of understanding which made for the contrasts of accounts offered in chapter four and five for the years between 1945 and 1956.

The remaining three chapters formed a distinct section and need to be taken together if a reasonable assessment is to be made. In order, they followed first the distress within the Communist Party during 1956, and particularly the arguments contained within *The Reasoner*. Chapter seven dealt with the response to the Suez invasion, the rise of the first Campaign for Nuclear Disarmament, the composition of the movement and its character. Finally, chapter eight addressed the new generation of socialists, the development of what became known as a New Left and an examination of the magazine *Universities and Left Review*. Together the three chapters recorded the moving out from the long period of division and distrust, which served as an experience of the cold war and the engagement with the rapidly developing culture of consumerism and welfare capitalism after the war. Yet I place the New Left into a longer history of radical thinking. The immediate presence of G. D. H. Cole in the middle-fifties and the return in articles in *ULR* to earlier sentiments, such as guild socialism via the formula of workers' control, afford two examples of this continuity.

The meeting up between the new radicals and Raymond Williams linked chapter eight with four where I stress that the major works; *Culture and Society* and *The Long Revolution*, were products of the long years of a thinking through of the idea of culture in the context of adult education teaching, and not the period of the New Left despite the apparent coincidence of timing when the dates are looked at retrospectively. The point once again is that what has rather ahistorically been presented as a sudden new departure after 1956, was in fact deeply informed by an existing political project. What the New Left represented was a political departure which encompassed that changing culture brought on by the advance of the welfare state and commercial capitalism, changes which a generation born between the wars had to adapt to and address, but which meant that the conditions out of which their political manner grew, no longer existed.

A number of biographical accounts cite the inaction of the national government in the thirties either against the advancement of fascism or to address the poverty of the unemployed, as a stimulation toward socialism, particularly in the organized form of the Communist Party. The drive to action was a sense of injustice and even more abhorrence of the perceived immorality of fascism against which they felt compelled to make a necessary even if failed protest. The theme connects chapter two with six and seven, when again the pressure towards public witness was overwhelming. In chapter six, the protest was against the perceived disregard of the Communist Party leadership for revelations and outrages in the supposed Communist part of the world. In chapter seven the protest invoked by the scandal of Suez, becomes channelled into a struggle for survival against an enemy which threatened the extinction of humanity itself. Chapter six refers to 'renewing the libertarian tradition', and had the development of the anti-nuclear campaign not got under way from that moment, something else would have had to have been invented. As it was, the bomb, of which previously people who had been members of the Communist Party had made very selective criticism, became the means by which people 'separate for a decade met ... up, in all sorts of ways' (Williams 1979a 361). In the thirties, the politics of protest against overwhelming odds had led to socialism and many into the Communist Party; in the fifties protest led people out and into a new unity of dissent.

To the themes of a changing culture and pressure of overwhelming odds against which a stand had to be made, must be added one last. Particularly present in chapters two and four is my contention that many of the people in this story came from backgrounds which were in some manner marginal to the dominant culture of England. This marginality could come from several sources. Origins were in some cases important, and could include such features as migration from Celtic periphery, imperial colony or European Jewry. Alternatively, beliefs could be important where these were informed by chapel or sect, as in the case of Harry Pollitt whose early learning was through a Moravian Sunday School. A third possibility was class, and the experience of entering into a body and experience dominated by a different culture from their own. An obvious example was Raymond Williams's encounter with Cambridge, both town and university. The particular male culture of this last, as late as the middle-fifties, meant women from similar backgrounds faced even greater impediment. My contention is that these experiences influenced responses to circumstance and made legitimate unorthodoxy, dissent and protest in the name of a liberty which may itself have been part of a person's earliest experience.

It is a conclusion of this work that the events in the CPGB around 1956 only necessitated a break which the changing culture of post-war Britain was already pressing. Older independent socialists and radicals would have linked up with the post-war generation and its politics regardless of events within the Communist world. The cushion of the welfare state, enhanced educational opportunity, and the peace movement which followed in the wake of the attempted invasion of Suez would have ensured that. Feuds within and between Communist parties were in that regard irrelevant. However, the coincidence of Hungary with Suez did give a direction to how events unfolded. The 'New' Left after 1956 was of a particular order because of the coincidence of the two outrages and the make-up of people who formed its ranks. That make-up was induced by the three dimensions outlined above; a changing culture, protest at a perceived overwhelming threat, and a sense of marginality induced by personal background and the dominant culture within which people found themselves. Together these made for a particular political and cultural formation. It is my contention that what then was perceived as an alternative, whether to a dominant culture, a terrifying threat, or a stand upon which to protest, in short a view of socialism, was contextually, and therefore historically, specific, and that in altered circumstance, this aspiration will in the words of the late Ralph Miliband have to be reinvented.

FURTHER READING

The following are selected references which provide further insight into the principal characters main themes of the book, or individual chapters. The references are deliberately a mix of works contemporary with the period and more recent publications. The place of publication is London unless otherwise stated.

One work which has very much served as a guide is *Politics and Letters*, Verso, 1979—the extended interview which Raymond Williams gave to three members of the editorial committee of *New Left Review*. However, the inspiration for the subject comes from Raymond Williams's part history, part argument, 'Adult Education and Social Change' reproduced in *What I came to say*, Hutchinson, 1989, which offers intriguing suggestions for future research, to which I fear no one book could give full justice. Also of importance is Tom Steele's *The Emergence of Cultural Studies*, Lawrence and Wishart, 1997, which in addition to offering a much needed corrective to the standard accounts of the field, covers the same period from a different though complementary perspective.

Contextualizing the period with an overview of the century is Eric Hobsbawm, *The Age Of Extremes*, Michael Joseph, 1994. However, readers wanting to gain a more precise sense of the historical context of Britain in the inter-war years should read Paul Addison's *The Road to 1945*, Quartet, 1977. For the cultural history of the years from 1939 to 1960 Robert Hewison's *Under Siege* published by Methuen, 1988, and *In Anger* published by Oxford NY, 1981, are both informative and enjoyable. Books on the left are numerous as 'members', however, Gary Werskey's *Visible College*, Free Association Books, 1988, is a rarity in being about scientists rather than the more usual cultural figures. For the Communist Party, Francis Beckett's *Enemy Within*, Merlin Press, Suffolk, 1998, is a readable and sympathetic treatment of its subject. For the party historians group, Raphael Samuel's 'British Marxist Historians I', *New Left Review* 120 1980, is a most evocative piece. A more critical view of the Left in the earlier part of the period is Ben Pimlott's *Labour and the Left in the 1930s*, Cambridge, 1977, while A. J. Davies's *To Build A New Jerusalem*, Abacus, 1996, offers a very readable critique covering the period as a whole.

Potentially, the largest number of books for further reading fall under the heading of autobiography and biography. Since only a small sample is referenced here, they will attempt to be varied in approach. Experiential accounts are many, however, together with Margaret Cole's *Growing up into Revolution*, Longmans, 1949, and *The Life of G. D. H. Cole*, Macmillan, 1971, offer background to two of the most influential figures in the intellectual left. Raymond Williams has offered autobiographical sketches in several books, however, his novels certainly provide the best insights into both his own experiences and the period, and of these, *Border Country*, Hogarth, 1988, and *Loyalties*, Hogarth, 1989, are perhaps the two most important. Three other autobiographical accounts covering the period are Mervyn Jones' *Chances*, Verso, 1987, Malcolm MacEwen's *The Greening of a Red*, Pluto, 1991, and John Harrison's *Scholarship Boy*, Rivers Oram, 1995. There are various writings on E. P. Thompson, but his own *Beyond the Frontier* published by Merlin in 1997, perhaps offers the most intimate account of the inspiration behind this extraordinary figure.

Of Williams's period in adult education, John McIlroy's and Sally Westwood (eds), *Border Country*, is invaluable and groundbreaking. Extending the theme are essays by John McIlroy and Roger Fieldhouse in John Morgan and Peter Preston (eds), *Raymond Williams: Politics, Education, Letters*, St Martin's Press, NY, 1993. Readers interested in the politics of adult education after the war should read Roger Fieldhouse's *Adult Education and the Cold War*, University of Leeds, 1985a.

The Campaign for Nuclear Disarmament has been the subject of many writers, however still the best inside account is Peggy Duff's *Left Left Left* published by Allison & Busby, 1971. Of other studies, Richard Taylor and Colin Pritchard, *The Protest Makers*, Pergamon Press, Oxford, 1980, is still valuable for its biographical notes of many of those involved. For the New Left, it is worth comparing the two volumes published under the title *Out of Apathy*. The first is a 1960 collection of essays by some of those most centrally involved at the time, while the second is a reflective view of the time by same of the same people, published in 1989.

Finally, two very different books are *Lifetimes of Commitment*, Cambridge, 1991, which should be read for accounts of activists while *Children of the Revolution*, Lawrence & Wishart, 1997, offers personal views of what its was like to grow up with them, as young people.

LETTERS, INTERVIEWS AND RECORDINGS

Interviews:
Anna Davin, 9 August 1993.
Jim Fyrth, 3 November 1993.
Douglas Hyde, 20 December 1993.
Martin Eve, 26 January 1994 and 28 October 1994.
Noreen Branson, 17 June 1996.
John Vickers, 12 May 1997.
Margaret McLean, 19 June 1997.

Correspondence:
Philip Corrigan, letter 21 September 1992.
Jim Fyrth, letters 2 September 1993, 28 February 1997, 1 April 1997, unpublished autobiographical extracts.
Lionel Elvin, letter 2 March 1997 and attached unpublished autobiographical notes.
John Vickers, letter 4 June 1997 containing autobiographical notes.
Martin Eve, letter n.d. and Publishers Directory extract on history of Merlin Press.
Victor Kiernan, letters of 22 August 1996 and 1 February 1997.
John Saville, letter 15 September 1993.
John McIlroy letter n.d. (probably early 1997).
Roger Fieldhouse letter 5 March 1997 with unpublished conference paper attached (for details see Fieldhouse 1996).
Raymond Williams to Tony McLean, letter 14 July (year not given but probably 1952 or 1953) contains outline of what became *Culture and Society* and part one of *Long Revolution*.

Recordings
Autobiography of Tony McLean recorded on cassette.
Workers Education Association South Eastern District Lectures and reminiscences in honour of Tony McLean entitled 'Adult Education and Social Change' recorded cassette.
Sixty years of Adult Education in Kent. Lectures recalling history of Oxford Extra-Mural Department and Workers' Education Association recorded on cassette.

Each of the above cassettes were kindly provided by Margaret McLean.

MEMORIALS, FUNERALS AND CELEBRATIONS

Douglas Hyde: A life of struggle Memorial Meeting Socialist History London School of Economics 12 April 1997.

Raphael Samuel: funeral Highgate Cemetery 18 December 1996.

Raphael Samuel 1934–1996: A memorial celebration Conway Hall 26 April 1997.

Raphael Samuel: A round table discussion London History Workshop 7 July 1997.

Public speeches and personal conversations at the above events deepened my understanding not only of the figures being celebrated but their time and context. I should like to record my thanks to all who took part.

PERIODICALS BIBLIOGRAPHY

Arena

Common Wealth Review

Essays in Criticism

Highway

Labour Monthly

Labour Review

The Left Book News/The Left News

New Left Review (1960–1962)

The Marxist Quarterly

The Modern Quarterly

New Reasoner

New Statesman

Penguin New Writing

The Plebs Magazine

Poetry and the People

Politics and Letters

The Reasoner

Scrutiny

The Tutors Bulletin of Adult Education

Universities and Left Review

World News (1956–1957)

BIBLIOGRAPHY

Published in London unless otherwise stated. Date of original publication in parenthesis:

Acland, Sir Richard *Unser Kampf* Penguin 1940.
    What it will be like Gollancz 1943.
    How it can be done Macdonald 1944.
Addison, Paul *The Road to 1945* Quartet 1977.
Adult Education Committee of the Ministry of Reconstruction *The 1919 Report* Department
    of Adult Education University of Nottingham 1980 (Nottingham 1919)
Ali, Tariq 'Professor Ralph Miliband' *Independent* 24 May 1994.
Allsop, Kenneth *The Angry Decade* John Goodchild 1985.
Anderson, Perry *Arguments in English Marxism* Verso 1980.
Andrews, Molly *Lifetimes of Commitment* Cambridge UP Cambridge 1991.
Arena *Britain's Cultural Heritage* Arena n.d.
    The American threat to British Culture Arena n.d.
Armstrong, J. R. 'Notes on town planning architecture and community' *Politics and Letters* 4
    Summer 1948.
Attfield, John and Stephen Williams *1939: The Communist Party and the War* L & W 1984.
Backstom, Philip *Christian Socialism and Co-operation in Victorian England* Croom Helm Kent
    1974.
Bailey, Stephen 'What Cole Really Meant' 1960 in Briggs and Saville (eds) 1960.
Bamford, Caroline *The politics of Commitment: the early new left in Britain 1956–1962* Univer-
    sity of Edinburgh unpublished thesis 1983.
Barker, Rodney *Education and Politics* OUP Oxford 1972.
Barnet, Anthony 'The keywords of a key thinker' *The Listener* 4 Feb 1988.
Barrow, Logie 'Socialism in Eternity' *HWJ* 9 Spring 1980.
Bevan, Aneurin *Why not trust the Tories* Gollancz 1945.
    In Place of Fear (1952) Quartet Books 1978.
Beddington, D. W. *The Nonconformist Conscience* Allen and Unwin 1982.
Benn, Tony *Writings on the wall* Faber and Faber 1984.
Blackburn, Robin 'Raphael Samuel: the politics of thick description' *NLR* 221 1997.
Blatchford, Robert *Merry England* Clarion 1895.
Blyth, John *English University Adult Education* Manchester UP Manchester 1983.
Bonner, Pauline and George 'Criticism not Stigmatism' Forum *Daily Worker* 29 May 1956.
Boune, H. 'The problem of unity' n.d.
Bourne 'Correspondence' *New Statesman* 30 November 1957.
Bowen, Roger (ed.) *E. H. Norman: his Life and Scholarship* University of Toronto Press Canada
    1984.
Brandon, Ruth *The Burning Question* Heinemann 1976.
Branson, Noreen *History of the Communist of Great Britain 1927–1941* L & W 1985.
    History of the Communist of Great Britain 1941–1951 L & W 1997.
——Bill Moore *Labour–Communist Relations 1920–1951 Part I: 1920–1935* CP History Group
    pamphlet 82 1990.
——Bill Moore *Labour–Communist Relations 1920–1951 Part II: 1935–1945* CP History Group
    pamphlet 83 1990.
Braybon, Gail and Penny Summerfield *Out of the Cage* RKP 1987.
Briggs, Asa and John Saville (eds) *Essays in Labour History* Macmillan 1960.
    Essays in Labour History 1886–1923 Macmillan 1971.
    Essays in Labour History 1917–1938 Macmillan 1977.
Brockway, Fenner *Socialism over sixty years* Allen and Unwin 1946.
Brooks, Stephen *Labour's War* Clarendon Press Oxford 1992.
Brown, Geoff 'Independence and incorporation' 1980 in Jane Thompson (ed.) 1980.
Brown, Ivor 'G. D. H. Cole as an undergraduate' 1960 in Briggs and Saville (eds) 1960.

Bryant, B. A. D. *The new left in Britain 1956–1968* University of London unpublished thesis 1980.

Burge, Alan and Keith Davies 'Enlightenment of the highest order' *Llafur* 7 1 1996.

Butler, David and Gareth Butler *British Political Facts 1900–1994* (seventh edition) Macmillan 1994.

Calder, Angus *The Common Wealth Party 1942–1945* University of Sussex unpublished thesis 1968.

> *A People's War: Britain 1939–1945* Jonathan Cape 1969.

> *The Myth of the Blitz* Pimlico 1992.

Callaghan, John *Ranjani Palme Dutt* L & W 1993.

Cambridge Journal of Economics 'Maurice Dobb' 2 1978.

Carpenter, L. P. *G. D. H. Cole, An intellectual biography* Cambridge UP Cambridge 1973.

Cato *Guilty Men* Gollancz 1940.

Caudwell, Christopher *Illusion and Reality* (1937) L & W 1973.

Centre for Contemporary Cultural Studies *Economy, Culture and Concept* sp 50 CCCS Birmingham 1977.

> *Working Class Culture* Hutchinson 1979.

> *Making Histories* Hutchinson 1982.

Chun, Lin *The British New Left* Edinburgh Press Edinburgh 1993.

Clark, Jon et al. (ed.) *Culture and Crisis in Britain in the Thirties* L & W 1979.

Coates, David et al. *A Socialist Anatomy of Britain* Polity Cambridge 1985.

Coates, Ken and Tony Topham (eds) *Workers Control* Panther Modern Society MacGibbon & Kee 1970.

Cockburn, Patricia *The years of The Week* (1968) Comedia 1985.

Cohen, Phil *Children of the Revolution* L & W 1997.

Cole, G. D. H. 'Collectivism, Syndicalism and Guilds' 1917 reprinted in Coates and Topham (eds) 1970.

> *The People's Front* Gollancz 1937.

> 'The watch on the home front' *Highway* xxxii November 1939.

> 'Sociology and Politics in the twentieth century' *Politics and Letters* 2 & 3 Winter–Spring 1947.

> *A Century of Co-operation* Allen & Unwin/Co-operative Union 1947.

> *A history of the labour party from 1914* RKP 1947.

> 'What Workers' Education Means' *The Highway* 44 October 1952.

> 'Some advice to the left' *New Statesmen* 21 Nov 1953.

> 'The future of socialism' *New Statesmen* 15 and 22 Jan 1955.

> 'World Socialism Restated' *New Statesman* 5 May 1956a.

> '3 Questions for Communists' *Daily Worker* 14 May 1956b.

> 'Reflections on Democratic Socialism' *Reasoner* 3 1956c.

> 'Midway thoughts on Suez' *New Statesman* 27 October 1956d.

> *The Post-War Condition of Britain* RKP 1956e.

> 'What is happening to British capitalism' *ULR* 1 1957.

> 'Next steps in British foreign policy' *New Reasoner* Summer 1958.

——Raymond Postgate *The Common People* (1938) Methuen 1961.

Cole, Margaret 'Communism and the Webbs' *The Highway* xxviii February 1936.

> 'What's an escapist?' *Highway* xxxii January 1940.

> *Growing up into Revolution* Longmans 1949.

> *The Life of G. D. H. Cole* Macmillan 1971.

> 'Guild Socialism and the Labour Research Department' in Briggs and Saville (eds) 1971.

Collins, Henry 'Literary Criticism in Adult Education' *Tutors Bulletin of Adult Education* November 1946.

> 'The open society and its enemies' *Politics and Letters* 1947–8.

> 'Working-Class Education and University Standards' *The Highway* 44 January 1953.

Communist Party of Great Britain *It can be done: Report of the Fourteenth Congress* Communist
Party 1937.

> *Report of the Central Committee to the 15th Party Congress* Communist Party 1938.
> *Marxist Study Themes: The Communist Party, Unity, and the Fight for Peace* Communist
> Party 1950.
> *The Communist Party 24th National Congress: The People Will Decide* Communist Party
> 1956.
> *The Communist Party 24th National Congress: Resolutions and Proceedings* Communist
> Party 1956.
> *The Communist Party 24th National Congress: Report of the Executive Committee* Com-
> munist Party 1956.
> *25th (Special) Congress of the Communist Party: The Report of the Commission on Inner
> Party Democracy* Communist Party 1957.
> *Report of the Commission on Inner party Democracy Amendments submitted by Party org-
> anizations for the Twenty-Fifth (Special) Congress* 20 April Communist Party 1957.
> *Communist Party of Great Britain 25th (Special) Congress of the Communist Party:
> Draft Political Resolution* Communist Party 1957.
> *Amendments to Political Resolution* 20 April Communist Party 1957.
> *25th (Special) Congress of the Communist Party: Draft Revised Text of The British Road to
> Socialism* Communist Party 1957.
> *25th Congress Report* Communist Party 1957.
> *Amendments to the British Road to Socialism* 20 April Communist Party 1957.
> *Amendments to Rules* 8 May Communist Party 1957.
> *26th Congress Report* Communist Party 1959.
> *The Communist Party 26th National Congress: Report of the Executive Committee* Com-
> munist Party 1959.
> *Twenty-Sixth Congress of the Communist Party: Report on New Rules* Communist Party
> 1959.

Communist Party Executive Committee *Lessons of the 20th Congress of the CPSU* 13 May 1956.

> Letter to Edwin Payne (Historians' Group) 16 May 1956.
> *Communist Party Executive Committee Statement on 'The Reasoner'* 13 September 1956
> (version subsequently published in *World News* 22 September 1956).
> *The Next Stage* October 16 1956.
> *'The Reasoner'* 10–11 November 1956.
> *The Twenty-fifth Congress* May 1957.
> *Report of the congress appeals committee to the 25th Congress of the Communist Party* (Peter
> Fryer) 26 April 1957.

Communist Party Historians' Group 'Political tasks confronting the Group' June 1951.

> 'Historians' Group 1955–1960'.
> 'Members May 1955'.
> *Speeches at the Memorial meeting for Leslie Morton* CP Historians' Group 1988.

Coombes, B. L. 'The Way We Live Now' *Penguin New Writing* 2 1941.

Corfield, A. J. *Epoch in Workers Education* WEA 1969.

Cornforth, Maurice *Communism and Philosophy* L & W 1980.

——(ed.) *Rebels and their Causes* L & W 1978.

Cox, Idris *Forward to a new life for South Wales* South Wales Committee of the Communist
Party Wales 1944a.

> *The fight for socialism in Wales* Welsh Committee of the Committee Party Wales 1948.
> 'Communist Strongholds in Inter-War Britain' *Marxism Today* June 1979.

——et al. n.d. *South Wales in the march of history* Rhondda Communist Party Wales.

Cox, John *Overkill* Pelican 1981.

Craig, F. W. S. *British Parliamentary Election Statistics 1918–1968* Political Reference Publications Glasgow 1968.

Craik, William *Central Labour College* L & W 1968

Crick, Bernard 'Socialist literature in the 1950s' *Political Quarterly* 32 1960.
　　George Orwell: A life Penguin 1982.
Croft, Andy 'Introduction' *Mean's Test Man* (1935) Spokesman Pamphlets Nottingham 1983.
　　Red Letter Days L & W 1990.
　　'Betrayed Spring' 1994 in Jim Fyrth (ed.) 1994.
　　'Writers, the Communist Party and the battle of ideas 1945–50' *Socialist History* 5 1994.
　　'Walthamstow, Little Gidding and Middlesbrough: Edward Thompson, Adult Education and Literature' *Socialist History* 8 1995.
　　'Culture or Snobology' Socialist History Society Conference `Getting the Balance Right' Birkbeck College 22 June 1996.
Crosland, Anthony *The Future of Socialism* Jonathan Cape 1956.
　　'On the Left Again' *Encounter* XV 4 October 1960.
Crossick, Geoffrey (ed.) *The lower middle class in Britain* Croom Helm Kent 1977.
Curtis, S. J. *History of Education in Great Britain* (seventh edition) University Tutorial Press Cambridge 1967.
——M. E. A. Boultwood *An introductory history of English education since 1800* (fourth ed.) University Tutorial Press Cambridge 1966.
　　Daily Worker 'This criticism strengthens us' 2 April 1956.
　　Daily Worker 'Call for unity to end Tory rule' 20 April 1957.
Davidson, Basil *Partisan Picture* Bedford Books Bedford 1946.
　　Special Operations Europe Gollancz 1980.
　　Guardian 5 February 1997.
Davies, A. J. *To Build A New Jerusalem* Abacus 1996.
Davies, Ioan 'Cultural Theory in Britain; narrative and episteme' *Theory, Culture and Society* 10 3 1993.
Dent, H. C. *Part-time education in Great Britain—an historical outline* Turnstile Press 1949.
Devereux, W. A. *Adult education in inner London 1870–1980* Shepheard-Walwyn/ILEA 1982.
Dimitroff, Georgi *The United Front* L & W 1938.
Dobb, Maurice 'Economics and the Economics of Socialism' *Modern Quarterly* 22 1939.
Dowse, Robert *Left in the Centre* Longmans 1966.
Duff, Peggy *Left Left Left* Allison & Busby 1971.
Dutt, Palme 'Steps to Labour unity in Britain' *World News* 3 16 21 April 1956.
　　'The British Communist Party' *Times Literary Supplement* 5 May 1966.
Dworkin, Dennis and Leslie Roman *Views Beyond the Border Country* Routledge 1993.
Eade, Charles *The war speeches of the Rt Hon Winston Churchill* volume one Purnell n.d.
Eagleton, Terry *Criticism and Ideology* NLB 1976.
　　'Criticism and Politics; the work of Raymond Williams's *NLR* 95 1976.
——(ed.) *Raymond Williams: critical perspectives* Polity 1989.
Edwards, Hywel 'A large shadow in history's fierce afterglow' *New Welsh Review* 31 Winter 1995–6.
Eldridge, John and Lizzie Eldridge *Raymond Williams making connections* Routledge 1994.
Electrical Trades Union *Educational Services* 1955 unpublished.
Eliot, T. S. *Notes toward the definition of culture* Faber and Faber 1948.
Evans, Bernard *Radical Adult Education* Croom Helm Kent 1987.
Fernbach, David 'Tom Wintringham and socialist defence strategy' *History Workshop* 14 1982.
Feinstein (ed.) *Socialism, Capitalism and Economic Growth* Cambridge UP Cambridge 1982.
Fieldhouse, Roger *Adult Education and the Cold War* University of Leeds Leeds 1985a.
　　'Conformity and Contradiction in English Responsible Body Adult Education, 1925–1950' *Studies in the Education of Adults* 17 1985b.
　　'Adult Learning—for Leisure, Recreation and Democracy' in Jim Fyrth *Labour's Promised Land* Lawrence and Wishart 1995.
　　'Oxford and Adult Education' in Morgan and Preston (eds) 1993.

A collective political biography of four influential British adult educators: W. Temple, R. H. Tawney, A. D. Lindsay, and G. D. H. Cole unpublished 1996.

Foot, Michael *Aneurin Bevan—volume 1* New English Library 1966.

Aneurin Bevan—1945–1960 Paladin 1975.

——Donald Bruce *Who are the patriots* Gollancz 1949.

——Mervyn Jones *Guilty Men, 1957* Gollancz 1957.

Fox, Pamela *Class Fictions* Duke University Press North Carolina 1994.

Frances, Hywel *Survey of miners' Institute and Welfare Hall Libraries, October 1972–February 1973* Coalfield History Project University College Swansea Wales n.d.

Against Fascism: South Wales miners and the Spanish Civil War L & W 1984.

——David Smith *The Fed: A history of the South Wales miners in the twentieth century* L & W 1980.

Fryer, Peter *Hungarian Tragedy* (1956) New Park Publications 1986.

'The Hungarian revolution' Correspondence *New Statesman and Nation* 24 November 1956.

Letter announcing the *The Newsletter* dated April 1957.

'They've stacked the cards against the CP rebels' *Tribune* 19 April 1957.

Fyrth, Jim 'Dr Henry Collins' *Bulletin of the Society for the Study of Labour History* 20 1970.

Autobiographical notes unpublished 1997.

——(ed.) *British Fascism and the Popular Front* L & W 1985.

——(ed.) *Labour's High Noon* L & W 1993.

——(ed.) *Labour's Promised Land* L & W 1995.

Gaitskell, Hugh 'At Oxford in the Twenties' 1960 in Briggs and Saville (eds) 1960.

Ginsberg, Morris 'Psycho-analysis and Sociology' *Politics and Letters* 2 & 3 Winter–Spring 1947.

Goldsworthy, David *Colonial issues in British Politics 1945–1961* OUP Oxford 1971.

Gollan, John *Democratic Centralism* 15 October 1956.

Letter to E. P. Thompson and John Saville unpublished n.d. Circulars 1956 Box CPGB Archive.

Gollancz, Victor *My Dear Timothy* Gollancz 1952.

More for Timothy Gollancz 1953.

Grant, Betty Letter on Working Committee of the Historians' Group dated July 1953.

The Present Position on Local History in Britain n.d.

Letter to John (Saville?) citing attached statement on local history 15 September n.d.

Graves, Robert and Alan Hodge *The Long Week-End: A social history of Great Britain 1918–1939* Readers' Union Limited 1941.

Green, Martin *A mirror for Anglo-Saxons* Longmans 1961.

Green, Michael 'Raymond Williams and Cultural Studies' *Cultural Studies* 6 1974.

Green, S. W. 'Correspondence' *New Statesman* 30 November 1957.

Gurney, Peter *Co-operative Culture and the Politics of Consumption in England 1870–1930* Manchester UP Manchester 1996.

Hall, Arnold *The adult school movement in the twentieth century* Department of Adult Education University of Nottingham Nottingham 1985.

Hall, Stuart 'A sense of Classlessness' *ULR* 5 1958.

'Some paradigms in cultural studies' *Annali Anglistica* 21 1978.

'The early new left' History Workshop seminar, 10 September unpublished 1985.

'The "First" New Left: life and times' in Oxford University Socialist Discussion Group (ed.) 1989.

'Raphael Samuel: 1934–1996' *NLR* 221 1997.

Harrison, J. F. C . *History of the Working Men's College 1854–1954* RKP 1954.

Learning and Living RKP 1961.

A Scholarship Boy Rivers Oram 1995.

Harrison, Stanley *Poor Men's Guardians* L & W 1974.

Harrop, Sylvia (ed.) *Oxford and working-class education* (second revised ed. 1909) Nottingham studies in the history of adult education University of Nottingham Nottingham1987.

Haqqi, S. Anwarul *The Colonial Policy of the Labour Government (1945–51)* Muslim University, Aligarh 1960.

Hawkins, T. H. and L. J. F. Brimble *Adult Education—the record of the British Army* Macmillan 1947.

Hayman, Ronald (ed.) *My Cambridge* Robson Books 1977.

Heinemann, Margot 1985 'The Peoples' Front and the Intellectuals' in Jim Fyrth (ed.) 1985.

——Noreen Branson *Britain in the Nineteen Thirties* Weidenfeld and Nicolson 1975.

Hemming, James 'Politics, the group and social function' *Politics and Letters* 1 Summer 1947.

Hewison, Robert *In Anger* OUP New York 1981.

    Under Siege Methuen 1988.

Higgins, Michael *The Migrant's Return: A personal reflection on the importance of Raymond Williams* NIACE Cymru and BBC Cymru 1996.

    Highway 'Notes and Comments' xxxii November 1939.

    'Education in the army' xxxii March 1940.

    'Notes and Comments' xxxii March 1940.

Hill, Christopher 'A Whig Historian' *Modern Quarterly* 1 3 July 1938.

    Lenin and the Russian Revolution (1947) Penguin 1971.

Hilton, Rodney 'The historians' Group and the British Tradition' (signed as Chairman of Historians' Group) n.d.

    'Christopher Hill: some reminiscences' 1978 in Donald Pennington and Keith Thomas (eds) 1978.

Hinton, James 'The Roots of British Communism' *NLR* 128 1981.

    Protests and Visions Hutchinson 1989.

Historians' Group of the Communist Party *Local History* Bulletin 1 October 1950.

    Local History Bulletin 2 November 1950.

    Local History Bulletin 3 January 1951.

    Local History Bulletin 4 February 1951.

    Local History Bulletin No. 10 n.d.

    Our History No. 1 n.d. but probably 1953.

    Our History No. 13 November 1954.

    Our History No. 18 April 1955.

    Our History No. 20 June 1955.

    Our History No. 22 September 1955.

History Workshop *Culture, Ideology and Politics* RKP 1982.

    Theatres of the Left 1880–1935 RKP 1985.

    Patriotism: volume 1 History and Politics Routledge 1989a.

    Patriotism: volume 2 Minorities and Outsiders Routledge 1989b.

    Patriotism: volume 3 National Fictions Routledge 1989c.

Hobsbawm, Eric *Primitive Rebels* Manchester UP Manchester 1959.

    'The Fabians Reconsidered' in *Labouring Men* Weidenfeld and Nicolson 1964.

    Bandits Weidenfeld and Nicolson 1969.

    'Maurice Dobb' 1967 in Feinstein (ed.) 1967.

    Revolutionaries Weidenfeld and Nicolson 1973.

    'The Historians' Group of the Communist Party' 1978 in Cornforth, Maurice (ed.) 1978.

    'Fifty Years of Peoples' Fronts' 1985 in Hobsbawm 1989a.

    Interview on 1956 *Marxism Today* November 1986.

    Politics for a Rational Left Verso 1989a.

    The Age of Empire Sphere 1989b.

    The Age of Extremes Michael Joseph 1994.

Hodgen, Margaret *Workers Education in England and the United States* Kegan Paul 1925.

Hodgkin, Thomas 'Objectivity, ideologies and the present political order' *The Highway* 42 January 1951.

Hogben, Lancelot 'The modern challenge to freedom of thought' *Modern Quarterly* 4 1 1938.

Hoggart, Richard *Uses of Literacy* Chatto & Windus 1957.

    Speaking to Each Other volume one: About Society Penguin 1970a.

    Speaking to Each Other volume two: About Literature Penguin 1970b.

    A Local Habitation. Life and Times volume I 1918–1940 OUP Oxford 1989.

    A Sort of Clowning. Life and Times volume I 1940–1959 Chatto & Windus 1990.

    An Imagined Life. Life and Times volume III 1959–1991 OUP Oxford 1993.

    An English Temper Chatto & Windus 1982 .

    The way we live now Chatto & Windus 1995.

    'Defending the faith' *Bookseller* 15 March 1996.

Hoggart, Simon and David Leigh *Michael Foot: a portrait* Hodder and Stoughton 1981.

Howard, Anthony *Crossman: The Pursuit of Power* Jonathan Cape 1981.

Howe, Stephen *Anti-colonialism in British politics: The left and the end of empire 1939–1964* University of Oxford unpublished thesis 1984.

——(ed.) *Lines of Dissent* Verso 1988.

Hudson, Kate *The double blow: 1956 and the Communist Party of Great Britain* University of London unpublished thesis 1992.

Hughes, Glyn *The new left in Britain 1956–64* University of Keele unpublished thesis 1973.

Hunter, Bill 'This was the real Harry Pollitt' *Labour Review* August 1983.

Hutt, Allen 'Dona Torr' *Labour Monthly* 37 3 March 1957.

Huxley, Aldous 'Free Discipline in Education' *The Highway* xxvi October 1933.

Hynes, Samuel *The Auden Generation* Bodley Head 1976.

Inglis, Fred *Radical Earnestness* Martin Robinson Oxford 1982.

    The Cruel Peace: everyday life and the cold war Basic Books New York 1992.

    Raymond Williams Routledge 1995.

    'The Figures of Dissent' *NLR* 215 1996.

James, J. G. et al. 'Correspondence' *New Statesman* 7 December 1957.

Jepson, Norman *The Beginnings of University Adult Education* Michael Joseph 1973.

Joad, C. E. M. 'I pontificate' *Tutors Bulletin of Adult Education* 86 April 1952.

Joannou, Mary 'Raymond Williams 1921–1988' *WEA News* Autumn 1988.

John Gollan—brief biographical details July unpublished 1966.

Johnson, Paul *The Suez War* MacGibbon & Kee 1957.

Johnson, Richard 'Thompson, Genovese, and socialist-humanist history' *HWJ* 6 1978.

    Three problematics: elements in a theory of working-class culture sp56 CCCS Birmingham 1979a.

    'Culture and the historians' 1979b in CCCS 1979.

Jones, Jean *The League Against Imperialism* Socialist History Society Occasional Papers 4 1996.

Jones, Mervyn 'The time is short' in MacKenzie (ed.) 1958.

    Chances Verso 1987.

Kaufman, Gerald (ed.) *The Left* Anthony Blond 1966.

Kaye, Harvey J. *The British Marxist Historians* Polity Cambridge 1984.

    Education of Desire Routledge 1992.

——(ed.) *The Face of the Crowd: selected essays of George Rudé* Harvester Hertfordshire 1988.

——(ed.) *Poets, Politics and the People: writings of V. G. Kiernan volume 2* Harvester Hertfordshire 1989.

——Keith McClelland (eds) *E. P. Thompson Critical Perspectives* Polity Cambridge 1990.

Kee, Robert *The world we left behind* Weidenfield and Nicolson 1993.

Kenny, Michael *The First New Left* L & W 1995.

Kettle, Arnold 'Rebels and their Causes' *Marxism Today* March 1958.

    'Culture and Revolution' *Marxism Today* October 1961.

Khrushchev, Nikita *Khrushchev Remembers* Sphere 1971.

Kiernan, Victor 'Culture and Society' *New Reasoner* 9 1959.

'Maurice Dobb: Random biographical notes' *Cambridge Journal of Economics* 2 1978.

'Herbert Norman's Cambridge' 1984 in Roger Bowen (ed.) 1984.

History, Classes and Nation-States Polity Press Cambridge 1988.

Kimber, R. and J. J. Richardson (eds) *Pressure groups in Britain: a reader* Dent 1974.

King, Francis and George Matthews *About Turn* L & W 1990.

Klugmann, James *History of the Communist Party of Great Britain: volume 1 Formation and Early Years 1919–1924* L & W 1969a.

History of the Communist Party of Great Britain: volume 2 The General Strike 1925–1926 L & W 1969b.

'The crisis in the thirties: a view from the left' in Clark et al. (eds) 1979.

Kozak, Marion 'How it all began: a footnote to history' *Socialist Register* 1995.

Krantz, Frederick (ed.) *History from Below* Concordia University of Montreal Canada 1985.

Kubal, David 1972 *Outside the Whale: George Orwell's art and politics* University of Notré Dame Press Philippines 1972.

Labour Party Research Department *Twelve wasted years* Labour Party 1963.

Labour Monthly June 1945.

Labour Monthly July 1945.

Labour Monthly August 1945.

Labour Monthly September 1945.

Labour Review 2 3 May–June 1957.

Labour Review 2 5 September–October 1957.

Landsbury, George *My England* Selwyn & Blount 1935.

Laski, Harold *Reflections on the revolutions of our time* Allen & Unwin 1943.

Layton-Henry, Zig and Paul Rich (eds) *Race, Government and politics in Britain* Macmillan 1986.

Lea, John Thomas and Clarice Lea *The history and development of the mechanics institutions* Research in Librarianship Lancashire 1968.

Leavis, F. R. *Education and the University* (1944) Chatto & Windus 1948.

'Left-wing intellectuals and working-class culture' *New Statesman* 9 March 1957.

Letters in Criticism Chatto & Windus 1974.

The Common Pursuit (1952) Penguin 1976.

Lee, Jenny *My life with Nye* Penguin 1981.

Lessing, Doris 'The small personal voice' 1957 in Maschler (ed.) 1957.

The Golden Notebook (1962) Paladin 1989.

Levy, Hyman 'A chapter in modern scientific history' *Modern Quarterly* 1 4 1938.

'The social conditioning of science' *Modern Quarterly* 2 2 1939.

Lewis, Jane *Women in England* Wheatsheaf Sussex 1984.

Lewis, John *The Left Book Club* Gollancz 1970.

Lewis, Peter *The Fifties* Heinemann 1978.

Lewis, Richard *Leaders and Teachers: Adult education and the challenge of labour in Wales 1906–1940* Cardiff University Press Cardiff 1993.

London District Communist Party *Bulletin* 11 January 1957.

MacEwen, Malcolm *The Greening of a Red* Pluto 1991.

Macfarlane, L. J. *The British Communist Party: its origins and development until 1929* MacGibbon & Kee 1966.

McGuigan, Jim 'Reviewing a Life' *NLR* 215 1996.

McIlroy, John 'Raymond Williams in Adult Education part I' *Studies in the Education of Adults* 22 2 October 1990.

'Raymond Williams in Adult Education part II' *Studies in the Education of Adults* 23 1 April 1991.

'Teacher, Critic, Explorer' 1993 in Morgan and Preston (eds) 1993.

——Sallie Westwood *Border Country: Raymond Williams in Adult Education* National Institute of Adult Continuing Education Leicester 1993.

Macintyre, Stuart 'Red Strongholds between the Wars' *Marxism Today* March 1979.
　　Little Moscows Croom Helm Kent 1980a.
　　A Proletarian Science L & W 1980b.
MacKenzie, Norman (ed.) *Conviction* MacGibbon & Kee 1958.
McKinnon, Alan 'Communist Party election tactics—a historical review' *Marxism Today* August 1980.
Mahon, John *Harry Pollitt* L & W 1976.
MAHRO *Visions of History* Manchester UP Manchester 1983.
Margolies, David 'Left Review and left literary theory' 1979 in Jon Clark et al. (ed.) 1979.
Marriott, Stuart *Extra-Mural Empires* Department of Adult Education University of Nottingham 1984.
Marquand, David 'The new left at Oxford' *Guardian* 18 August 1957.
　　'England, the Bomb, and the Marchers' *Commentary* 29 May New York 1960.
Martin, David and David Rubinstein *Ideology and the Labour Movement* Croom Helm Kent 1979.
Martin, Kingsley *Laski* Johnathan Cape 1969.
　　Editor: a second volume of autobiography 1931–45 Hutchinson 1968.
Maschler, Tom *Declaration* MacGibbon & Kee 1957.
Matthews, George 'Stalin's British Road' Supplement *Changes* 14–27 September Democratic Left 1991.
May, Daphne 'Work of the historians' group' *Communist Review* May 1949.
Meacham, Standish *Toynbee Hall and Social Reform 1880–1914* Yale UP New Haven 1987.
Meredeth, F. W. 'Aerial Warfare in its Social Implications' *Modern Quarterly* 1 3 1938.
Miles, Robert and John Solomos 'Migration and the state in Britain; an historical overview'' in Charles Husband (ed.) *Race in Britain* Hutchinson 1987.
Miliband, Ralph *Parliamentary Socialism* Merlin 1972.
　　'John Saville: a presentation' 1979 in David Martin and David Rubinstein 1979.
　　'Harold Laski: an exemplary public intellectual' *NLR* 200 1993.
　　'Thirty years of the Socialist Register' *Socialist Register* 1994.
　　'A re-thinking sermon' *New Statesman* and *Society* 27 May 1994.
　　'Harold Laski's socialism' (1958/59) *Socialist Register* 1995.
Millar, J. P. M. *Education and Power* NCLC Publishing Society n.d.
　　The Labour College Movement NCLC Publishing Society n.d.
Monkhouse, Elizabeth 'The Future of Adult Education' in Workers' Education Association (ed.) 1983.
Moore, Bill *Labour–Communist Relations 1920–1951 Part III: 1945–1951* CP History Group pamphlet 84/85 1991.
——George Barnsby (eds) *The anti-Fascist people's front in the armed forces* CP History Group pamphlet 81 1990.
Morgan, John and Peter Preston *Raymond Williams: Politics, Education, Letters* St Martin's Press New York 1993.
Morgan, Kenneth O. *Labour in Power 1945–1951* OUP Oxford 1984.
Morgan, Kevin *Against Fascism and War* Manchester UP Manchester 1989.
　　Harry Pollitt Manchester UP Manchester 1993.
Morning Star 'Veteran Andrew Rothstein dies' 25 September 1994.
Morton, A. L. 'The writing of Marxist history' *Communist Review* July 1949.
　　A People's History (1938) L & W 1954.
　　History and the Imagination L & W 1990.
Morris, William *Journalism Contributions to 'Commonweal' 1885–1890* Theommes 1996.
Muggeridge, Malcolm *The Thirties* Collins 1967.
Mulhern, Francis 'The Moment of "Scrutiny" ' *NLB* 1979.
　　'The Cambridge Affair' *Marxism Today* March 1981.
　　'A Welfare Culture? Hoggart and Williams in the Fifties' *Radical Philosophy* 77 1996.

Murry, Middleton 'The need of an English Communism' *Highway* xxv October 1932.

Nayar, Radhakrishnan 'Our Best Man' *Times Higher Education Supplement* 17 November 1995.

The New Fabian Essays Turnstile Press 1952.

New Left Review (ed.) *Exterminism and the cold war* Verso 1982.

'Tributes to Edward Thompson' *NLR* 201 1983.

New Statesman and Nation *Keep Left* 1947.

Keeping Left 1950.

Newman, M. *Socialism and European Unity* Junction Books 1983.

Newton, Kenneth *The sociology of British Communism* Allen Lane 1969.

Niel, A. S. 'Discipline in a Modern School' *The Highway* xxvi December 1933.

Norris, Christopher (ed.) *Inside the Myth* L & W 1984.

O'Connor, Alan *Raymond Williams* Blackwell Oxford 1989.

Orwell, George *Inside the Whale and other essays* Penguin 1962.

The Lion and the Unicorn Secker & Warburg 1962.

Homage to Catalonia Penguin 1966.

The Collected Essays volume 1 An age like this 1920–1940 Penguin 1970.

The Collected Essays volume 2 My country right or left 1940–1943 Penguin 1970.

The Collected Essays volume 3 As I please 1943–1945 Penguin 1970.

The Collected Essays volume 4 In front of your nose 1945–1950 Penguin 1970.

Osmond, John *Creative Conflict* RKP 1977.

The Divided Kingdom Constable 1988.

Oxford English Limited *News From Nowhere Raymond Williams Third Generation* 6 1989.

Oxford University Socialist Discussion Group *Out of Apathy* Verso 1989.

Palmer, Bryan *The Making of E. P. Thompson* New Hogtown Press Toronto 1981.

E. P. Thompson: Objections and Oppositions Verso 1994.

Panitch, Leo 'Ralph Miliband, Socialist Intellectual 1924–1994' *Studies in Political Economy* 45 Fall 1994.

'Ralph Miliband, socialist intellectual 1924–1994' *Socialist Register* 1995.

Pankhurst, Sylvia 'The Threat of War' *The Highway* xxvii March 1935.

Parkin, Frank *Middle Class Radicalism* Manchester UP Manchester 1968.

Passerini, Luisa 'Work ideology and consensus under Italian Fascism' *HWJ* 6 1979.

Paynter, Will *My Generation* Allen & Unwin 1972.

Pearce, Brian 'The Communist Party and the Labour Left 1925–1929' (1957) *Reasoner Pamphlet 1* republished in Woodhouse, Michael and Brian Pearce 1975.

Peers, Robert *Adult Education: a comparative study* RKP 1959.

Pelling, Henry *The British Communist Party* Adam & Black 1958.

Pennington, Donald and Keith Thomas (eds) *Puritans and Revolutionaries* OUP Oxford 1978.

Pimlott, Ben 'The socialist League—intellectuals and the labour left in the 1930s' *Journal of Contemporary History* 6 3 1971.

Labour and the Left in the 1930s Cambridge 1977.

Pitcairn, Lee 'Crisis in British Communism: an insiders view' *NLR* 153 1985.

Poetry and the People editorial 7 January 1939.

Politics and Letters 'Editorial For Continuity in Change' 1 summer 1947.

'Critic and Leviathan' 1 summer 1947.

'Critic and Leviathan: A Comment' 1 summer 1947.

'Editorial Culture and Crisis' 2 & 3 winter–spring 1947.

'Critic and Leviathan: Literary Criticism and Politics' 2 & 3 winter–spring 1947.

'Critic and Leviathan: David and Goliath' 2 & 3 winter–spring 1947.

'Commentary: The Bureau of Current Affairs' 2 & 3 winter–spring 1947.

'Correspondence' 2 & 3 winter–spring 1947.

'Critic and Leviathan: Writers and Leviathan' 4 summer 1948.

'Correspondence' 4 summer 1948.

Pollitt, Harry *Looking Ahead* Communist Party 1947.
    Communism and Labour Communist Party 1949.
    Letter to Edwin Payne (Historians' Group) 13 April 1956.
Priestley, J. B. 'Britain and the Nuclear Bombs' *New Statesman* 2 November 1957.
Pritchard, Gwynn 'The people's remembrancer' *New Welsh Review* 31 Winter 1995–6.
Radical History Review 'Edward Thompson' *Radical History Review* 3 1976.
Raven, Charles *Christian Socialism 1848–1854* (1920) Frank Cass 1968.
Raybould, Sydney 'On objectivity and ideologies' *The Highway* 42 February 1951.
——(ed.) *Trends in English adult education* Heinemann 1959.
Redfern, Gordon 'The real outrage' *ULR* 5 1958.
Rich, Paul *Race and empire in British politics* Cambridge UP Cambridge 1990.
Ried, Betty 'The Left Book Club in the Thirties' 1979 in Jon Clark et al. (eds) 1979.
Robertson, Terence *Crisis: The Inside Story of the Suez Conspiracy* Hutchinson 1964.
Roberts, Elizabeth *A Woman's Place* Blackwell Oxford 1984.
Robson, William (ed.) *The Political Quarterly in the 1930s* Penguin 1971.
Rolph C. H. *Kingsley* Gollancz 1973.
Rowbotham, Sheila *Hidden from History* Pluto 1973.
    'Travellers in a strange country' *History Workshop Journal* 12 1981.
    'E. P. Thompson: a life of a radical dissident' *New Statesman and Society* 3 Sept 1993.
    'Some memories of Raphael' *NLR* 221 1997.
Rowley, Eve n.d. *A history of the WEA in Longton* WEA and Wedgwood Memorial College Staffordshire n.d.
Rushdie, Salman 'Outside the Whale' *Granta* 11 1984.
Russell, Bertrand 'Open Letter to Eisenhower and Khrushchev' *New Statesman* 23 November   1957.
Russell, Sam 'Tito' *Marxism Today* July 1980.
Rust, William *The Story of the Daily Worker* People's Press 1949.
Rustin, Michael 'The new left and the crisis' *NLR* 121 1980.
    For a pluralist socialism Verso 1985.
    'Raymond Williams (1921–1988)' *Radical Philosophy* 49 1988.
Sampson, Anthony *Anatomy of Britain* Hodder and Stoughton 1962.
Samuel, Raphael 'Class and Classlessness' *ULR* 6 1959.
    'British Marxist Historians I' *NLR* 120 1980.
    'The lost world of British Communism' *NLR* 154 1985.
    'Staying Power: The lost world of British Communism part two' *NLR* 156 1986.
    'Class Politics: The lost world of British Communism part three' *NLR* 165 1987.
    'Ralph Miliband 1924–1994' *HWJ* 38 1994.
    'Making It Up' *London Review of Books* 4 July 1996.
    Raphael Samuel tributes and appreciations 1997.
Sartre, Jean-Paul 'Commitment in Literature' *Politics and Letters* 2 & 3 Winter–Spring 1947.
Saville, John (ed.) *Democracy and the Labour Movement Essays in Honour of Dona Torr* L & W 1954.
    'The XXth Congress and the British Communist Party' *Socialist Register* 1976.
    'May Day 1937' in Briggs and Saville (eds) 1977.
    The Labour Movement in Britain Faber and Faber 1988.
    'The Communist Experience: a personal appraisal' *Socialist Register* 1991.
    'Parliamentary Socialism Revisited' *Socialist Register* 1995.
Schneer, J. 'Hopes deferred or shattered: The British labour left and the third force movement 1945–1949' *Journal of Modern History* 56 2 1984.
Schwarz, Bill 'The people in history: the Communist Party historians' 1982 in CCCS 1982.
Scruton, Roger *Thinkers of the new left* Longman Harlow 1985.
Shearman, Harold *Adult Education for Democracy* WEA 1944.
Simon, Brian *Education and the Labour Movement 1870–1920* L & W 1974.
——(ed.) *The search for enlightenment* NIACE Leicester 1992.

Lady Simon 'Education and the Ray Report' *The Highway* xxv January 1993.
Sinfield, Alan *Society and Literature 1945–1970* Holmes & Meier New York 1983.
    Literature, Politics and Culture in Post-war Britain Basil Blackwell Oxford 1989.
Sinnot, Diana 'Our historical tradition' *Arena* June/July 1951.
Smith, Dai 'Relating to Wales' in Eagleton (ed.) 1989.
    'The history of Raymond Williams's *New Welsh Review* 12 1993.
    Aneurin Bevan University of Wales Press Cardiff 1993.
    'Gwyn A. Williams 1925–1995' *HWJ* 41 1996.
Snee, Carol 'Working-class literature or proletarian writing' in Clark et al. (eds) 1979.
Snow, Edgar *Red Star Over China* Gollancz 1937.
Socialist History Society (Our History) *The Communist Party and 1956* Social History Society
    1993.
Socialist Register 1973 Merlin.
Socialist Register 1976 Merlin.
South Wales District of the Communist Party *A programme of health and work* n.d.
Squires, Mike 'CPGB Membership during the Class Against Class Years' *Socialist History* 3
    1993.
    The Aid to Spain Movement in Battersea 1936–1939 Elmfield 1994.
Steedman, Carolyn 'Raphael Samuel, 1934–1996' *Radical Philosophy* 82 March–April 1997.
Steele, Tom *The Emergence of Cultural Studies: Adult Education, Cultural politics and the
    'English' Question* L & W 1997.
Stevens, Philip Jones *Education, culture, politics: the philosophy of education of Raymond
    Williams* Institute of Education unpublished thesis 1992.
Stocks, Mary *The Workers Education Association, the first fifty years* Allen & Unwin 1953.
Strachey, John 'Mr J. M. Keynes and the Falling Rate of Profit' *Modern Quarterly* 1 4 1938.
Strachey, Ray 'The Women's Movement' *The Highway* xxvi October 1933.
Summers, Anne 'Thomas Hodgkin' *HWJ* 14 1982.
Swindells, Julia and Lisa Jardine *What's left: women in culture and the labour movement* Rout-
    ledge 1990.
Tanner, Duncan 'New Liberalism' *Modern History Review* April 1993.
Tatton, Derek 'Raymond Williams, the WEA and "Towards 2003" ' *Workers' Education*
    Autumn 1988.
Tawney, R. H. 'The School Leaving Age Bill' *The Highway* xxii February 1930.
    'The WEA in wartime' *The Highway* xxxii November 1939.
    The Radical Tradition Allen & Unwin 1964.
Taylor, Barbara *Eve and the New Jerusalem* Virago 1983.
Taylor, Charles 'Alienation and Community' *ULR* 5 1958.
Taylor, Richard and Colin Pritchard *The Protest Makers* Pergamon Press Oxford 1980.
Thames, Richard *Ernest Bevin* Shire Buckinghamshire 1974.
Thomas, Hugh *The Spanish Civil War* Eyre & Spottiswoode 1961.
    The Suez Affair Penguin 1970.
Thomas, J. E. *Radical Adult Education: theory and practice* Department of Adult Education
    University of Nottingham 1982.
——J. H. Davies (eds) *A select bibliography of adult continuing education in Great Britain*
NIACE   Leicester 1984.
Thompson, Dorothy 'The personal and the political' *NLR* 200 1993.
    'Introduction' in *Outsiders Class, Gender Nation* Verso 1993
    'On the Trail of the New Left' *NLR* 215 1996.
Thompson, Edward P. 'Mr Cameron' *The Highway* 40 April 1949.
    William Morris romantic to revolutionary L & W 1955.
    'Through the Smoke of Budapest' *Reasoner* 1 1956.
    'Commitment in politics' *ULR* 6 1959.
    'The New Left' *The New Reasoner* 9 1959.
    'Outside the Whale' in Thompson (ed.) 1960.

'Revolution' *NLR* 3 1960.

'Revolution Again! Or shut your ears and run' *NLR* 6 1960.

'Homage to Tom Maguire' in Briggs and Saville (eds) 1960.

'Long Revolution part I' *NLR* 9 1961.

'Long Revolution part II' *NLR* 10 & 11 1961.

The Making of the English Working Class Gollancz 1963.

'Peculiarities of the English' *Socialist Register* 1965.

'Organizing the Left' *The Times Literary Supplement* 19 February 1971.

'Recovering the Libertarian Tradition' *The Leveller* 27 January 1972.

The Poverty of Theory Merlin 1978.

'The Nehru Dynasty' in Thompson 1980.

Writing by Candlelight Merlin 1980.

'Overture to Cassino' in *Double Exposure* Merlin Suffolk 1985.

Witness Against the Beast Cambridge 1993

——John Saville Letter to John Gollan 7 October unpublished Circulars 1956 Box CPGB Archive.

——Dorothy Thompson *Beyond the Frontier* Merlin Suffolk 1997.

——(ed.) *The Railway: an adventure in construction The British-Yugoslav Association* 1948.

——(ed.) *Out of Apathy* New Left Books 1960.

Thompson, G. H. 'Beehive incident' *Highway* xxxii December 1939.

'What sails shall be set' *Highway* xxxii February 1940.

Thompson, Jane (ed.) *Adult Education for a change* Hutchinson 1980.

Thompson, Paul *The Edwardians* Weidenfeld and Nicolson 1975.

The voice of the past: oral history OUP Oxford 1978.

Thompson, T. J. and E. P. Thompson *There is a Spirit in Europe: A memoir of Frank Thompson* Gollancz 1947.

Thompson, Willie *The Good Old Cause* Pluto 1992.

The Long Death of British Labourism Pluto 1993.

The Left in History Pluto 1997

The Times *The Times House of Commons 1945* n.d.

Tribune *One way only* n.d. (probably 1950).

Tribune at Forty Quartet Books 1977.

60 not out: Tribune anniversary special issue 28 February 1997.

Upward, Edward *The Rotten Elements* Penguin 1972.

Vaizey, John 'The bogey of monopoly capitalism' *The Highway* 43 December 1951.

Veldman, Meredith *Fantasy, the Bomb, and the Greening of Britain: Romantic Protest, 1945–1980* Cambridge 1994.

Vernon, Betty *Ellen Wilkinson* Croom Helm Kent 1982.

Margaret Cole 1893–1980 Croom Helm Kent 1986.

Wainwright, W. Letter to Joan Simon 14 November 1958

Walter, Nicolas 'Secularism and British Marxism' *NLR* 126 1981.

Warburg, Fredric *An Occupation for a Gentlemen* Hutchinson 1959.

Ward, J. P. *Raymond Williams* (Writers of Wales) University of Wales Press Cardiff 1981.

Webb, Beatrice *Our Partnership* Longmans 1948.

The Diary of Beatrice Webb volume three 1905–1924: The Power to Alter Things Virago 1984.

Webb, R. K *The British Working Class Reader* (1955) Augustus Kelley New York 1971.

Webb, W. L. 'A thoroughly English dissident' *Guardian* August 1993.

Weiler, P. N. 'British labour and the cold war' *Journal of British Studies* 26 1 1987.

Welsh Committee of the Communist Party *Wales in the new world* 1944.

The flame of Welsh freedom 1944.

Communist policy for the people of Wales 1945.

Werskey, Gary *The Visible College* Free Association Books 1988.

Westwood, Sallie and J. E. Thomas *Radical Agendas? The politics of adult education* NIACE Leicester 1991.

Whale, Gwendolyn 'Christopher Hill: some reminiscences' in Donald Pennington and Keith Thomas (eds) 1978.

Wiener, Martin *English Culture and the Decline of the Industrial Spirit 1850–1980* Cambridge UP Cambridge 1981.

Widgery, David *The left in Britain* Penguin 1976.

Williams, Gwyn *When Was Wales* Penguin 1985a.

Williams, Joy and Raymond Williams (eds) *Lawrence on Education* Penguin 1973.

Williams, Merryn 'Raymond Williams 1921–88' *Planet* 68 April–May 1988.

Williams, Raymond 'Commentary' *Cambridge University Journal* April–November 1940.

    'The Soviet Literary Controversy' *Politics and Letters* 1 Summer 1947.

    'The State and Popular Culture' *Politics and Letters* 4 Summer 1948.

    Reading and Criticism Fredrik Muller 1950.

    'Stocktaking' *Use of English* 1 3 1950.

    'The Teaching of Public Expression' *The Highway* April 1952.

    'The Idea of Culture' *Essays in Criticism* III 3 1953.

    'The new party line' *Essays in Criticism* 7 1 1957.

    Culture and Society Chatto & Windus 1958.

    'Culture is ordinary' in MacKenzie (ed.) 1958

    Border Country Chatto & Windus 1960.

    'The new British left' London Letter *Partisan Review* 27 2 Spring 1960.

    The Long Revolution Chatto & Windus 1961.

    Communications (first edition) Penguin 1962.

    'The Deadlock' *Encounter* 18 1 January 1962.

    Drama from Ibsen to Eliot (1952) Penguin 1964.

    Second Generation Chatto & Windus 1964.

    'Affluence after Anger' *The Nation* 19 Dec 1966.

    'The Left in the Thirties' *Guardian* 22 March 1968.

    Drama from Ibsen to Brecht Penguin 1973.

    Marxism and Literature OUP Oxford 1977.

    Politics and Letters Verso 1979a.

    Modern Tragedy Verso 1979b.

    Fight for Manod Chatto & Windus 1979c.

    The Welsh Industrial Novel University College Cardiff Press 1979d.

    'The Bloomsbury Fraction' in Williams 1980.

    'The Writer: commitment and alignment' *Marxism Today* June 1980.

    Problems in Materialism and Culture Verso 1980.

    'The Robert Tressell Memorial Lecture' *HWJ* Autumn 1983.

    Keywords Fontana 1983.

    'Adult education and social change' in Workers' Education Association (ed.) 1983.

    Towards 2000 Chatto & Windus 1983.

    Orwell Fontana 1984.

    The Country and the City Hogarth 1985.

    'Preface' *Culture and Society* Hogarth 1987.

    What I came to say Hutchinson 1989a.

    Resources of Hope Verso 1989b.

    Loyalties Hogarth 1989c.

    Writing in Society Verso 1991.

——(ed.) *George Orwell: A collection of critical essays* Prentice Hall New Jersey 1974.

——Michael Orram *Preface to Film* Drama Limited 1954.

Wilmot, Peter and Michael Young *Family and Kinship in East London* Penguin 1957.

Wilson, Edmund 'Marxist History' *New Statesman* 15 October 1932, in Howe (ed.) 1988.

Wintringham, Tom *New Ways of War* Penguin 1940.

Wollheim, Richard *Socialism and Culture* Tract 331 Fabian Society 1961.

Wood, J. *The Labour Left in the CLPs 1945–51* Warwick unpublished thesis 1977.

Wood, Neal *Communism and British Intellectuals* Columbia UP New York 1959.

Woodhams, Stephen 'Against the Wisdom of the Age' *Socialist History* 5 1994.

'Lin Chun, The British New Left' *Socialist History* 7 1995.

'Raymond Williams: Culture and History' *Socialist History* 8 1995.

'Raymond Williams: Retrospect and Prospect' *Contemporary Politics* 3 1 1997.

'Adult education and the history of cultural studies' *Changing English* 6 2 1999.

'George Orwell; Orwell, England and Empire' in Chandramohan, Balasubramanyam (ed.) *Explorations in Post-colonial Theory and Practice* forthcoming.

Woodhouse, Michael and Brian Pearce *Essays on the history of Communism in Britain* New Park New York 1975.

Woolford, Jack 'Tony McLean: A Memoir' in Workers' Education Association (ed.) 1983.

Wootton, Barbara 'The New Deal at the Cross Roads' *The Highway* xxvii February 1935.

In a world I never made Allen & Unwin 1967.

Workers' Education Association *The WEA Education Year Handbook 1918* Department of Adult Education University of Nottingham Nottingham 1981.

Adult education and social change South Eastern District 1983.

Central Executive Committee 'Educational Policy in Wartime' *The Highway* xxxii January 1940.

Worswick, G. D. N. 'Cole at Oxford 1938–1958' in Briggs and Saville (eds) 1960.

Wright, Anthony W. *G. D. H. Cole and socialist democracy* OUP Oxford 1979.

R. H. Tawney (Lives of the Left) Manchester UP Manchester 1987.

Wykes, David *A preface to Orwell* Longman Harlow 1987.

Yeo, Stephen *Religion and Voluntary Organizations in Crisis* Croom Helm Kent 1976.

'A New Life, The Religion of Socialism' *HWJ* 4 Autumn 1977.

Young, Nigel *An infantile disorder* RKP 1977.

Zilliacus, Konni 'Correspondence' *New Statesman* 16 November 1957.

INDEX OF NAMES

SELECTED SUBJECT INDEX